How to Write Better Resumes

Completely Revised and Updated

GENE CORWIN
DIRECTOR,
Career Blazers Resume Services
Boca Raton, Florida

GARY JOSEPH GRAPPO
FOUNDER AND FORMER PRESIDENT
CareerEdge

ADELE LEWIS
FOUNDER AND FORMER PRESIDENT,
Career Blazers Agency, Inc.
New York City

McGraw-Hill
New York   Chicago   San Francisco   Lisbon   London   Madrid
Mexico City   Milan   New Delhi   San Juan   Seoul
Singapore   Sydney   Toronto

1 2 3 4 5 6 7 8 9 0   QPD/QPD   0 9 8 7 6 5 4 3

ISBN 0-07-142232-3

McGraw-Hill books are available at special quantity discounts to use as premiums and sales promotions, or for use in corporate training sessions. For more information, please write to the Director of Special Sales, McGraw-Hill, Two Penn Plaza, New York, NY 10121-2298. Or contact your local bookstore.

Contents

Introduction

If you are reading these words in a bookstore or library, trying to decide whether this book is worth your time and money, let us help you decide. We assume that, having turned to this page, you are interested in improving or changing your position. We also assume you know that a powerful, effective resume is one essential tool toward accomplishing that goal.

You probably want to continue working in your current career area; or you are changing career fields but know precisely in what new area you want to apply past career interests, skills, and achievements. From these assumptions, we frame our entire universe of prospective readers, and we welcome you among them. This book will show you how to apply your skills to finding the job that satisfies you most.

In looking for a job, you should always aim for the very best and try to avoid settling for less. Be sure, however, that you maintain an open and realistic attitude, evaluating each opportunity with a flexible, far-sighted view. It is also our belief that you should take the job where you'll be happiest. Every job has psychological fringe benefits, and these, in the long run, can more than counter what might be viewed as a slight initial salary deficiency. If you are happy in your job, you'll do better work (and conversely, if you do better work, you'll be happy). Soon you will receive tangible recognition of that work. The contentment in your work will spill out into other areas of your life and is, therefore, an important and vital job asset. May this book ultimately bring you happiness.

1

The Art of Job Hunting

Whether you're unemployed, just starting out, or simply looking for greener pastures, your job hunt can be either a triumphant experience or a complete catastrophe. From our long experience in dealing with a variety of job seekers, we've come to realize that there is a definite skill to looking for and getting jobs. We call this skill self-marketing, the ability to sell one's self. For those lucky few who intuitively possess self-marketing ability, job hunting is an exhilarating, rewarding experience. Conversely, for those not possessing this skill, job hunting can be a depressing, traumatic task. Fortunately, learning to sell one's self can be mastered. It is rarely innate, never offered as part of an educational curriculum, and hardly ever recognized as an independent skill. It requires lots of thought, a dedication to assume new, *positive* attitudes, self-discipline, and lots of perseverance before it can be mastered. Once acquired, self-marketing ability will stay with you for the rest of your life and serve as a tremendous source of security in a variety of situations. You are always selling something—a thought or an idea—and in a job search, you are selling the benefits of hiring you over the competition. Self-selling skills are even important after you get a job, to help keep it.

Part of being a good salesperson means you must always maintain a cheerful, optimistic, and *positive* attitude. Keep in mind that you will get a job, whether it's this week or next month. When you consider that you spend more than 70,000 hours of your life on the job, doesn't it make sense to be generous with the time allotted to secure one?

Give up all *negative* attitudes, such as "I can't; it's impossible," as well as negative presuppositions about the job market: "It's not what you know; it's who you know," "No one over 40 stands a chance of getting a good job," "You have to have the exact experience they're looking for," "They never hire anyone who's been fired," "Large employment gaps are the kiss of death," and "It's impossible to change careers."

Anyone involved in recruiting will tell you that there is some validity to these beliefs, but they are not insurmountable. No matter what you think your disadvantages and hindrances are, acknowledge them and then be determined to overcome them. The best way to do this is to have an attack plan for handling your specific problem throughout your job search. For instance, some people in their 40s and beyond may feel they are too old and, therefore, unemployable. An attack plan for these individuals may include improving their wardrobe (for men, buying some new ties), updating their resume to a computerized format, and possibly even shedding a few pounds if necessary to appear healthy, athletic, and fit. After all, according to research, image is 93 percent of your message. At Career Blazers, we constantly place people over age 40 in excellent positions in prestigious companies. We continually have job listings for persons interested in changing fields or careers. If it were true that it's not what you know but whom you know, there would be no employment agencies, no executive search firms, and no ads in the paper. Our placement files prove that "exact" experience is rarely a requirement. Employers are flexible, and although initially they might ask for certain qualifications, they tend to lose their rigidity and hire the person who best convinces them that he or she is right for the job.

People involved in hiring are relatively sophisticated; they don't automatically prejudge anyone who has been fired. They know that a person fired from a particular position at a different company might be extremely valuable to their company. They realize that because changing jobs is such a stressful experience, many people are willing to stay in intolerable situations rather than face the great unknown. Company A's loss may very likely be Company B's gain.

It is true that large gaps in employment history may require additional effort in job hunting. However, those people who remain confident and true to themselves as well as others will ultimately meet with success.

People are constantly changing careers. A person with a scientific background has excellent prospects for a career in technical sales. We've seen engineers become salespersons, teachers metamorphosed into publishers' reps, copywriters filling slots in marketing areas.

Dwelling on the negative has no validity. Every negative thought or disadvantage can be overcome. A positive attitude yields positive results. To be successful, you must focus on the positive aspects of your work history and accentuate the positive skills you have acquired. Most important, if you believe you can, you will.

Even if you are employed or underemployed, you can still make the contents of this book work for you, although your job is still to show up for work every day. Utilizing evenings and weekends, make a commitment now, today, to begin to change your current job to a fresh new one that will be more challenging and interesting. You don't have to be a slave to your current employer if for good reasons you are unhappy there. Begin now with a plan that includes updating your resume, updating your cover letter, networking in your evening hours, and answering ads and sending out mailings on weekends. Return phone calls on breaks and lunch breaks if you are currently employed. It can be done. You just have to manage time more effectively and be more organized. Remember, you can achieve whatever it is that you desire in the way of new employment.

Looking for a job requires a great deal of effort, much insight, a high frustration tolerance, and a strong determination not to become discouraged and negative. Our vast experience in helping people find jobs tells us that a negative attitude is a luxury no job seeker can afford. This has become one of our favorite mottos, and we believe every job seeker should incorporate it into his or her personal philosophy.

THE SKILL OR ART OF JOB HUNTING—A FOUR-STEP CAREER STRATEGY

Step I is to start your job hunt with a little research. Make sure your salary requirements are in line with those currently offered. The classified section of your local newspaper offers a wealth of such information. A few calls to appropriate search firms is another simple method of learning a great deal about market conditions, along with surfing the Internet.

You know exactly the kind of job you're looking for. You are qualified (both in terms of education and work history). And your salary expectations are realistic. You are well on your way.

Step II is your resume. You know there are jobs available. You must now let the world know you are ready, willing, and available. You want to put your credentials on display and broadcast the fact that you are up for hire. Your resume is the best possible vehicle for this information. It must look good, be easy to read, and—most important—create interest in its product: you. After all, you are the greatest product you will ever sell. To be successful, your resume must totally and instantly convince the reader that you are, indeed, a person of substance and should be interviewed. Chapters 2 and 3 will show you, using a logical, step-by-step approach, just how this can be accomplished.

Step III follows with how to circulate your resume most effectively. Chapter 5 gives you a crash course in cover letters that get the reader's attention and maximize the impact of your resume in order to prompt interviews. Chapter 6 discusses networking and job sources for effective career strategy.

Step IV is changing an interview into an offer. Chapter 8 discusses the skills of self-marketing at an interview. You'll learn the necessary ingredients of effective self-selling, how to handle multiple interviews, and the proper techniques for salary negotiations. You'll learn how to control the interview and, finally, how to convert that interview into a solid job offer. We are convinced that once these basic skills have been mastered, you will find job hunting to be a positive, uplifting experience.

Go for it!

2

Contents and Style of a Resume

There was a time when job seekers could simply visit a potential employer and be interviewed, but that time has long since passed. In this complex world where distance, time, and sheer numbers discourage personal involvement, the resume has become the most essential ingredient in both the job search and hiring process. As such, your resume must represent you in the clearest, most forceful manner possible. In essence, your resume becomes an embodiment of you and will serve as your representative when you are not there to speak for yourself. The success of your job campaign is completely dependent on the effectiveness of your resume. A good resume results in interviews; an inferior one is simply discarded.

Employers tell us it is not unusual for them to receive hundreds of resume each day. Under these circumstances, no more than 10 or 20 seconds are given to scan each resume before allowing time for a thorough read-through. If a resume is more than two pages long, it will be immediately rejected, as will those that appear cluttered and don't invite easy reading. Spelling or grammatical mistakes are never tolerated. In order to warrant a thorough read-through, your resume must show *immediately* that you have the ability to organize information and present it in a clear, concise manner. You must instantly communicate to the reader that you know where you are going with your career and that you have just the right background to make you a valuable staff addition.

Resumes are sales presentations designed to sell you to a prospective employer in the same manner that any product is sold in a newspaper or magazine ad, whether it's a refrigerator or an automobile. In this instance you are advertising yourself to catch someone's attention and interest in wanting to see you, utilizing the same advertising techniques to maximize your credentials. The three essential elements in a strongly written resume are (1) **skills and abilities,** (2) **experience,** and (3) **achievements.** The last item is perhaps the most important because employers want to know not only what you did, but how well you did it. Achievements are generally what sets you apart from other applicants.

Skills and abilities are those aptitudes that have become an integral part of you. Such things as organizational ability, communication, or interpersonal skills follow wherever you go, to whatever job you do, whether a salesman, a teacher, or a fireman. Experience, on the other hand, is specific knowledge gained from exposure to a specific product, service, or industry. This may, or may not, have carryover value from one job to another.

But let's begin with the basics. Every resume must identify and describe the writer. It **must** include:

- Your name, address, and telephone number
- A description of your educational history
- A description of your work history
- Work-related honors or citations
- Publications, if any

It **may** also include:

- A summary of qualifications
- Your job objective or career goal
- A capsule description of your work history
- Memberships in any professional organizations
- Foreign languages, if any
- Information on hobbies, only if they relate to your career choice or show personal success, such as an award or outstanding achievement
- Military service, if any
- Security clearance, if any (technical sales)
- Willingness to travel or relocate

It should **not** include the following information:

- Reasons for leaving past jobs
- Past salaries or present salary requirements
- Personal data—age, height, weight, marital status, number of children
- Health status
- Names of spouse or children
- A photograph of yourself
- Names and addresses of references

RESUME STYLES

Although every resume should contain a brief, concise summary of your work history and educational background, the style or approach differs in the arrangement of this data. Though there are two basic resume styles, we believe the chronological is the most effective, but the functional format has gained in popularity over the past few years. As a matter of fact, what has emerged on the evolutionary trail as the most accepted resume trend is a combination resume that is both chronological and functional. A chronological/functional resume allows for very strong opening paragraphs summarizing your entire career, emphasizing those areas most material to your current career path. If you can immediately establish relevancy to the position for which you are applying, chances of catching the attention of the reader is greatly enhanced. These opening paragraphs are, therefore, better served by the functional format, after which a detailed itemization of work experience can follow in chronological format.

We will discuss and evaluate the two styles, with consideration of their usefulness. Despite minor variations, the two basic styles or approaches are:

- Chronological (historical)
- Functional

THE CHRONOLOGICAL (HISTORICAL) RESUME

As the name implies, this style presents the information in chronological sequence. The succession of facts must be presented in **reverse** chronological order, starting with the present or most recent experience and moving backward in time.

As with any resume, start with your name, address, and phone number. It is traditional in some industries to list your education first. There are no hard-and-fast rules about this, and certainly if you have a good, solid background of experience but have not completed your degree, then it makes sense to place the education at the end of the resume instead. Usually, however, your most advanced degree is shown first, followed in reverse order by all other degrees. Again, dates should always be used. State the name of the university, city, state, degree earned, and the dates attended. Academic honors would be included in this grouping.

If you have opted to use a career objective or resume capsule, place it near the top of the first page. Keep it brief and realistic.

Your work history should list each job (in reverse chronological order), specifying your job title, the name of your employer, the address (city and state, number, and name of street are not necessary), and a summary of your duties and responsibilities. These summaries should be brief but specific. Always include dates; they can be in vertical columns to the left of the other information, on a line before the description of each job held, or included as an integral part of the paragraph. Generally, placing the dates in a vertical column is preferable, as employers like to be able to determine at a glance the times involved.

The chronological resume should be brief and fill no more than two pages. This type of resume offers a clear, concise picture of you, and it is probably the easiest to assimilate in a quick reading.

THE FUNCTIONAL RESUME

As its name implies, the functional resume emphasizes the applicant's qualifications and abilities. This approach rejects a chronological sequence of employment and educational history, and provides analysis of particular professional strengths. The employment strengths or skills are the important facts in this style of resume.

Your work history, volunteer experience, and educational record are fragmented into significant talents, and each skill is listed separately. Because these functions or responsibilities usually have crossed over a number of jobs, the sequence of job history has been sacrificed to emphasize ability. Names of employers and dates are omitted from this section of the resume because the expertise has been gained from more than one position.

The functional resume should be brief, concise, and well structured. It should start with your name, address, and phone number, your job objective, and a resume summary (if needed). The body of the resume should consist of four or five paragraphs, each one heading a particular area of expertise or involvement.

The skills paragraphs should be listed in order of importance. We define the most important skill as the function that is most similar to your present career goal or job objective.

Typical headings might be Marketing, Legal Secretarial, Research, Sales Management, and so on; a brief summary of your accomplishments in each category would follow.

Though this type of resume has gained in popularity over the past few years, very few employers approve of this approach. Our employment experts tell us that they become very suspicious of a total functional resume. They feel it is often used to cover up a spotty work record (for example, seven jobs in four years or a long period of unemployment), to exaggerate certain abilities, or to disguise some "whole truth." One corporate executive put it succinctly when he said, "It raises more questions than it answers."

The only situation that lends itself to the functional resume is one in which you are attempting a career change. In that case, this style of resume may be advantageous because it shows at a glance the kinds of jobs within your capacity. Because most resume readers feel that resume lose their effectiveness if dates or names of employers are not shown, you should overcome this by adding a very concise historical (always in reverse chronological order) listing of employers, job titles, and job descriptions with the appropriate dates. This history should follow your description by function.

THE IMAGINATIVE/CREATIVE RESUME

You may feel that an imaginative, highly unusual approach is the ideal thing to shake loose your resume from the pack. Using artwork, illustrations, cartoons, or a unique format may very well create an impression, but not necessarily a good one.

We have received resumes that were over 2 feet long, wound up like a scroll; very, very small ones put together to resemble a passport (the print so reduced you would have to use a magnifying glass to read it); resumes in the formats of menus, playbills, calendars, stock certificates, and even a summons. True, these resume s caught the eye. They amused and charmed us, but they did not sustain enough interest to become effective. Such resumes are usually difficult to read, unprofessional, and impossible to file. Corporate employers share our opinion that a resume is a business matter and, accordingly, should be presented in a businesslike, professional manner.

THE ELECTRONIC RESUME

Creating an electronic resume for posting on-line is a simple thing to do, and every job seeker should have a printed version (hard copy), and a corresponding electronic file of the document. This is an ASCII text resume without fancy formatting such as bold face, italics, certain fonts, and sizes over 12 point. It is advantageous because it is recognizable by nearly every application and every computer, even though it is not the prettiest format. Simply save as "text only" and you will have an electronic format. Electronic resumes provide employers with the ability to search for prospective employees through the use of electronic scanners.

However, unless specifically requested, go the old-fashioned route and mail, fax, or e-mail your standard format resume.

Sites to See

- The Riley Guide—http://www.jobtrak.com/jobguide
- JOBTRAK—http://www.jobtrak.com
- The Monster Board—http://www.monster.com/home.html
- FedWorld—http://www.fedworld.gov
- CareerPath—http://www.careerpath.com
- JobBank USA—http://www.jobbankusa.com
- On Line Career Center—http://www.occ.com

But how effective is an electronic resume? According to *Career-Mosaic*, "real people find real jobs on-line." One newly employed graduate wrote, "I responded to an ad under your J.O.B.S. database and I started my job within two weeks." Another person states, "*CareerMosaic* was invaluable in finding me my new job. [After posting the resume] recruiters were calling me daily." Recently, we assisted placing a candidate with a major hotel company for a managerial position upon discovering his resume on-line.

Here are some key tips to help guide you when creating an electronic resume:

ELECTRONIC RESUME TIPS

Use Nouns

Traditional resume rely on descriptive words and action words. For an electronic resume, use lots of nouns instead. Remember, computers search for key words such as bio-tech, engineer, programmer, and administrator.

Use Keywords

Think about the top ten keywords that someone would use to find you if they typed in a word search string. Integrate all of those words into your resume. For instance, if you are a food and beverage manager, your keywords may be: restaurant, bar, food service, hotel, banquets, dining, menu, cuisine, food manager, and beverage manager.

Keep It Simple

You've heard this before, but the same holds true for electronic resumes. Avoid decorative typefaces and too much underlining. In cyberspace, just include the facts!

Name and Contact First

You're selling yourself, so keep your contact information prominent in the resume.

Use Jargon

The use of acronyms and industry lingo are often used by employers, who store all resumes received in complex databases to identify ideal candidates who list these words in their resumes.

White Spaces

Like traditional resumes, electronic resumes should have lots of white space to be reader friendly.

One-Page Resume

One-page resumes work better for recent college graduates. Two-page resumes work for executives and people with three or more years of career experience.

USE CAUTION IN POSTING RESUMES

Be cautious when posting your resume if you are currently employed. Registering your resume with an on-line career site exposes you to the risk that your current employer will read your posting. The more broadly you distribute your resume, the more likely it will come back to your boss. Also, some candidates who posted a resume two years ago and are now happily employed still continue to get calls (some unwanted) because their resumes are floating in cyberspace.

One way to avoid this is to list your resume only with an on-line database that promises anonymity. In this case, your resume is accepted for distribution without your name and address. Companies will be able to reply to you via some type of e-mail address or registration number.

3
Putting Yourself on Paper

When preparing your resume, always keep in mind the purpose of that resume—to serve as a personal advertisement, generating enough interest in you to secure an interview. As an effective advertisement, it should be attractive, easy to read, concise, and informative. Because the chronological resume is the most preferred style, we will use this approach in showing you how to write your resume.

The information contained in the resume should be presented in the following order:

- Identifying information
- Summary or resume capsule (optional)
- Career or job objective (optional)
- Employment history
- Educational history
- Honors or citations, if any
- Publications, if any
- Membership in professional organizations (optional)
- Military service

Including mention of hobbies, knowledge of foreign languages, willingness to travel or relocate, and other personal information is appropriate only if it is relevant to the position you are applying for. When used, this information should appear near the end of the resume.

In deciding whether to include a job objective and/or a job summary, consider that your present or most recent job description should be on the first page. If your objective and/or summary are too long, it may be better to shorten both or omit one of them.

IDENTIFYING INFORMATION

Always start with your identifying material in a conspicuous position, either flush left (leaving room for the margin) or on the top center (again, leave about ¾ to 1½ inches for the margin). Give your complete name, street address, city, state, zip code, and phone number, complete with area code. If you can be reached at the office, that number should also be listed.

The use of the summary, also called resume capsule, is optional, and mainly used by candidates with at least five years of experience. To be effective, it must include information indicating that you are indeed qualified for the position sought. Although optional, we have been told by more than one personnel director of an important company that this is the first piece of information they scan. If the summary, essentially a digest of the resume, sustains their interest, they will continue to read the resume in its entirety. The beauty of the summary is that it gives you the power of the functional resume with none of the disadvantages. Here is your opportunity to combine and build on similar aspects of your background that may have been acquired over a period of many years in a number of different positions.

Suppose one of your accomplishments occurred in an early job. If you were using a straight reverse-chronological style presentation, this important information might not be noticed by the reader. It probably would appear near the bottom of the page or possibly on the second page, and would very likely be missed. The summary allows you to emphasize it at the beginning. It is the space where you can list the highlights or whatever else you might consider your biggest career accomplishment, regardless of when that was.

The summary should consist of one strong sentence, three or four at the most. Those sentences should be enough to highlight the aspects of your background that will most appeal to a potential employer.

Here are some samples of summary paragraphs:

"Seventeen years of sales growth achievement in the medical field, having established strong rapport with professional practitioners."

"More than five years' involvement in HTML and Java for Web site design. Programming both for internal requirements and external clients. Thoroughly experienced in graphic design, content, layout, and implementation.

"Fifteen years' experience in Nuclear Power Plant Engineering, including start-up, modifications, construction, installation, and testing of ASME Code Class I, II, and III Systems."

We suggest that you write down every skill, responsibility, job duty, and accomplishment that will qualify you for your next position. Think of every problem you had some part in solving, any new idea you contributed to that was ultimately used by your employer, any achievements or capabilities you have that would demonstrate or suggest that you can do the job better than anyone else.

Study your list and pare it down to five or six points. Combine those that are similar in function so that you can write a brief narrative that has a convincing tone to it. Be brief, and choose your words carefully.

You may have to write several drafts—shortening sentences, changing a word here and there, deleting unnecessary adjectives or phrases that might be repetitive. Work on it until you have it perfect.

The summary or capsule resume is the best way to emphasize solid work background and highlight specific qualifications to a targeted employer. Although it often involves retyping the resume for each potential employer, the capsule resume can be the only part of your resume that does have to be adjusted to suit different employers' needs.

JOB OBJECTIVE OR CAREER GOAL

As with the summary, the use of a job objective or career goal is strictly optional. It is usually used when an individual has a background in more than one area and has preference in a particular direction.

We've seen excellent results with resumes that include objectives; those that omit this information fare just as well. The purpose of the objective is to describe succinctly the position you want by job title, function, and/or industry. The job objective must logically connect with the balance of your resume. The contents of your resume must demonstrate that you are indeed qualified for the position you are seeking. You should avoid stating objectives that are too confining; you don't want to cancel out opportunities that might be of interest to you. On the other hand, be careful of clichés ("a position that is both rewarding and stimulating;" "a challenging position that offers growth potential"). Such statements are meaningless and the reader may infer that you either lack direction or are unsure of what your career goals are. The following are clear and concise examples.

"A position with management potential in the system software area in a technically advanced environment."

"Seeking corporate position where my expertise in editorial design will be employed in communications media for both external and internal circulation."

EMPLOYMENT HISTORY

The heart of your resume is the section that describes your experience or employment history. It is important to remember that your resume must be honest as well as logical. Never put anything in your resume that is not 100-percent true. Stay with the truth, even if you feel that a small exaggeration or distortion might make you more marketable. Any information that is not true can become an insurmountable liability. Employers usually expect that a new employee will require some training, and they are quite willing to do so. If, however, you claimed certain strengths and are unable to demonstrate those abilities, you can be sure your credibility on all other matters will be questioned.

Begin your employment history with your present or most recent experience. Work backwards, treating each position as an independent entry. Each job mentioned should include the name and address (city and state, no streets or numbers) of the employer, the dates involved (month and year), and a concise description of your responsibilities. If you are presently employed, use the present tense in describing your current position and, obviously, the past tense for former jobs. Use only implied pronouns in crisp, simple language. Writing in the third person (he/she) is stylistically objectionable, as well as suggesting a certain detachment. Using the first person (I) is redundant; plainly the person reading the resume is aware that you are the subject of your own resume. For example, compare the following "bits" of information:

"She/he was responsible for creation of marketing concepts"

"I was responsible for creation of marketing concepts"

"Responsible for creation of marketing concepts"

Always give the name of each company you have worked for, including your present employer, even though you may wish this to be considered confidential. You will weaken your resume by not including specific names. Once we received a resume without any company identifying information, and decided we were not interested in that candidate. Luckily, he followed up with a phone call. It was only when he told us the name of the company, which happened to be a direct competitor, that we realized his experience was exactly what we were looking for. It is understandable that you might be circumspect about the fact that you are looking for a job. However, all agencies and employers treat this information as confidential.

Your goal in this section of the resume is to make as much as you can of each position you've held, while keeping the descriptions as brief as possible. Describe your major responsibilities, while concentrating heavily on the accomplishments you can legitimately own or share.

Always be as specific as possible and avoid generalizations or long descriptions of the company you worked for. Describe exactly what you did and what your responsibilities were. Think of as many problems as you can that you were able to solve. Our questionnaire in Chapter 4 will help you to organize these thoughts. Mention any improvements you were responsible for, any ideas adopted by your employer. Don't be shy; never be humble. But never be arrogant, either. Be proud of your achievements.

Remember that although it is important to list accomplishments, the job description also has to paint an accurate picture of what your daily routine included.

You may assume that an interviewer's interest will be piqued by each of your employment history entries, and you will be asked to elaborate on them in the interview. View each bit of information you provide as the basis of a future leading question. It's a good idea to mentally rehearse your responses as you write your job description.

Use active verbs; they give a certain power to your resume. And choose your words carefully; make each word count. Avoid being flowery; too many adjectives, especially an overabundance of superlatives, lessens the impact of your resume.

Always keep in mind that you're aiming for a one-page, maximum two-page, resume. It has been our experience that using a short, one-page resume works best when responding to a newspaper ad or conducting a mass mailing. A longer resume, with two or more pages, is effective in situations where you have been personally referred to someone. In this case, the person generally will take the time to read a longer resume and give you adequate consideration. Because of this, it is a good practice to have two versions of your resume stored in your computer and to use them appropriately. Be brief **and** concise. Keep narratives describing each position succinct—no more than 5 to 10 lines. Each accomplishment should be broken up into bite-sized entities for the reader to spot and digest quickly. Information concerning past positions should **not** be as long as current or recent ones. Avoid repetition—if your job responsibilities were similar in more than one job, describe in detail only the most recent position. Also, it is not necessary to use complete sentences. Indent and use "banner" statements to emphasize accomplishments. Start such entries with an asterisk(*) or bullet (•) so they appear to "pop" out.

Rewrite your first draft. It may be necessary to rewrite it several times, striking out unnecessary words and phrases and tightening sentences until they say exactly what you mean. Reread it several times, checking for spelling and grammatical errors. After several readings, have a friend or colleague scan it. Another person may pick up errors that you have missed and possibly suggest some additional qualifications.

EDUCATIONAL HISTORY

Start with your most advanced degree and include the name and location of the college or university you attended, the degrees you earned, and the year you graduated. Mention your major field of study and all career-oriented scholarships and academic awards. Thereafter, list all other degrees in reverse chronological order until you reach your B.A. or B.S. Include the same information for each as described for the advanced degree. Though abbreviations generally should not be used in resumes, it is acceptable and correct in listing your degrees, for example, Ph.D., M.S., B.A., B.S. If you have attended college, it is not necessary to include information concerning high school.

A recent graduate should mention his or her grade point average if it is 3.5 or higher. Obviously, there is no point in calling attention to a C average. If you were a member of Phi Beta Kappa, or graduated summa cum laude or magna cum laude, or if you received other high academic honors, no matter what your level of experience, by all means mention it.

PROFESSIONAL SOCIETIES AND PUBLICATIONS

List all career-oriented professional associations and organizations. Your membership in such groups implies dedication to your field and an ability to get along with others. If you are or have ever been an officer in any organization, be sure to mention that fact.

PERSONAL INFORMATION

Remember a very simple rule: *Personal information should never be included in your resume.* Never put in writing or discuss at an interview such personal matters as your height, weight, marital status, number of children, and so on.

Remember, your resume should include only information describing your qualifications; any other information is considered inappropriate and unprofessional.

Because of the passage of employment laws that have made it illegal for an employer to question an individual as to his or her age, sex, race, or religious preference, such information does not belong on a resume.

Your state of health (it's always "excellent" anyway) is superfluous. If, however, you have a disability and feel that you want the potential employer to know about it before the interview, mention it in your cover letter, *not* in the resume. Bear in mind that your resume should emphasize your *abilities,* not your disabilities.

Should you include your hobbies and leisure-time activities? Again, the answer is usually no. The only time these should be put into a resume is in the case of an award for outstanding achievement. A track star or swimmer who wins a major award in his or her sport should include this noteworthy event on a resume. It indicates to an employer that you have the personal drive and potential to be successful at anything you do. Keep in mind that every word in your resume should be there for a reason, and there is no place for a description of your nonprofessional or non-work-related interests.

REFERENCES

Never supply the names of your references on your resume. Not only is it unprofessional, but it can cause a lot of bother to those individuals listed. Simply state, as the last entry on your resume, "References on Request" or "References will be furnished upon request."

Always get permission from those individuals you wish to use as references. Don't put yourself or them in the position in which any calls will come as a surprise to them. Try, if possible, to get references that can be reached quickly. For that reason, it is preferable to list persons who can be reached by phone rather than by mail. Make certain that you have all of their current addresses and phone numbers. If you are giving a person's business phone, check to see if he or she is still employed by the same company.

If your name has been changed through marriage or for any other reason during your work or educational history, be sure that your references know you by your new name. It is wise for women who have married and adopted their husband's name to indicate their maiden name as well. Give permission to call your references only when an employer has indicated that you are under serious consideration.

PHOTOGRAPHS

Never include photographs unless you are looking for a job as a model. Not only are photographs on resumes unprofessional, but their legality is questionable. If an employer kept resumes containing photographs on file, that action could be considered a covert form of racial, sex, or age discrimination and, as such, could be considered illegal. But more important to you, don't prejudice your chances by sending a photo.

REASONS FOR LEAVING PAST JOBS

Your resume should be a businesslike summary of your talents, qualifications, goals, work history, and education. Because the reasons you left previous employers do not add to that summary, they should **not** be included in your resume.

SALARIES, PAST AND PRESENT

Neither your present minimum salary nor your past earnings should be discussed or listed in your resume. A potential employer will probably arrange a series of interviews, and the subject of salary will most often be discussed close to or at the final meeting.

Every employer we've had contact with considers salary a most confidential matter. It is considered extremely unprofessional as well as indiscreet for employees to discuss salaries among themselves. Your resume will be seen by many individuals in the company who normally would not and *should not* know your salary range, so no indication of it should appear in your resume.

Should you at least include your salary requirement? No. Including your salary requirements might eliminate you from certain positions in which the remuneration has not yet been decided, or it might preclude you from obtaining a certain position with an already established higher salary. As indicated above, reserve your discussion of salary for the final interview.

RESUME APPEARANCE

Visualize an employer who, after placing an ad, receives more than 200 resumes. He or she is also developing new systems, planning programs, and has a desk filled with other projects demanding attention. He or she is now faced with selecting the resume to read more closely. Obviously, the first step is to scan. This is why I recommend a one-page resume. They are read more often than multipage resumes. As we've indicated before, our inquiries have shown that an average recruiter rarely gives more than 10 seconds of attention to a resume in deciding whether it merits a complete reading.

Although initially sending a one-page resume is in your best interest, there is a place for an expanded two- or three-page resume. Utilize a one-page resume for cold leads. For instance, a newspaper ad is considered a cold lead. A mass mailing is also the perfect situation for a one-page resume. Send a one-page resume to companies with which you have had no personal contact.

Utilize an expanded two- or three-page resume for warm leads. For example, a referral to a hiring manager friend by a family member is a warm lead. Send the two- or three-page resume to individuals and companies that you are personally referred to and that you know will give it personalized attention. The expanded two- or three-page resume makes a great "leave behind."

Put yourself in the reader's position. Do you actually read every word in every newspaper or magazine you look at? We're sure the answer is no. In this fast-paced world, who has the time or even the interest? Rather, you automatically scan the material to decide which articles, advertisements, or stories are worth your time for a thorough read-through. The print media has proven that "eye appeal" is as important as content; people simply discard what is difficult to read. And we are aware that many staff managers and employers discard resumes containing excellent material because they were poorly presented. Remember—to do its job, your resume must pass the "quick scan test."

To pass this test, your resume must be visually inviting. Start by selecting a format. In Chapter 4 you will find some samples that have been successful. Whether you choose one of these samples or create your own, be sure that the total effect is pleasing to the eye. Be equally sure that it is easy to read, and that the different sections are clearly separated from one another.

Separate thoughts into paragraphs with pleasing white space between them. There is nothing more difficult to scan than a long, solid block of text, with no breaks or indentations. Even better, itemize and highlight thoughts with dashes or asterisks. At the very least, separate each job by white space, providing different sections to the resume.

Use good-quality paper in a professional printer. The printer should be of laser quality with a minimum rating of 300 dpi (dots per square inch); 600 to 1200 dpi is even better. If you are unable to access a quality printer, copy your resume to disk and have it printed at a professional business center (such as Kinkos) in your local neighborhood.

Use standard 8½-by-11-inch bond paper. It is a professional size, is easily handled, and is convenient to file. Avoid legal size paper, plastic sheet covers, or report folders—again, all too difficult to file. Stay away from unprofessional visual effects: photographs, illustrations, wild formats, or too many mixed-type styles.

Aim for one or a maximum of two pages of typewritten material. Use only one side of the paper, and, if the resume is more than one page, staple the pages together, making sure that your name appears on each page.

GIVING YOUR RESUME "EYE APPEAL"

A professional layout should be subtle and unobtrusive, but at the same time it should direct the reader's eye to the most important information. You can accomplish this by using proper width margins, combining uppercase and lowercase, and underlining special items.

Use the ground—the white space on your paper—effectively. Use your margins imaginatively; use wide margins to lend importance to the information on the page and, at the same time, to provide a restful, easy-on-the-eye appearance. Create white space by double or triple spacing between blocks of information.

Be selective in your use of uppercase; perhaps reserve it for job titles or names of employers. You might underline major accomplishments, but this, too, should be done sparingly. Avoid allowing your resume to look too "busy," which is often the result when you use too many typefaces and a plethora of underlines.

REPRODUCTION

In general, employers expect your resume to be reproduced by a high-quality copier on white linen paper. It is unacceptable to submit your resume on standard white bond copier paper. Stay clear of eye-catching colored papers unless you are in the fashion industry or the arts. Never send copies that were produced by the following: a typewriter, draft-quality printers, or carbon paper. Only a professional, computerized reproduction process that turns out clear, sharp copies may be used.

Because the success of your job campaign very likely may hinge upon the appearance of your resume, it is important that you have a superior product. Printing and copying services are listed in the telephone Yellow Pages under the heading of "Printers." Other services under the headings of "Resumes" will be able to retype your resume, assist you with the layout, and provide a choice of typefaces.

THE USE OF COMPUTERS

What did we ever do before computers? Designing and printing your resume from a computer is now the standard in writing resumes and cover letters. With bold, attractive fonts, it permits perfect typesetting and creates instant eye appeal and emphasis for key professional achievements and headlines.

Computers bring many advantages to the job-search process. Utilizing a popular word-processing program, MS Word, on a PC provides you with the ability to quickly create and edit a basic resume. Changes and major edits are free of the laborious problems of complete typing and retyping.

Further, your resume stored in MS Word allows you to select various print-shop-quality fonts for your resume and cover letter. Your documents will have the competitive edge with font selections, ranging from Bookman and Arial to Times Roman Italic, Times Roman Bold, and Helvetica. On a computer, a professional typeset look is a simple series of a few keystrokes for a complete document. In a few seconds, you have a print-shop-quality resume and cover letter.

A program such as MS Word also provides even more advanced applications for the job seeker. Utilizing the "copy file" feature, you can instantly manufacture dozens of resumes for each position you are applying to. With a few simple on-screen edits, you can tailor your resume and cover letter to accentuate the skills that a particular company is looking for. Targeting your resume and fulfilling a specific need for a particular company can only increase your chances for an interview.

One final note on the subject of computers. Computers equipped with a fax modem, or stand-alone facsimile machine, are an integral part of an effective job-search campaign. You should always fax your resume with your cover letter. When you telemarket yourself, ask for the fax number of the person to whom you wish to send your fax. Send the original copy of the resume and cover letter in the same day's mail. Mailing the originals works in your favor; you benefit from more contact with the key recruiter and, in a sense, "double advertise" yourself. You have achieved more name recognition.

One individual in New York City received a well-paying job within days of his campaign. In a single morning, he sent out almost 20 cover letters and resumes directly from his computer to a targeted list of hiring managers. By midafternoon, he received three phone calls for interviews. Three weeks later, he was completely settled into a new job.

4
Organizing Your Thoughts

Before you sit down to actually write your resume, it is imperative that you organize all of your information in terms of dates, education, courses, employers, job responsibilities, and all the other data that will be included. We've found that the most difficult part of writing a resume is putting your thoughts and data into a meaningful form. To help you accomplish this, we have provided a series of workspaces: forms and worksheets that will force you to analyze your data and organize it to correspond with the standard resume formats. Using these worksheets will force you to examine the natures of your previous jobs and your particular skills and strengths, and will pay off tremendously later on when you begin writing your resume and have your job interviews. This chapter actually becomes a skeleton version of the first draft of your resume.

RESUME WORKSPACE

Use the space that follows to provide the information indicated.

Identifying Information

Complete the following information.

Name: _____
(If a married woman, include married and maiden names.)

Address: _____
(Street and number, city, state, and zip code)

Home Phone: _____
(Be sure to give area code.)

Business Phone: _____
(Be sure to give area code.)

Note: If your business phone is confidential, state that; for example: Business phone: (212) 555-1280 (confidential).

Resume Capsule

The resume capsule, as with the job objective, is an optional feature. However, one or the other must be used if you are trying to change careers. Use this space to write a resume capsule, whether you decide to use it on your final resume or not.

_____

_____

_____

_____

Job Objective

Remember, the job objective is **optional.** If used, keep it brief. The only time it **must** be used is if you are trying to change careers.

_____

_____

_____

_____

Employment History

Your employment history should be listed in **reverse chronological order.**

Name of Company: _____

Address of Company: _____

_____

Job Title: _____

Dates: Description of Responsibilities: _____
From   To
(Month/Year)   (Month/Year)
                                _____

_____   _____   _____

                                _____

                                _____

                                _____

Name of Company: _____

Address of Company: _____

_____

Job Title: _____

Dates: Description of Responsibilities: _____
From   To
(Month/Year)   (Month/Year)
                                _____

_____   _____   _____

                                _____

                                _____

                                _____

Name of Company: _____

Address of Company: _____

_____

Job Title: _____

Dates: Description of Responsibilities: _____
From   To
(Month/Year)   (Month/Year)
                                _____

_____   _____   _____

                                _____

                                _____

                                _____

Educational History

List your education as you did your employment history, in **reverse chronological order:** your most advanced degree or your most recent education is first. Be sure to list all pertinent details—dates, degrees earned, educational institutions attended, and so on.

Advanced Degree

Dates:

		_____
		(Name of university)
From	To	_____
(year)	(year)	(Address of university)
_____	_____	_____
		(Degrees or credits earned)

Undergraduate Degree

Dates:

		_____
		(Name of university)
From	To	_____
(year)	(year)	(Address of university)
_____	_____	_____
		(Degrees or credits earned)
		_____
		(Major) (Minor)

Personal Information

Publications and Major Achievements: _____

_____

_____

Foreign Languages or any other special skills:_____

_____

Associations

_____

_____

_____

_____

References

Though the names of your references should **never** be included on your resume, it is a good idea to assemble your data at the time you are preparing your resume Have a minimum of three people as references. It is advisable to include a statement that references will be furnished upon request.

Note: List the complete address—street and number, city, state, and zip code. Give area code with telephone number.

Name of Reference: _____

Position: _____

Company Affiliation: _____

Company Address: _____

_____

Business Phone and Extension: _____

Name of Reference: _____

Position: _____

Company Affiliation: _____

Company Address: _____

_____

Business Phone and Extension: _____

Name of Reference: _____

Position: _____

Company Affiliation: _____

Company Address: _____

_____

Business Phone and Extension: _____

Name of Reference: _____

Position: _____

Company Affiliation: _____

Company Address: _____

_____

Business Phone and Extension: _____

Action Words

Linked with identifying your responsibilities and portraying your previous jobs is the matter of using strong, descriptive words to describe those activities. Look over the list of words below to help you identify ones that reflect or describe your job responsibilities and/or accomplishments. Use these words as needed to complete the Employment History Worksheets.

A
accomplish	appraise
account	approve
accumulate	arrange
acquire	assign
activate	assist
adhere	assume
administer	assure
advertise	audit
advise	augment
allocate	authorize
analyze	automate

B
brought	built
budget	

C
catalog	consider
change	construct
code	consult
collect	continue
communicate	contract
compare	contribute
compile	control
complete	cooperate
compose	coordinate
compute	correct
conceive	correlate
concentrate	create
conduct	credit
configure	

D
debug	develop
decrease	direct
define	disperse
delegate	display
delete	distribute

design	document
determine	

E
edit	establish
educate	examine
emphasize	execute
employ	exercise
engage	expand
engineer	expedite
enhance	extend
enlarge	evaluate
ensure	

F
fix	function as
forecast	furnish
format	

G
generate	graph
grant	guarantee

H
head	hire
help	

I
implement	instruct
improve	integrate
include	interfere
increase	interpret
inform	interview
initialize	invent
initiate	investigate
inspect	involve
install	issue

J
join	justify
judge	

L   lease   load
      lessen

M   maintain   meet
      manage   modify
      market   monitor
      master   motivate
      measure

N   negotiate   normalize
      neutralize   notify

O   open   order
      operate   organize
      orchestrate

P   participate   produce
      perform   program
      persuade   project
      plan   promote
      post   propose
      prepare   protect
      present   provide
      process   publicize
      procure   purchase

Q   qualify   quantify

R   reclaim   requisition
      recommend   research
      reconstruct   reshape
      recruit   responsible for

release   retain
report   retrieve
represent   review
request   revise
require

S   schedule   stimulate
      screen   strengthen
      secure   structure
      select   subcontract
      sell   submit
      serve   succeed
      set objectives   summarize
      set up   supervise
      solve   supply
      sort   support
      specify   synthesize
      staff   systematize
      standardize

T   teach   train
      test   transfer
      trace   translate
      track

U   underscore   upgrade
      update   utilize

V   validate   visualize
      verify

W   weigh   write
      word process

SAMPLE LAYOUTS
SAMPLE RESUME LAYOUT #1

Name
Street Address
City, State, Zip Code

Home Phone #
Business Phone #

Employment History

_____   Job Title
From (date) _____   Name of Company
to present _____   Address of Company

_____   Write out duties and responsibilities of job in question.

_____   Job Title
From (date) _____   Name of Company
to (date) _____   Address of Company

_____   Write out duties and responsibilities of job in question.

_____   Job Title
From (date) _____   Name of Company
to (date) _____   Address of Company

_____   Write out duties and responsibilities of job in question.

Educational History
From (date) _____   Name of College
to (date) _____   Address of College
_____   Degree Earned

References: On Request

SAMPLE RESUME LAYOUT #2

Name _____

Street Address _____

City, State, Zip Code _____

Home Phone # _____

Business Phone # _____

Employment History

_____   Job Title

From (date) _____   Name of Company

to present _____   Address of Company

_____   Duties and responsibilities of job written out.

_____   Job Title

From (date) _____   Name of Company

to (date) _____   Address of Company

_____   Duties and responsibilities of job written out.

Educational History

From (date) _____   Name of College

to (date) _____   Address of College

_____   Graduate Degree

From (date) _____   Name of College

to (date) _____   Address of College

_____   Undergraduate Degree

References: Available on Request

SAMPLE RESUME LAYOUT #3

Name _____

Street Address _____

City, State, Zip Code _____

Home Phone # _____

Business Phone # _____

<u>Career Objective</u>

　　To use the experience gained in . . .

<u>Educational History</u>

Name of College _____ From (date) _____

Address of College _____ to (date) _____

Advanced Degree _____

Name of College _____ From (date) _____

Address of College _____ to (date) _____

Bachelor's Degree _____

<u>Employment History</u>

<u>Job Title</u>

Name of Company _____ From (date) _____

Address of Company _____ to present _____

　　Description of duties and responsibilities in the above company.

<u>Job Title</u>

Name of Company _____ From (date) _____

Address of Company _____ to (date) _____

　　Description of duties and responsibilities in the above company.

<u>Job Title</u>

Name of Company _____ From (date) _____

Address of Company _____ to (date) _____

　　Description of duties and responsibilities in the above company.

<u>References</u>: Available on Request

SAMPLE RESUME LAYOUT #4

_____ Name

Street Address
City, State, Zip Code
Home Phone #
Business Phone #

Employment History

    <u>Job Title</u>
    Name and Address of Company_____

    Description of job, giving duties and responsibilities.

                      From (date) to present _____
    <u>Job Title</u>
    Name and Address of Company_____

    Description of job, giving duties and responsibilities.

                      From (date) to (date) _____

<u>Educational History</u>
    Name and Address of College_____
    Degree Received   From (date) to (date) _____

<u>References</u>: Available on Request

SAMPLE RESUME LAYOUT #5

Name

Street Address   Home Phone #
City, State, Zip Code   Business Phone #

Career Objective   To work as a . . .

Employment History

From (date) _____   Job Title—Name of Company _____
to Present _____   Address of Company _____

                          Description of duties and responsibilities in
                          this position.

From (date) _____   Job Title—Name of Company _____
to (date) _____   Address of Company _____

                          Description of duties and responsibilities in
                          this position.

From (date) _____   Job Title—Name of Company _____
to (date) _____   Address of Company _____

                          Description of duties and responsibilities in
                          this position.

Educational History   Degree—Name of College _____
                                   Address of College _____

References   Furnished on Request

5

The Cover Letter

A cover letter should be enclosed every time you send out or fax your resume. In the case of a fax, a fax cover sheet is not necessary. The cover letter is sufficient. Its enclosure is not only an act of courtesy but a means of adding a personal touch. It gives each individual you approach an indication of your personal attention to his or her situation—which would not be the case if the resume arrived unaccompanied. The cover letter also neutralizes the tone of the impersonal, reproduced resume.

This is your chance to let your individual style, personality, and unique strengths stand out from the crowd. Don't be afraid to "sell" yourself here by describing some unique incident or experience. If you wish to do something flamboyant, the cover letter, rather than the resume, is the place to do it.

Our corporate experts tell us they are much more likely to read a resume accompanied by a cover letter than one received without a letter. The letter removes the look of a mass mailing.

It doesn't matter whether you are sending your resume in answer to an ad, to an employment agency, or as part of your personal mailing campaign. The cover letter will always follow the same, simple rules. It should be brief—limited to one page and no more than four paragraphs. Needless to say, it should be neatly typed and conform to the standards of business correspondence.

Whenever possible, address your cover letter to a particular individual in the company, preferably by name and title. If it is impossible to ascertain the name, address the letter to "Personnel Director" or, by title, to the head of the department in which you are hoping to work. In answering an ad, however, address your letter as the ad indicates. If there is no more than a box number, simply address it to that box number and start with the salutation, "To whom it may concern."

An effective cover letter is a very calculated self-marketing tool and follows key guidelines. A cover letter has three paragraphs with three distinct objectives:

1. Get the reader's attention.
2. State professional experience and accomplishments along with the benefit to the company.
3. Close for the reader to take action and call you.

The purpose of the first paragraph is to get the reader's attention. This is where you interject a few outstanding facts or features about yourself. A student once applied this advice after one of my college seminars. He had cleaned pools all through school. He felt that there was nothing about cleaning pools that would get anyone's attention in his cover letter. In actuality, he increased his customer base from 35 to 50 over the years. That should get anyone's attention. He also remained a faithful and loyal employee all through college. He put these "attention getters" in the first paragraph of his cover letter. Not too long after that, he began to get interviews and landed a job with a major telecommunications company making $50,000 a year! As you can see, it's not always what you did, but it's how you perceive yourself and how you say it.

The first paragraph of your letter determines whether or not the reader continues to read. Just as in a newspaper article, the first sentence or "lead" should be original and informative, and it should set the tone for the rest of the letter. It should tell why you are writing to that particular person or company. If it is an answer to an ad, say so, and give the name and date of the publication where the ad appeared. If the letter is part of your direct mail campaign, explain in two or three lines either why you would like to work for that particular company or why you feel their hiring you would be in their company's best interest. A frequent mistake in cover letters is to describe why the job is in the candidate's best interest, rather than to stress what the candidate can do for the employer. For example, to say "I believe your firm can offer me the dynamic challenges and responsibilities I seek" does not convince a recruiter of what you have to offer that company.

If you have a friend inside the company who suggested you contact this particular company, you should give the name, title, or job category, and the department where the friend is employed.

Some typical opening lines are:

"Dorothy Johnson, a programmer in the systems programming department, suggested that I write to you."

"I am replying to your ad, which appeared in The New York Times *on Sunday, May 12."*

"Your recent acquisition of Zebulon Textiles Company led me to believe that you might be interested in my nine years of experience as a marketing manager with extensive industry experience."

The second paragraph of a cover letter should tell the manager or recruiter the benefits of hiring you. Don't just give him or her the facts. State the benefits about these facts and how the facts relate to the company. It is not sufficient to say you have received extensive training. Give the benefit, too. Explain that as a result of this training, there will be minimal learning time and immediate results. Now the recruiter can visualize what your training will mean once you are employed. Don't always assume that the reader or listener will make this correlation. You have to do it for him or her. Without stating a benefit, the person you're writing to or speaking with has no clue how it will profit him or her. This same technique can be used effectively at an interview.

Be absolutely positive that you understand how to utilize this technique. It is extremely valuable. Complete the following worksheet. It will be good practice. The first two are done for you.

PERSONAL STATEMENTS AND BENEFITS WORKSHEET

Statement	Benefit
1. I have extensive computer and word-processing experience.	1. You will save both time and money because I will need little or no training.
2. My organizational skills are exceptional.	2. Because I am so organized, I am usually able to provide my manager with information quickly, saving time and minimizing problems.
3. I get along with others very well.	
4. At my previous place of employment, I had perfect attendance.	
5. Working long hours and sticking with a task until completion is how I get things done when necessary.	
6. It is my belief to always deliver more than what is expected.	
7. In my free time, I like to play sports and volunteer at the local Rescue Mission.	
8. I am always eager to learn to try new things.	
9. My friends and co-workers always comment on how reliable and punctual I am.	
10. I am career oriented and take my work seriously.	

Use the cover letter to describe special projects in which you played a key role, or the unusual features of a program you worked on. Another frequent use of the cover letter is to summarize your achievements in a somewhat more readable form than the optional summary portion of the resume.

Because different aspects of your resume are highlighted in each cover letter, the same resume can be used to pursue different job opportunities. The cover letter stresses your most appropriate skills and talents and can be geared uniquely to each particular company that will receive your resume.

The third paragraph is very easy to construct and is the most important in many ways. However, many individuals just seem to have a hard time doing it. Close for action! Get the reader to call you. The companies that send you marketing mail know the value of closing for action. They want you to call them and order. You want the reader to take action, to pick up the phone and call you. Write, "When can we arrange an interview? I can be reached at . . . [and give them your telephone number]."

Do not make statements such as: "Hope to hear from you soon. [or] Thank you for your consideration. I'll be calling you next week." The first phrase sounds weak. The second phrase sets you up for a secretary who is going to make sure that you don't get through. You are in a better position to interview and negotiate if they call you.

When an employer calls you, it means that they have a sincere interest in you. This places you in a much better position to sell yourself at the interview and, later, to negotiate your salary. If you must call them, don't announce it in your letter. Just call them a week to 10 days after your letter was sent.

Do not try to get a job with only your resume and cover letter! Companies do not hire someone because a resume and cover letter looked good. Companies do set up *interviews* for people with good resume and cover letters. The interview is where you actually sell yourself and get a job offer.

TYPES OF COVER LETTERS

There are several situations that require you to mail your resume and cover letter. These are:

- A response to an ad
- An unsolicited inquiry to a targeted employer as part of your direct mail campaign
- A letter to an employment agency
- A letter to a friend or colleague who might offer assistance in a job search

RESPONSE TO AN AD

Read the ads carefully, marking or clipping those of interest to you. Examine the requirements thoroughly. Employers advertise for the "ideal" candidate and, more often than not, actually hire an individual not possessing every qualification listed in the original ad. For that reason, it is a good idea to reply not only to those ads that fit you perfectly, but also to those for which you meet just some of the requirements.

Now reread each ad you intend to answer. Study each separately. Assume that the requirements are rank ordered, and deal with each as sequenced in the ad. List on a piece of scratch paper every qualification, skill, strength, or accomplishment you possess relevant to the particular advertisement. If you don't have all the requirements, make a note of any experience in either your education or work history that demonstrates other capabilities that would make you an asset to that particular company. Write and rewrite this information until you have eliminated all excess words. Communicate your strengths clearly and succinctly. Work on your letter until each idea flows effortlessly to the next. Let's look at a typical ad and consider how to respond to it.

Sales Manager/Travel

Famous-brand "Last Ever" sporting goods offers excellent opportunity. Territory includes N.Y., Mass., Vt., N.H., Me. Must have previous sales and travel experience. Salary, commission, bonus. Car & travel expenses plus complete benefits. Write Box 6214.

An appropriate reply can be found later in this chapter. Address your letter to the company and person listed in the ad, or simply to the Personnel Director if no individual's name is listed.

It's a good idea to research each company whose ad you intend to answer, and then include in your letter any new information you have become aware of: an expansion, a recent or imminent merger, an acquisition, or new product developments or services. Mention how you would be able to help the organization implement or maximize its current goals. (Obviously, if the ad lists only a box number, this will not be possible.)

Don't be discouraged if you don't get an immediate response. We've found that it is not unusual for a recruiter to hold resumes for more than six weeks or longer before setting up interviews.

This is one situation where you must not be shy. Don't be afraid to take the initiative; telephone the recruiting director or even the department manager, if you know his or her name, to arrange a time for a personal interview.

DIRECT MAIL LETTER

A successful technique in a job campaign is to select a number of employers of your choice and simply send each a copy of your resume with an individually written cover letter. Compile a list of prospective employers using professional journals, business directories, and other references. Learn as much as possible about the companies you have chosen. Address the letter to a specific person. Call the company and ask for the name of the personnel manager. Be sure to have the name spelled correctly.

Don't let this research overwhelm you; you're looking for a minimum of facts. If you are planning to send out 50 or more letters, research the 10 or 12 companies in which you have the most interest. For the remaining organizations, it is enough to simply address the letter to the appropriate person and then mention the company name once or twice in the body of your letter. In essence, you are trying to make the letter appear as personal as possible, bearing in mind that most people don't read form letters.

In each letter, point out the particular strengths and accomplishments that would be of interest to the reader and indicate where they are described in your resume. The tone of the letter should generate interest in you. Refer to a particular qualification that will demonstrate why it would be particularly advantageous to the potential employer to add you to its staff. Always discuss how you can be of value to them rather than how they can help you.

LETTER TO STAFFING SERVICES

Start by calling each target employment agency and executive search firm in your area, and talk with—or get the name of—the highest-ranking individual. In some cases, you might set up a meeting; in other instances, you'll get "permission" to send your resume. For out-of-town agencies or persons whose names are unavailable, simply address your cover letter to the president.

The purpose of your letter is to set up a conversation with the appropriate recruiter in each agency—best done in person, second best by phone. Request that your resume be kept on file so that you can be notified of any suitable job openings. Though we recommend that you discuss your feelings concerning relocation, the covering letter is not the place to mention salary requirements. You should keep your cover letter brief, but at the same time make reference to your strengths.

Frequently, executive recruiters rewrite resume (not always to the candidate's advantage). You must ask them to show you your "rewritten" resume before it is sent to a potential employer. We cannot emphasize this too strongly!

The last paragraph, similar to the other types of cover letters, should include an indication that you will phone in a week or so to set up either a phone or a personal interview.

LETTER TO COLLEAGUE OR FRIEND

Colleagues, friends, or relatives can often be an excellent source of leads. For that reason, you should give them a copy of your resume. When sending your resume, include a short, informal note instead of a businesslike covering letter. The note should simply say that you're in the process of seeking employment or attempting to change jobs and would appreciate any suggestions he or she can offer. You might mention how you feel about relocation. Also let them know if your job search is confidential.

Don't discuss your salary requirements, but you might ask if it would be useful to send additional resumes.

SAMPLE COVER LETTERS

On the following pages are sample cover letters. You may wish to use one as an example to follow, or parts from different letters. Never copy them exactly. Use these samples as guides to create your own letter that will reflect your own style and personality. Then use your cover letter to point out your unique strengths and why the company would benefit from hiring you.

16 4th Street
Ft. Lauderdale, Florida 33311
(954) 162-4690

April 19, 20XX

Mr. James Arter
Personnel Director
Sun & Tan, Inc.
1200 Biscayne Blvd.
Miami, Florida 33125

Dear Mr. Arter:

Please find the enclosed resume in response to your advertisement for Sales, which appeared in the *Miami Herald* on Sunday, April 13, 20XX.

I have had eight years' experience selling cosmetics and hair products for Jackson and Andrews. In this position, I was responsible for the Florida, Alabama, and Georgia territory.

Realizing that this summary, as well as my resume, cannot adequately communicate my qualifications in-depth, I would appreciate having the opportunity to discuss with you in person how I might become an asset to your company. When can we set up an appointment for an interview? I look forward to meeting you.

Sincerely,

Amy Lawson

Amy Lawson

Encl.

RESPONSE TO AN AD

200 Erie Avenue
Rochester, N.Y. 14610
(716) 681-1144

May 12, 20XX

Box 6214
Rochester Times
10 Broad Street
Rochester, N.Y. 14610

To Whom It May Concern:

I enclose my resume in response to your Last Ever sales advertisement in the *Rochester Times* on Sunday, May 4.

My sales/marketing background includes an eight-year association with Gordon's Sporting Goods, Inc., where I was in charge of developing the New England territory. This involved recruiting, training, and working with the sales force. It was also my responsibility to develop and implement sales/marketing plans and strategies in support of the field sales effort.

I am presently employed as Sales Manager of Woodrow and Martin, Inc., a men's clothing manufacturer. I am very eager to return to the sporting goods industry.

In my present position, I call on, sell, and service mass merchandisers, retail chains, department stores, and military exchanges. I achieved success in these and other related activities, and enjoy the fine rapport and reputation developed through my ability to communicate and work with people on all levels.

I am a results-oriented manager who enjoys traveling and working with people, motivating them, and developing their skills to maximum potential. It would be difficult to indicate every area of expertise in my resume; therefore, I would appreciate meeting with you to discuss my qualifications for this position in greater detail.

I may be reached at the above phone number to set up an appointment for an interview.

Sincerely,

Harry Ellis

Harry Ellis

29 Ridge Road
Elmira, New York 10623
Phone (607) 439-2343

April 14, 20XX

Box X3349
New York Guardian
749 East 56th Street
New York, New York 10022

Dear Sir:

I am replying to your advertisement of this date offering a position as copy editor on a sports car publication.

As my resume demonstrates, I have my B.S. in journalism and have been working as copywriter and assistant copy editor on magazines for the past six years.

Your ad specified an interest in and knowledge of sports cars. I did not feel it appropriate to mention it in my resume, but I am the owner of one of the few surviving Type 57 Bugattis in this country, and have rebuilt and maintain the car myself. The car is registered with the Bugatti Club of America, to which I also belong. As you can see, I have established credentials as a sports car enthusiast.

Please contact me at your convenience to explore my background further.

I appreciate your consideration.

Yours truly,

Anthony Lo Bello

Anthony Lo Bello

Encl.

RESPONSE TO AN AD

16 Chilton Street
Cleveland, Ohio 40612
Phone: (216) 223-3344

April 9, 20XX

Mr. George Teasdale
Personnel Manager
United Chemical Corporation
452 Sorrent Drive
Teterbora, New Jersey 11402

Dear Mr. Teasdale:

I am replying to your advertisement in the April issue of *Cosmetic Chemistry*.

My work with Basic Pharmaceutical's Anesthetic and Analgesic Division consisted primarily of developing and testing non-oleaginous bases for topical anesthetics. The bases, of course, had to be broadly anti-allergic if they were to be of commercial value and were tested for same. Our procedures, in both development and testing, were similar to those used in the cosmetic industry, and our tests were at least as rigorous.

My resume also shows, as your ad requested, heavy quantitative analysis and quality control experience.

We should speak further. I will be in New York for the Pharmaceutical Chemists' Society meeting next month. When can we arrange an interview for that time?

Thank you for your consideration.

Yours truly,

John Villiers

John Villiers

Enclosure

320 Garrity Drive
Chicago, Illinois 11625
Phone: (312) 996-6421

May 24, 20XX

Mr. Henry Wilford
President
Seafarer's Museum
Xenobia, Maine 10874

Dear Mr. Wilford:

I am applying for a position with your museum as I feel my experience in developing a museum sales department will be of interest to you.

As my resume indicates, I held the position as Sales Manager of Woodbury Reconstruction Company for six years. In this capacity, I developed a mail order sales department and created a successful bookshop specializing in native crafts.

I expect to be in the vicinity of Xenobia in the first week of July. When could we arrange an interview for that time? As I am currently employed, I would appreciate this be kept in confidence.

Your consideration is greatly appreciated.

Sincerely yours,

Richard Shelton

Richard Shelton

Enclosure

14 Seagate Avenue
Grand Rapids, Michigan 49505

September 3, 20XX

Mr. Ernest Chapman
Vice President for Marketing
Cargon & Fuller, Inc.
280 Wall Street
Grand Rapids, Michigan 49505

Dear Mr. Chapman:

I believe my 10 years of solid marketing background would be an asset to Cargon & Fuller, Inc.

In my association with General Dynamics, Inc., I was responsible for increasing sales of a $40 million product line between 15% and 34% in 20 markets after years of consistent decline. I also reversed continual losses of what once was a $150 million profit center and restored profitability to several smaller operations scheduled for write-offs. In addition, I have been successful in opening market areas previously unknown to the company.

As you will see from the enclosed resume I am also experienced in new product development, acquisitions, licensing, and export. When can we set up an appointment to discuss a sales or marketing position with your firm? I may be reached at 616/757-7775.

Sincerely,

Samuel Davis

Samuel Davis

2121 Toronto Street
Buffalo, NY 14229

May 19, 20XX

Mr. Arthur Bigelow
Personnel Director
Niagara Industries, Inc.
10 Chambers Street
Buffalo, NY 14281

Dear Mr. Bigelow:

In September 20XX, I will receive my Bachelor of Arts Degree in Marketing from the University of Buffalo, and I am interested in obtaining an entry-level position with your company. Friends have told me about Niagara, Inc., and I understand you have a superior marketing department.

My undergraduate studies covered a wide range, with concentrations in statistics, economics, and law as well as in marketing. As such, I believe I have a strong business background and would work well in your organization.

I have enclosed my resume showing my work experience during summers and part-time employment while in college. From this information, you will see that I am an active, motivated person and will continue this aggressiveness with your organization.

I look forward to meeting you. When can we set up an appointment for an interview? I may be reached at 716/225-4422.

Sincerely,

Caroline Houston

Caroline Houston

DIRECT MAIL CAMPAIGN

26 James Street
Chicago, Illinois 60602
Phone: (313) 656-4399

April 6, 20XX

Mr. John Anderson
Personnel Director
Digital Corporation
Detroit, Michigan 51073

Dear Mr. Anderson:

I am a graduate student in Computer Science at Yale University, and I will be awarded an M.S. degree in June 20XX. I am currently looking for a position related to Database/Graphics Package Design in the research and development department of a major company.

Before coming to Yale, I designed, supervised, and completed a CAD system. The function covers vector, character and curve generation, windowing, shading, and transformations.

At Yale, my research work involves Compilation of Relational Queries into Network DML. To enhance my background, I have taken some courses in computer graphics and databases, and I have experience in and an understanding of the design of databases. With this strong background, I certainly believe that I am competent to meet challenging tasks and can make a good contribution to your company.

Enclosed is my resume, which indicates in some detail my training and experience. I sincerely hope that my qualifications are of interest to you and that an interview might be arranged at your convenience.

Thank you for your consideration. I look forward to hearing from you soon.

Sincerely yours,

Martha Levine

Martha Levine

Encl.

19 Bayside Lane
Bethesda, MD 21058

July 21, 20XX

Mr. Robert Nash
Vice-President of Sales
Nelson & Murphy Inc.
2100 Broad Street
Baltimore, MD 21245

Dear Mr. Nash:

I am applying for a position as Sales Manager with your company, as I feel my background in developing a sales department will be of interest to you.

As my resume indicates, I joined Kobin, Inc., in the capacity of a trainee and moved up the ladder to my current position of Sales Manager. In each year of my employment, I was successful in opening new accounts, penetrating existing ones, and reopening closed businesses. As a result, I was responsible for sales increases of 20% to 25%.

As sales manager I was involved in recruiting, training, and supervising a staff of 120 salespeople and was responsible for sales worldwide.

I am looking forward to meeting you. When can we set up an appointment for an interview? I may be reached at 301/665-6728.

Sincerely,

James Wilson

James Wilson

DIRECT MAIL CAMPAIGN

1900 Hillside Terrace
Boston, MA 02126
Phone: 617/778-9086

April 15, 20XX

Mr. Donald Reed
Personnel Director
Chase & Morris, Inc.
615 Main Street
Boston, MA 02120

Dear Mr. Reed:

I am writing to you today in hope you will read my resume and consider me for a marketing position with your company.

I was very interested in the article about your company that appeared in *The New York Times* on April 1, 20XX. Your paternalistic policy, which involves a "no turnover" company, complies with both my short-term and long-range goals, as I am really interested in a stable opportunity.

As my resume indicates, I offer 12 years of solid marketing experience. In my association with Stanley, Inc., my present employer, gross sales have increased by $15 million due to a concentrated Product Marketing Plan I introduced.

I was also responsible for the development of strategies and implementation of a direct mail strategy for seven new packages and five offers, which resulted in a package that beat the control by 250%.

Please call at your convenience to set up an interview. Your consideration is greatly appreciated.

Sincerely yours,

Adam Stane

Adam Stane

Encl.

DIRECT MAIL CAMPAIGN

1800 Harrison Road
Los Angeles, CA 90063

April 30, 20XX

Martha Livingston
Personnel Manager
Vogue Patterns, Inc.
100 Pace Street
Los Angeles, CA 90002

Dear Miss Livingston:

I believe my 10 years of accounting experience might be an asset to Vogue Patterns and therefore I have enclosed my resume for your consideration.

I seek a stable opportunity and strongly identify with your firm's mission to keep employee turnover low, while rewarding strong performance and productivity. My own work ethic is modeled after this same value system.

In my 10-year association with Helene Curtis, I was fully responsible for the preparation of monthly consolidated financial statements for management and public reporting—Forms 10K, 10-2, and the Annual Report to Shareholders—and shared responsibility with the Corporate Controller in maintaining operating units compliance with the FASB and SEC pronouncements.

When can we set up an interview? I may be reached at 310/223-2260. Your consideration is greatly appreciated.

Sincerely,

Anita Parsons

Anita Parsons

Encl.

110 Tenth Ave.
New York, NY 10011

May 10, 20XX

Miss Anne Tully,
Personnel Director
Deeth & Johnson, Inc.
165 Madison Avenue
New York, NY 10016

Dear Miss Tully:

In June 20XX, I will receive my Bachelor of Arts degree from Columbia University and I am interested in obtaining an entry-level accounting position with your company.

As you will see from the enclosed resume, I majored in accounting, minored in economics, and maintained a 3.2 grade average from my freshman through senior years. For the past three summers, I have been employed as a temporary accounting clerk by Career Blazers Temporary Personnel, Inc., and my assignments have included such agencies as Benton & Baroles, Cunningham & Walsh, and B.B.D. & Gray. These assignments convince me that my ultimate career goal lies in the advertising industry.

Not noted in my resume is my intention of returning to Columbia University's evening sessions to pursue an MBA in accounting and business.

I will call early next week to set up an appointment for an interview. I am confident that I have the qualifications to become an asset to Deeth & Johnson.

Sincerely,

Karen Reed

Karen Reed

106 East End Ave.
New York, NY 10028
(212) 874-3614

January 16, 20XX

Walker Associates
517 Fifth Ave.
New York, NY 10017

Gentlemen:

I would appreciate it if you would place my enclosed resume in your files.

I graduated from Ohio State University in 1990 and my 10 years of financial experience consist of 4 years as controller of a ladies' ready-to-wear manufacturer, three years as assistant controller in a sportswear firm, and 3 years as an accountant with a book publisher.

My "hands-on" operations experience has included developing professional accounting, reporting, and data processing functions. My strengths include problem-solving, producing order out of confusion, and getting things done.

I would like to discuss my salary requirements when we meet at a personal interview. Because my time is flexible, I am available to meet you at your convenience. I shall call early next week to set up an appointment.

Sincerely,

Kenneth Newman

Kenneth Newman

18 Dogwood Lane
Hastings, NY 10706

June 16, 20XX

Mrs. Dorothy Mitchell
Career Blazers Agency, Inc.
590 Fifth Ave.
New York, NY 10036

Dear Mrs. Mitchell:

Thank you for taking the time to discuss opportunities available to me through Career Blazers. As I mentioned in our conversation, I have nearly as much paralegal as legal secretarial experience. However, my interest at this time lies in the area of paralegal.

I am enclosing 10 copies of my resume as you suggested. You will notice that I have emphasized my paralegal expertise. I am particularly interested in a position in the metropolitan area and would consider a temporary assignment if it had potential to become permanent.

I expect to be in New York City in early July. Let's get in touch before then to set up another meeting. I may be reached at 914/536-2909.

Sincerely,

Allen Oxman

Allen Oxman

Enclosure

14 Sommers St.
Newburgh, NY 12550

May 10, 20XX

Miss Lynn Brown
Career Blazers Agency, Inc.
590 Fifth Ave.
New York, NY 10036

Dear Miss Brown:

I've been told by several personnel directors in the publishing field that Career Blazers specializes in placing recent college graduates. I will receive my Bachelor of Arts degree in English from Skidmore College in September 20XX, and am interested in obtaining an editorial position with a book or magazine publisher.

As my resume indicates, I maintained a 3.5 average for my four years in college and worked as an Administrative Assistant for the Skidmore Office of University Systems for three years (1996–1998), part-time during school and full-time through the summers and other vacations. I am an excellent typist, and though I am not looking for a secretarial position, I would be willing to exchange my typing skill and secretarial expertise for an entry-level position with potential.

I am looking forward to meeting you in the near future and will call you early next month to set up an interview.

Yours truly,

Nancy Hanks

Nancy Hanks

1900 Driftwood Drive
No. Miami Beach, Florida 33160

August 25, 20XX

Ms. Nola Chestor
Management Recruiters, Inc.
180 Collins Avenue
Miami, Florida 33139

Dear Ms. Chestor:

I am enclosing a copy of my resume in hopes that your firm may assist me in locating a position as Corporate Controller with a Fortune 500 company.

As my resume indicates, I have 10 years' experience in Financial Management and Control, having served in the past as Treasurer, Controller, Corporate Accountant, Consolidation Manager, and Director of Financial Planning. In my present position at Thompson Chemical Corp., I initiate, develop, and supervise all internal audits.

As I have not yet given notice, I would appreciate your discretion in this matter.

I am looking forward to meeting you in person, at which time I can explain in depth both my qualifications and aspirations. I will call early next week to set up a personal meeting.

Yours truly,

Warren Barth

Warren Barth

16 South Street
Darien, Connecticut 06490

February 8, 20XX

Ms. Patricia Schwartz
Taft Computer Company
1800 Broad Street
Philadelphia, Pennsylvania 20171

Dear Patricia:

It was a very pleasant surprise running into you at the Philadelphia Computer Show this morning. I have enclosed my resume so that it may be circulated to the appropriate department heads when you contact them.

As we discussed today, I am interested in working for Taft in the Philadelphia area and in dealing with customers. An experienced software specialist, I have proposed, planned, designed, managed, developed, and delivered major software systems to users. Project management of a multiperson effort has been the primary responsibility of my latest job. In addition to having management and technical skills, I enjoy people, giving presentations, and consulting. Taft appears to offer opportunities in marketing, customer support, and development that would use my computing expertise, along with my verbal abilities.

Having recently delivered a significant software application, I would like to begin a new challenge as soon as possible.

Talking with you was a pleasure and has given me a very positive impression of Taft Computer Company.

When can we meet again to further explore the next step in our discussion? I may be reached at 203/561-3426.

Yours truly,

Carl Ferguson

Carl Ferguson

encl.

474 Hardscrabble Road
Millville, New York 10901

April 4, 20XX

Ms. Bernice Luddington
Art Director
Abington's Department Store
1502 Mamaroneck Avenue
White Plains, New York 10603

Dear Ms. Luddington:

The controller of your Paramus branch, William Scott, who is a neighbor of mine, has told me that you have an opening for a display designer in your White Plains store.

As you can see from my resume, I had extensive experience in the field prior to the birth of my first child. While I have been unable to seek employment in the field for several years, I have kept my hand in by designing displays of art and handicrafts as a volunteer at our local library.

My youngest child is now in high school and able to take care of himself. In addition, my sister lives nearby and has agreed to take care of any emergency that might arise; so, I will be able to devote myself wholeheartedly to my job.

I would welcome an opportunity to speak with you. When can we meet? Please call 914/989-3214 at your convenience.

Thank you for your consideration.

Yours sincerely,

Helen Fries

Helen Fries

Enclosure

95 Valentine Lane
Melville, NY 11747
Phone: (516) 894-3241

June 8, 20XX

Ms. Jane Raymond
Personnel Director
North Bank of America
White Plains, NY 10603

Dear Ms. Raymond:

Mr. John Smith, an executive in your Manhattan office who is a friend of my father, suggested I write to you about the possibility of an opening in your international department.

As you can see from my resume, I am a French major and Spanish minor and am very interested in a position where I can use my knowledge of languages. I have worked as an office temporary for the past three summers and some of my assignments were in the banking field. I am proficient in several software packages, including MS Word, Excel, and Power Point, and would be willing to use these skills in an administrative capacity, as long as there would be an opportunity to move into a more challenging role once I have proven my capabilities and value to the organization.

I would like very much to meet you and am available for an interview any time convenient to you.

Sincerely yours,

John Osterio

John Osterio

3200 Bayview Drive
Scarsdale, NY 10583

April 11, 20XX

Ms. Claire Lunt
Beacon Press, Inc.
16 W. 49th St.
New York, NY 10020

Dear Ms. Lunt:

Rita Marks, an editorial assistant with your company, told me of your plans to expand your accounting department. For that reason, plus my avocational interest in books, I am enclosing a copy of my resume in hopes that my background will be of interest to you.

I am a graduate of Columbia University (June 1995) with a degree in accounting and economics, which emphasized taxation and managerial accounting. I will receive a Master of Business Administration from Columbia University in June 2002. For the past three summers I worked as an accounting clerk with Shiller & Rogers and, because some of their clients are involved in publishing, I have gained some actual experience in accounting for the book industry.

I have the education, experience, potential, and enthusiasm to be successful with your firm and would appreciate an opportunity for a personal interview. When can we set up a time to meet? At your convenience, I may be reached at 914/998-7456.

Sincerely,

Lillian Robbins

Lillian Robbins

119 Grattan Ave.
Oyster Bay, NY 11771
Phone: (516) 295-3344

December 19, 20XX

Roger Smaridge, Controller
General Rent-A-Car, Inc.
118 W. Second Avenue
Dayton, OH 45424

Dear Mr. Smaridge:

Nadine Foster, an attorney with your company and a longtime friend, recently told me about an opening for a tax accountant at General Rent-A-Car, Inc. I feel that I am extremely qualified for that position and I have enclosed a resume for your consideration.

As you can see from my resume, I have over 10 years' experience in the area of tax accountancy. In my present position with the Whitney Bowes Credit Corporation, I am heavily involved in property and sales tax research, which includes finding solutions to problems unique to the leasing industry. I am also responsible for any property tax appeals and audits that might affect Whitney Bowes. I have also gained expertise in the preparation of income and franchise tax in selected states.

I would appreciate an opportunity for a personal meeting, at which time I hope I can explain why I would be a very important asset to General Rent-A-Car.

When can we set up an interview? I may be reached, at your convenience, at the above phone number.

Yours truly,

Patrick Johnson

Patrick Johnson

41 Cumberland Drive
Scarsdale, New York 10583

September 18, 20XX

Mr. Bob Brody, President
Walker Brody Personnel, Inc.
509 Fifth Avenue
New York, New York 10017

Dear Mr. Brody:

Bill Lewis of Career Blazers Personnel Services, Inc. suggested you might be of assistance to me in my desire to find new employment. I became acquainted with Bill while I was Assistant Controller at Parker Press.

As you can see from my enclosed resume, all of my accounting experience has been in publishing. I started with R. R. Majors, Inc., then Parker Press, and am presently employed as Controller in Walker & Walker & Co. As you've probably heard, Walker & Walker is moving to Washington, DC, and because it is now imperative that I remain in the metropolitan area, I am available for a new position. Bill spoke very highly of you and I am looking forward to getting together with you to discuss my background and qualifications in depth.

Let's get in touch at your convenience to arrange a meeting. I can be reached at 914/567-7255.

Yours truly,

Bob Miller

Bob Miller

1440 N.W. 56th Ave.
Tampa, FL 33610

July 17, 20XX

Dear Mike,

I'm finally taking your advice and have decided to pull up stakes and make the move to New York City.

Just last week I gave notice at Peat & Marvich, and I think we actually found a buyer for our condo down here. We plan to move in with Jan's mother and then slowly look for either a co-op in the city or ultimately buy a house in Westchester County.

As you probably remember, all of my experience has been in public accounting, but I would consider any opportunity that offers both stability and potential.

I'd really appreciate any suggestions you might have that could be helpful in finding a job. If you know any employment agencies or executive recruiters that specialize in financial personnel, please let me know of them.

I'm enclosing a few copies of my resume. Because I've already given notice, please feel free to circulate them.

We should be in New York in mid-September and will call as soon as we get settled. Jan and I are looking forward to seeing you and Louise again.

Yours truly,

Bill

19 Seneca Lake Avenue
Elmira, NY 14901

November 19, 20XX

Ms. Phyllis Grey
General Elevator, Inc.
1200 Meadow Drive
Elmira, NY 14901

Dear Ms. Grey,

John Evans, a programmer with your company, suggested I send my resume to you. John and I met while we attended Hobart College.

As my resume indicates, I have solid background in sales and though I haven't had industrial experience, I minored in electrical engineering and feel I have an aptitude in any technical area. I understand that you are expanding your sales staff, and I would greatly appreciate your consideration.

I look forward to meeting you in the near future and getting in touch early next week.

Yours truly,

George Clancy

George Clancy

140 Wenkover Road
Cleveland, Ohio 44112
March 30, 20XX

Dear Yvette,

I ran into Dick Smith last week and he suggested I get in touch with you. Gene has been transferred to Dallas, so I have decided to leave Pacific Records and try to get a job in that area.

Since I last saw you, I've been promoted to a marketing position but will consider any opportunity in either marketing or sales. I would prefer a job without a lot of travel but will consider any opportunity as long as it is based in the Dallas area.

I'd really appreciate any suggestions you might have that could be helpful in finding a job. If you know of any employment agencies that place sales and marketing people, please let me know about them.

I'm enclosing six copies of my resume. Since I've already given notice, feel free to circulate them as you see fit.

We should be in Dallas by July. I'm looking forward to seeing you and Jim, and once again being neighbors.

Sincerely,

Margo

1400 State Street
Albany, New York 18246

May 15, 20XX

Dear Ruth,

As you probably know, Paris Records has been sold to National Records and I've been merged out of a job. Though there are a few possibilities in this area, I think this might be the perfect time for me to relocate to Florida. It would be great to be near my old friends and, as you know, I've always loved the warm weather.

I'm hoping that one of your firm's clients has an opening that fits my qualifications. I'm enclosing several copies of my resume for you to circulate at your discretion. Should you need more resumes, please let me know.

I'd really appreciate any suggestions you might have that could be helpful in my finding a job. Can you recommend any search firms/agencies that service the financial field?

I plan to be in Ft. Lauderdale in early July, but could fly down earlier if necessary.

I'm really looking forward to seeing you soon and am grateful for anything you might do.

Love,

Marge

6

Where Do You Find Work?

LOOK AROUND YOU

A job search, like charity, begins at home. Of all the various job sources, the most convenient—and, at times, the best—are your relatives, friends, and neighbors. Almost anyone you know may be able to furnish you with the lead you've been looking for. So if you're in the job market, don't keep it quiet; part of your campaign is to let as may people as possible know that you are job hunting.

Don't be embarrassed about spreading the word. Your friends, too, have been in your position and know that any help is welcome. Were the positions reversed and a friend asked you for help, wouldn't you be eager to assist in any way you could?

Often people who are employed hear of job openings in their companies before the jobs are advertised or listed with employment agencies. Not only are they the first to know about the vacancies, but companies do tend to give preference in hiring to people recommended by their own employees rather than to a complete stranger. At my agency, when following up one of our applicants, we have often found out that the job went to a friend of an employee even though we knew our applicant was a perfect fit with both the job and the company.

Even though a "friend at court" is no guarantee of getting a job, it is far more likely that you will reach the interview stage if recommended by an employee of that company than would someone answering an ad or sent by an agency. In job hunting, you always have to contend with human nature. An employer feels more secure about a prospect referred by someone he knows than about a complete stranger. Wouldn't you?

If you believe that someone you know is going to be instrumental in finding you a job, you might wonder if you shouldn't put off preparing a resume until it's needed. Don't! You should always have an updated resume, even when you are employed. As the old saying goes, "A wise man always keeps his options open." Professionals in any field must be able to supply their credentials at a moment's notice. You never want to miss out on an unforeseen opportunity. If a friend or relative suggests your name to his company, it is almost certain that he or she will get back to you and say, "I've told them about you and they're interested, but first they want to see a resume."

It is often a good idea to give the people you know copies of your resume. It helps them in talking about you to people they think can help you, and in addition, they can speed up the decision process by handing in the resume for you.

Networking is a process that job seekers have used since we evolved from feudal times and individuals sought employment. It is a method of creating an ever-expanding network of people who can help each other accomplish a specific goal, whether it be making a sale, finding an apartment, building a roster of clients, or finding the right job.

Go about your networking in a professional, organized fashion. Start out by making a list of anybody who might supply you with leads: acquaintances of your spouse, people you know from school, adult education courses, PTA, clubs, volunteer or religious groups, and even your doctor, lawyer, or stockbroker. Expand your network by including fraternity brothers or sorority sisters, co-workers, and members of your alumni association.

In addition, put yourself in situations where you are likely to meet people who can help you—political organizations, community groups, class reunions, and professional associations. (To get information about organizations in your field, ask your librarian for such reference books as *Gayles' Encyclopedia of Associations* and the *National Trade and Professional Associations,* Columbia Books, Inc., Washington, DC.)

CLASSIFIED ADS

Read the ads! There is a wealth of information in the classified columns of your newspaper. You may not find the job of your dreams (although you might), but you can learn much about the job market by going over the classified ads. You will see what kinds of jobs are open and can get an idea about salaries in the various fields. Through the ads, you have a means of testing whether the salary you're hoping for is in line with reality, or, for that matter, whether your job expectations are realistic.

When searching the ads, consider all job titles. An opening for a bookkeeper, for example, may be listed under "Accounting;" an administrative assistant's position could be advertised as "Executive Secretary." Don't let the job titles mislead you; read the entire body of the ad. The duties required and the qualifications desired give much more information about the job than its title can. The vocabulary of job hunting can overwhelm you with its confusion. An assistant to an editor might be advertised as "Editorial Assistant," "Secretary to the Editor," "Administrative Assistant," or even "Publishing Assistant."

Be careful not to ignore a good opportunity simply because the job title is not what you might have expected. Be sure to read the classified section carefully and respond to every ad that might be a "possible." Remember, too, that salaries are approximate. Very often jobs are filled at salaries higher or lower than those offered in the ads. Ultimately, salary depends upon the qualifications of the person selected. For this reason, it is advisable to answer all ads (with which your qualifications coincide to some degree) even if the salary offered is in the extreme lower limit of your range. A job listed at $22,000 might be filled eventually at a salary of $25,000, or one advertised as "to $28,000" might go only to $26,000. In addition, a job listed at a salary less than you had anticipated could offer so much growth and opportunity that it might bear investigation.

Because you are looking for the best possible job, it is advisable to explore as many opportunities as possible, to present yourself at as many interviews as you can, and to learn as much about each job offered as you are able. Then, after careful consideration of each job with all of its opportunities, benefits, and ramifications, you accept the one that most closely resembles what you are looking for.

Be sure to follow the directions given in each particular ad. If a phone number is listed and it is requested that you call for an appointment, do so; don't arrive without warning. Some job seekers think that an unannounced arrival shows great enthusiasm. It doesn't. What it does is waste both your time and the interviewer's, and it creates hostility. If a box number is listed, reply by sending your resume with a cover letter as discussed in Chapter 5.

Don't be discouraged if you don't get immediate results. At times, as much as three months can elapse before you receive a response to your resume. Remember that job hunting is harder and more frustrating than working, but once you have had a success in your search, the weeks or even months of anxiety and anguish will be forgotten very quickly.

PRIVATE STAFFING SERVICES

Anyone out job hunting should consider the services of the private staffing services. Their business consists of trying to find the right people for the jobs and the right jobs for the people. They might be able to offer you the help you need. The private agencies recruit and screen applications for many different firms and, therefore, are in a position to introduce you to a number of prospective employers.

Therefore, going to a staffing service is equivalent to applying for a variety of job openings. The agency can describe every opening that it has listed that could be filled by a person with your qualifications and leave you the choice of which ones you want to investigate further. Effectively, the agency does your legwork for you and will keep you informed of new job openings as they arise. Most agencies require resume, and you should be prepared to give them several copies.

Finding the appropriate agency is a very important consideration on the job hunt. Most agencies specialize in certain fields or professions; so, be sure that the agencies you register with handle your skills or professional qualifications. If you are a graduate engineer, there is no point in registering with an agency that specializes in accountants and bookkeepers. Study the agencies' ads in the classified columns of the newspaper; the types of jobs they advertise will generally indicate their area of specialization.

Because employment agencies are completely involved in recruiting, they can be helpful in advice about current job trends and market conditions. Quite often, too, they are able to assume some of the functions of the trained guidance counselor. Because they are in continual touch with the job market, they are able to see that your particular skills may be appropriate to an industry that you had never considered worth investigating.

A few years ago, our agency interviewed a young man who was what is often called "overqualified." He had a Ph.D. in Romance Languages, was completely bilingual in Spanish and English, and had reading and writing ability in French and Italian. He did not want to teach and had followed up what he considered to be every lead for a person of his training—United Nations, foreign embassies and consulates, import-export firms, multinational corporations, and so on. He had refused the offers he had received because he felt that the salaries were completely unrealistic. We agreed with him, but didn't feel we could do anything for him at the moment. His resume was passed around the office and our law desk called one of her accounts that had a heavy international practice. Unfortunately, the applicant needed a law degree to go with the bilingualism. Three days later, however, the law firm called back suggesting we contact an underwriter at a large marine insurance company. The outcome was that the applicant found a job at the managerial level and commensurate pay in a field that he had never considered.

EXECUTIVE RECRUITERS

If you are at a high management level, you may want to check out executive recruiters, who are likely to have positions available in your field and at your level. They differ from staffing services in that they usually only handle positions for midmanagement levels and up. You can purchase a reference book entitled "Directory of Executive Recruiters" in the business sections of most bookstores, or search a copy in the reference section of your public library.

It contains a list of executive recruiters (some with offices all over the world), including their addresses, phone numbers, fields covered, minimum salaries of positions handled, and an indication as to whether each accepts resumes or is willing to set up an interview regarding opportunities in general.

Once you have a list of the agencies you feel can be helpful to you, make an appointment, either by phone or with a letter, for a personal interview at the agency. It is more important to establish a rapport with a few agencies than to make a career of interviewing with many agencies.

The agency will describe every opening they have currently listed that would be relevant to a person with your background. They will leave you the choice of which ones you want to investigate further. Effectively, the agency does your legwork for you and will keep you informed of new job openings as they arise. Most agencies expect and need resumes, and you should be prepared to give them several copies.

Almost every agency will, at a minimum, recopy your resume onto their own letterhead. Many will make helpful suggestions about the content or style of your resume, and frequently they will change the format to one that is standard for their agency. There are pluses and minuses when this happens. Since the agency uses its own paper and format, there will be nothing to distinguish your resume from any other sent out by this agent. So forget about that special paper you may have picked out or the particular type font you may have planned to use. In some cases, agents have actually hurt a candidate's chances by changes they have made on the resume. In one extreme case, the candidate's last name was omitted! In another case, the contents of the resume was changed so radically that it no longer described the candidate. During the interview, one employer asked about something mentioned in the resume and received the reply, "Oh, does it say I did that?"

On the other hand, a good agent can play a critical role in improving your resume and getting that resume in front of a prospective employer. The most important rule to follow when you work with an agent is to make sure that you see and approve the resume that will actually be sent to the prospective employer.

Once the agent presents you with some leads for job openings, it's a good idea to be flexible in terms of which opportunities you are willing to investigate. For example, even though your background may be entirely research oriented and your intention is to continue in this direction, you may find an opportunity in the commercial world much more interesting than you imagined. In fact, frequently if the employer likes the applicant, the job might be redefined in terms of qualifications or salary. Of course, if you don't go on the interview, that can never happen.

It is very important to check back with your counselor after every job interview. This will help the agent have more insight into your unique needs and requirements.

The agent can also play a large role in the salary negotiations once a job offer is to be made. It is always easier to have a third party represent you in negotiations for a higher salary or better conditions.

As mentioned earlier, the agency fees in specialty fields are generally paid by the employer. However, don't hesitate to ask the agency interviewer to clarify any questions about your obligations. As with any other business arrangement, it is best to have a complete understanding of the terms at the very beginning of your relationship.

For an agency to find a job in this manner—where an employer who is unable to take an applicant suggests that the agency try to place him with another company—is not unusual. You have to consider your counselor at the agency as your ally. The agency wants to place you in the best job available for you. That is its function; if the agency wants to stay in business, it must perform it.

STATE AND GOVERNMENT EMPLOYMENT AGENCIES

Another fine source of job leads is the state or government employment agency. Unlike private commercial agencies, government agencies charge no fee to either the job applicant or the employer. Their functions are supported by the government.

If you are serious about your job search, you should visit your local government employment office to avail yourself of its services. In addition to advising you of job openings in the immediate vicinity, the counselors at these agencies can also give you information on obtaining a government job.

GOVERNMENT JOBS

Don't overlook the possibilities that government can offer. The U.S. government employs more than 17 million Americans. One out of six employed persons serves either federal, state, or local governments. The federal government employs 2.8 million, the state government employs 4 million, and local government over 8 million. U.S. government agencies hire 13,000 to 18,000 recent college grads a year. These statistics represent a significant portion of the workforce and, therefore, a government position is an option that should be taken seriously.

The range of job offerings is tremendous. Doctors, attorneys, secretaries, and clerks are employed by the government, as well as teachers, engineers, gardeners, and chauffeurs. Think of a job classification and rest assured that the government employs people in that category. Many people feel that the government jobs offer the most security (or did until the last recession), the best health plans, the most liberal vacations, and the most extensive retirement plans.

The government, perhaps, is the only employer that is not interested in your resume. Governmental positions have precise and inflexible educational and experiential requirements that must be met in order to apply for a given job. All that meeting these requirements entitles you to is the opportunity to take an examination for the job. The examination is both determinative and competitive. That is, you must achieve a certain grade in order to be eligible for the job, but the job will be offered first to the person who achieved the highest score on the test. Depending upon the job, the test may be written, practical, or physical. A sanitation engineer must be strong enough to lift a garbage pail, and a chauffeur must be able to drive, not merely know the traffic rules and the simple repair of a car.

Should you take a test for a government job and not score high enough to fill one of the immediately available openings, you may be eligible for subsequent openings. Usually, each "class" taking the examination retains its eligibility for a certain period of time, and during that time no additional examinations are given. Customarily, examinations are given every six months, every year, or every two or three years. As a rule, if you are still interested in a position when an examination occurs again, you must retake the exam to determine your eligibility.

If you are interested in government employment, you must be very methodical in seeking it out. You must find out what the offerings are that might be available immediately and in the future at every government level. There is no single office that takes care of federal, state, county, and municipal employment; each has to be applied for in its appropriate office.

On the municipal level, a call to your city or town hall will tell you where to go and who to see. For county employment, another phone call will start the ball rolling. On the search for employment with your state government, you should check the phone book to see if there is an office of the State Civil Service Commission (or Personnel Board) near you. If not, you should write to the State Civil Service commission requesting a list of current examinations and job openings.* You should also ask to be put on their regular mailing list, so that you can obtain continuous up-to-date information. On the federal level, surf the net at usajobs.opm.gov.

The main post office in your town will have some information on examinations and openings in the Federal Civil Service. More complete information may be obtained from the nearest local office of the Federal Civil Service Commission or from the main office in Washington, DC. Again, you should request to be put on the regular mailing list. It is worth noting that U.S. government jobs are available abroad as well as within the United States.

If you are interested in government work, read all of the literature available—your local library is a fine source. Take all tests for which you are eligible. There are enormous opportunities in government, and it is likely that your perseverance will get you the job you want.

CHAMBER OF COMMERCE

Your Chamber of Commerce can be extremely helpful in your job search by supplying you with a list of all of the companies in your area. Such a list would be excellent for your personal direct mail campaign. The Chamber of Commerce might also be able to tell you of actual job openings and which companies would be most interested in your skills and qualifications.

TEMPORARY SERVICES

Temporary services can be extremely useful. Not only are they a means of supporting yourself during your job campaign, but they can even help you in getting the kind of job you really want. They are especially valuable to beginners, people in the intermediate level, and those returning to the job market after an absence.

*See also Barron's *How to Prepare for Civil Service Examinations* (Clerks, Typists, Stenographers, and Other Office Positions).

Most job seekers tend to overlook this source. They feel that, as their goal is a *permanent* position, they have nothing to gain by taking temporary employment. On the surface this would appear logical, but it does not consider the fact that a temporary position can be the "foot in the door" you need to get the perfect job opportunity. Quite often, my agency has found that while our permanent division is recruiting for a specific job, our temporary division has sent a "temp" to cover the position until it was filled. We have become accustomed to learning that the "temp" was hired on a permanent basis.

It makes sense. Whereas temps are often hired to provide extra help during an occasional surge in a company's workload or to fill in for a sick or vacationing employee, they are also called in to keep the work from piling up on a desk that has unexpectedly become vacant. Although the original intention is to interview other people to fill the job, the temp is on the spot demonstrating a capability on the job. No longer an unknown applicant, the temp often will be hired ahead of a person replying to an ad offering the permanent position. Often, too, the temp—being a proven worker—will find the salary offer to be higher than that listed in the "specs" for the permanent position.

We had interviewed a highly experienced copywriter who had lost his job because of a slow advertising market. As our permanent division had nothing to offer him at the time, he asked if our temporary division could find him something—*anything*. As he explained, he was basically a lazy person and felt that any length of time collecting unemployment insurance would be psychologically disastrous for him. He also preferred to work as an office temporary rather than be overqualified in a permanent position.

Our temporary division sent him to a major oil company as a data entry clerk. As the gesture wouldn't cost him anything, he took his resume along and left it with personnel. After working a few weeks doing data entry, he was hired for an editorial position on the company's house organ (internal newsletter). This position was not even known to us, as the oil company hadn't gotten around to listing it!

A young woman came to us a few years ago with aspirations of getting into the publishing field. She had no previous experience, having just graduated from college, and in addition, she was job hunting at a time when most publishing houses were cutting back on staff. Desperate for work, she took temporary assignments, going from one company to another working as a word processor. While filling in at the offices of a professional engineering society, she was offered a job as an editorial assistant in their publications department. She called us a short time ago asking us to recruit an editorial assistant for her; she had been promoted to a full editorial position. The most remarkable part is that if we had received a call for an editorial assistant from the engineering society, we never would have sent that woman. In our previous dealings with them, they had always insisted on some engineering background for employees in their publications department. This woman, however, being on the spot, was able to demonstrate that her other skills and her intelligence more than made up for the deficiency in her background.

In the job search, it is always advisable to take an opportunity that lets you get your foot in the door and prove your capabilities. In addition,

Where Do You Find Work?

it also permits you to expand your network by meeting new people. It is not unusual for your supervisor on a temporary job, impressed by your work and having learned that you are marking time until you can find a permanent position, to suggest possibilities and leads that you wouldn't have found otherwise.

Therefore, while working as a temp, it is important to do the best job you can and to let everyone you meet know that you're looking for a permanent position. You never know who will introduce you to your new employers, so bring copies of your resume with you and leave one or two with anyone who shows interest in helping you.

Another advantage of temporary services is that they can be extremely helpful to beginners or to persons who are not yet sure where their interests lie. Temporary work lets you experiment, maybe spending a few days in an advertising agency, perhaps a week or so in an art gallery, or possibly a month with a nonprofit organization. It is a way of seeing how each field works and helping you collect information necessary for a wise and considered career choice.

Working on temporary assignments brings no guarantee of a permanent job offer, but there is a guarantee that you'll meet a variety of people, be exposed to many different kinds of businesses, and experience various distinctive working conditions. Most important of all, you will be gaining additional experience—all of this while getting paid for it! By all means, give serious consideration to doing temporary work while on your quest for a permanent job.

VOLUNTEER WORK

It may seem strange, but occasionally it can be profitable for you to work for nothing. Volunteer work, like temporary work, is a way of meeting people. As we cannot stress enough, the more people you meet, the greater the possibility that someone will be able to point you in the direction of your dream job. Volunteer work can also give you the opportunity to improve skills that are not yet sufficiently developed for remunerative employment.

One of the unexpected delights about volunteer work is that you never know with whom you might be working. Some of those people you see answering the phones on educational television stations during fundraising campaigns are very high-salaried executives of established companies. One of New York's leading industrial designers spends his Saturdays with three other volunteers at the sales desk of a New York museum. The wife of the owner of one of New York's finest French restaurants spends her Wednesday evenings in the company of 10 to 12 other people—most of whom couldn't afford a meal in her husband's establishment—stuffing envelopes for a nonprofit organization.

Not only can you meet people who might help you find a job, but, at times, the volunteer work itself can become a paid position.

The woman who directs the display department of a large upstate New York museum first started with them 10 years ago when it was only a *small* upstate New York museum. Growing nonprofit organizations often recruit new employees from the ranks of their volunteers.

Even if your volunteer work does not lead directly or indirectly to a job, it is a way to spend your free time, and it can possibly fill other voids in your life. You meet people who share interests similar to your own, as well as people who range across a far wider social economic scale than you would normally meet. Even if you ignore the fact that you are doing a "good deed," it is not time wasted.

JOB FAIRS

Attend all job fairs. Job fairs can save you both time and money, and you can literally meet and interview with numerous companies that attend the fair. Usually a hotel ballroom, convention center, or college gymnasium is set up like a trade show. Here, many companies will have a display booth with recruiters available to answer your questions about potential career opportunities. Bring plenty of resumes, dress professionally, and plan on spending the day.

Job fairs are usually announced in the Sunday employment section of your local newspaper. The fairs are sponsored by a number of private job fair companies, local newspapers, and area colleges. To participate in a college job fair, call the college's career office to request the date of their next job fair. They are held twice a year, one in the fall and another in the spring.

Upon arriving early, take your time and network. Keep in mind that you will have to come across as professional and articulate. Every encounter you have with a recruiter becomes the equivalent of a prescreen interview. Use common sense and get names and contacts if a particular recruiter is not currently hiring for the position you are interested in.

WORK-STUDY PROGRAMS

Recently, a man working on his M.B.A. called to request permission to observe our company for a class project. He arrived a few weeks later with his laptop computer and set up shop on one of the break tables. For four weeks, he arrived at 9 A.M. and departed at 5 P.M. just as if he was one of the employees. In fact, his enthusiasm, professional style, and willingness to help out led us to "adopt" him as an employee in this short time. As a result of this endeavor, he is now a top candidate for a specialized position that will become available when he graduates.

Whether or not you are in school, it is a good idea to get involved in your own personal work-study program. Call the human resources director of the company you are interested in and explain that you are on a career fact-finding mission. Make yourself available to assist one of their departments on a voluntary basis for a few weeks. Many hospitals, hotels, and other large companies would welcome your help and enthusiasm. After time spent exhibiting a professional image, demonstrated qualifications, and a good work ethic, you are in a good position to be considered for future positions. Through such a program, it is very likely that you will gain top-level contacts who may even refer you to colleagues in other companies for interviews and potential employment opportunities.

You cannot claim to have done all that is possible to find work if you have not conducted a direct mail campaign, including e-mail. Obviously, your resume will be an integral part of this campaign, so once you have prepared the best possible resume, you are ready to start.

Your next task is to compile a list of possible employers. If you want to work where you live or within commuting distance of your hometown, the Yellow Psges of your telephone directory is one of your best possible sources. If you are willing to relocate, the reference librarian at your local library can refer you to the books you need to compile your list. As a rule, you are not allowed to withdraw these books, but will have to prepare your list in the library's reference room. Because you will probably find that you need other information as you go along, this is not a great inconvenience.

The list does not have to be sent out all at one time. Using a computer-based approach, as we discuss in Chapter 3, you can send out 25 to 50 letters a week. Because a project such as this will take some time, plan on doing it in the evening or on a weekend. Keep your Monday through Friday business hours free for networking and making phone calls to prospective employers. Because every company on the list is going to be sent a cover letter with your resume, you must determine the names and titles of the persons to whom you plan to write. Reference books such as Standard and Poor's can give you this information. Again, the reference librarian can help you.

If you are willing to relocate, do not hesitate to write companies at a distance from your home. Most companies, when approached by a really "hot" applicant, will either send someone to interview the applicant or pay for the applicant's trip to their main offices. If you are willing to relocate, you should say so on your resume; otherwise, the company is apt to assume that you are looking for an opening in their office near your home.

Your cover letter should be brief and written in a conversational but not "cute" tone. Simply say that you are enclosing your resume and would like to be considered for a position in that company. Also, include a short statement indicating why you feel your qualifications will interest the firm. Because you are enclosing a resume, which gives a detailed description of your talents and skills, there is no need to be too verbose in your cover letter.

The letter should never exceed four paragraphs. Your final paragraph should state a "close for action" such as "When can we discuss this further? I may be reached at 212/289-4210." If after a week to 10 days you do not receive a phone call, by all means call and attempt to arrange an interview. The closer you come to personal contact, the closer you are to a job offer.

I cannot overemphasize the need to type *individually* every cover letter. This is why it is to your advantage to utilize a computer in your job search. You may reproduce your resume; never your letter. The letter should have the format of a standard business letter with sufficient margin all around to present an attractive appearance. Don't forget that it is your first introduction to a prospective employer.

7
Following Through

KEEPING A RECORD

Keep a record of each resume sent and note the dates of your calls and interviews. Also, indicate the results of each call and interview, and remember your follow-up letters. Don't leave anything to your memory; maintain a written record.

The simplest way to maintain a record of your direct mail campaign is to make a photocopy of each letter as you finish it. On the bottom of the copy, you can note the date and result of your phone call, date of interview, result of, and follow-up note. These can be kept in a file folder with a separate sheet—or calendar page—with dates and times of interviews noted. It would be disastrous to set up two interviews for the same time.

A second system is to set up a large sheet of paper with column headings across the top of the sheet. The information, of course, would be the same as that maintained by using photocopies. Below is the suggested heading for each column. The headings would be separated by lines drawn vertically down the full length of the sheet, and horizontal lines would be drawn, each about 2 inches below the other, to separate the entries for each company contacted.

Resume Mailing	Follow-up Phone Call	Interview	Thank-you Letter
NAME _____	DATE _____	DATE _____ TIME _____	DATE _____
			Job Offer
TITLE _____	RESULTS _____	INTERVIEWER _____	☐ YES ☐ NO
COMPANY _____	_____	RESULTS _____	**Confirmation or "No Thank-you" Letter**
ADDRESS _____	_____	_____	
_____	_____	_____	DATE _____
_____	_____	_____	☐ CONFIRMED
DATE SENT _____		_____	☐ NO THANK-YOU

Note that record-keeping sheets of this type have been provided on pages 87 through 89 for your convenience.

The third system involves the use of 4-by-6-inch index cards. Again, the information is the same as the other systems. Below is a sample layout for the card:

Mr. Richard Rowe   Mailed 3/22/97
Chief Draftsman
Systems, Inc.
424 Park Place
Buford, PA 21370

Phone Call: _____
                         (indicate date)

(Note results) _____

Interview: _____
                    (indicate date, time, and interviewer)

(Note results) _____

Thank-you Letter _____
                              (indicate date)

Job Offer _____

Confirmation or "No Thank-you" Letter _____
                                  (indicate date and letter type)

This system is the best for a very large mailing. We suggest that you have the index cards printed up cheaply rather than trying to type them yourself.

A direct mail campaign is not an inexpensive way of looking for work, but no way really is. Direct mail involves an expenditure of money—for reproduction of resumes, envelopes, postage, and phone calls—and time. But any other method involves as much time. The difference is that the direct mail time is spent in the comfort of your home instead of on buses, on the pavement, and in waiting rooms. If you are pounding the pavement looking for work, you also have expenses for car fare, lunches, and the continual cups of coffee. We point this out mainly to remind you that the job hunt is going to cost you regardless of how you do it. You've got to spend in order to earn.

On the following pages, you will find sample follow-up notes. Use them as a guide in creating your own personal responses.

May 7, 20XX

Mr. Richard Trump
Director of Social Work
Rockland Hospital
Rockland, Connecticut 06013

Dear Mr. Trump:

I regret that your job offer came a day too late. Just yesterday, I accepted a job as a social worker for another hospital. I am really sorry because I was impressed with your institution and probably would have fit in very well.

As I am not at all sure how my new job is going to work out, would you please be kind enough to keep my application on file and contact me if there is another opening in the next few months?

Thank you for your offer, and again, I am sorry I have to refuse it.

Sincerely,

Anne Paulson

Anne Paulson

SAMPLE FOLLOW-UP NOTES

79 Coastal Highway
Miami Beach, Florida 33110

September 7, 20XX

Mr. Marc Thomas
Leisure Realty Corporation
Miami, Florida 33133

Dear Mr. Thomas,

I just wanted to write to tell you how pleased I was to meet with you last Wednesday.

I was particularly impressed with the quality of homes you are constructing in Glen Garry and Boca Raton, and the total-market concept your organization has used to shape these developments.

Thank you for considering me for the position of Sales Agent at Leisure Realty.

I look forward to hearing from you.

Sincerely,

John Villiers

John Villiers

September 22, 20XX

Ms. Joanna Crosley
Marketing Director
The Johnson Crumpf Company
1435 Commonwealth Avenue
Boston, Massachusetts 02117

Dear Ms. Crosley:

I am delighted to confirm my acceptance of the job as Senior Marketing Analyst. As you already know, I am not going to report for another two weeks. But I have just given my present firm two weeks' notice, and will report to you on October 4.

Let me reiterate how pleased I am at getting this job. I was hoping that I would, as I feel that it is the perfect job for me and I know that I will fit into your company well.

I look forward to working with you.

Sincerely,

Barton Rockwood
Barton Rockwood

Resume Mailing	Follow-up Phone Call	Interview	Thank-you Letter
NAME _____ TITLE _____ COMPANY _____ ADDRESS _____ _____ _____ DATE SENT	DATE _____ RESULTS _____ _____ _____	DATE ___ TIME ___ INTERVIEWER ___ RESULTS ___ _____	DATE _____ **Job Offer** ☐ YES ☐ NO **Confirmation or "No Thank-you" Letter** DATE _____ ☐ CONFIRMED ☐ NO THANK-YOU

Resume Mailing	Follow-up Phone Call	Interview	Thank-you Letter
NAME _____ TITLE _____ COMPANY _____ ADDRESS _____ _____ _____ DATE SENT	DATE _____ RESULTS _____ _____ _____	DATE ___ TIME ___ INTERVIEWER ___ RESULTS ___ _____	DATE _____ **Job Offer** ☐ YES ☐ NO **Confirmation or "No Thank-you" Letter** DATE _____ ☐ CONFIRMED ☐ NO THANK-YOU

Resume Mailing	Follow-up Phone Call	Interview	Thank-you Letter
NAME _____ TITLE _____ COMPANY _____ ADDRESS _____ _____ _____ DATE SENT	DATE _____ RESULTS _____ _____ _____	DATE ___ TIME ___ INTERVIEWER ___ RESULTS ___ _____	DATE _____ **Job Offer** ☐ YES ☐ NO **Confirmation or "No Thank-you" Letter** DATE _____ ☐ CONFIRMED ☐ NO THANK-YOU

Resume Mailing	Follow-up Phone Call	Interview	Thank-you Letter
NAME	DATE	DATE TIME	DATE
TITLE	RESULTS	INTERVIEWER	**Job Offer**
			☐ YES ☐ NO
COMPANY		RESULTS	**Confirmation or "No Thank-you" Letter**
ADDRESS			
			DATE
			☐ CONFIRMED
DATE SENT			☐ NO THANK-YOU

Resume Mailing	Follow-up Phone Call	Interview	Thank-you Letter
NAME	DATE	DATE TIME	DATE
TITLE	RESULTS	INTERVIEWER	**Job Offer**
			☐ YES ☐ NO
COMPANY		RESULTS	**Confirmation or "No Thank-you" Letter**
ADDRESS			
			DATE
			☐ CONFIRMED
DATE SENT			☐ NO THANK-YOU

Resume Mailing	Follow-up Phone Call	Interview	Thank-you Letter
NAME	DATE	DATE TIME	DATE
TITLE	RESULTS	INTERVIEWER	**Job Offer**
			☐ YES ☐ NO
COMPANY		RESULTS	**Confirmation or "No Thank-you" Letter**
ADDRESS			
			DATE
			☐ CONFIRMED
DATE SENT			☐ NO THANK-YOU

Resume Mailing	Follow-up Phone Call	Interview	Thank-you Letter
NAME _____ TITLE _____ COMPANY _____ ADDRESS _____ _____ DATE SENT _____	DATE _____ RESULTS _____ _____ _____ _____	DATE _____ TIME INTERVIEWER _____ RESULTS _____ _____ _____ _____	DATE _____ **Job Offer** ☐ YES ☐ NO **Confirmation or "No Thank-you" Letter** DATE _____ ☐ CONFIRMED ☐ NO THANK-YOU

Resume Mailing	Follow-up Phone Call	Interview	Thank-you Letter
NAME _____ TITLE _____ COMPANY _____ ADDRESS _____ _____ DATE SENT _____	DATE _____ RESULTS _____ _____ _____ _____	DATE _____ TIME INTERVIEWER _____ RESULTS _____ _____ _____ _____	DATE _____ **Job Offer** ☐ YES ☐ NO **Confirmation or "No Thank-you" Letter** DATE _____ ☐ CONFIRMED ☐ NO THANK-YOU

Resume Mailing	Follow-up Phone Call	Interview	Thank-you Letter
NAME _____ TITLE _____ COMPANY _____ ADDRESS _____ _____ DATE SENT _____	DATE _____ RESULTS _____ _____ _____ _____	DATE _____ TIME INTERVIEWER _____ RESULTS _____ _____ _____ _____	DATE _____ **Job Offer** ☐ YES ☐ NO **Confirmation or "No Thank-you" Letter** DATE _____ ☐ CONFIRMED ☐ NO THANK-YOU

8
Winning Interview Techniques

The interview has been set up. Finally, the efforts of your job campaign have come to fruition—you have been granted an interview. You know the time, the place, the importance of doing well. Suddenly, you have an attack of nerves. You're both eager and anxious.

How will it go? Will you be able to convince the interviewer that not only can you do the job, but, indeed, you are absolutely the best person for it? You feel a little insecure. Will you be able to adequately articulate your qualifications?

What is happening to you happens to almost every job hunter: You're having a slight case of interview jitters. Don't worry; you're in good company. No matter how high up one is on the corporate ladder, being placed in the proverbial "hot seat" can be an unsettling experience. Our experience, as well as that of our colleagues all over the country, confirms that the great majority of job seekers find the interview the most stressful part of job hunting.

There are ways, however, of lessening that stress. The first step is to view the interview realistically. In most cases, job candidates tend to view the interview as an acid test of their abilities and self-worth. Such an attitude is extremely anxiety-producing and is guaranteed to elicit a negative response from the interviewer. But viewed realistically, the interview is simply a meeting between two equals—a buyer and a seller—to explore what each has to offer. Always keep in mind that feeling of equality between you and the interviewer.

The person conducting the interview is also under pressure. The interviewer must have the judgment to choose the most qualified candidate and at the same time must generate enough enthusiasm about the employer that when an offer is made, it will be accepted. Just as you are in competition with many other applicants, companies recruiting employees are similarly in competition with other employers trying to hire just the right person.

You were asked to be interviewed because someone in the company—an executive, an officer, the personnel director, or another representative of the employer—felt that the company's best interests would be served by knowing more about you. Your resume generated interest in you. It indicated to them that you are qualified; now they are trying to determine if you are the best qualified.

With this in mind, you must now convince them that it is in their best interests to hire you. You must present yourself in such a manner that your assets and abilities are superior to any other candidate.

We are not surprised to find that the job does not always go to the most qualified person. It is possible to predict with a high degree of reliability which candidates will receive not one, but many job offers. We have analyzed the common denominator, the quality that these winners possess. It is that they give a first impression that projects honesty, sincerity, and enthusiasm. Given several candidates with virtually identical credentials, the job will almost invariably go to the individual projecting the most positive and enthusiastic attitude and image.

The interview, no matter how you describe it, is purely a selling situation and you are the product. Life in general is selling. We are all selling something—an idea to our children, a special date to a friend, or ourselves to the reservationist at an already overbooked airline.

Your first goal in selling yourself is to get the interviewer to like you. This can be done by offering a sincere compliment—commenting about the beautiful artwork in the lobby or praising the cordial and helpful receptionist. Do not offer personal compliments. Stay clear of commenting on personal photos on the desk or, if you are a man, the jewelry a female interviewer may be wearing.

Another way to build an immediate friendship with this new person is to mention the name of anyone you both may know, or have in common. Name dropping is always effective. It creates friendship and a sense of common ground. Name-dropping can and should be used at any time throughout the interview.

POSITIVE ATTITUDE

A positive attitude is the single most important quality an individual could have to be successful at an interview. Simply stated, if you think you can't, you won't, and if you think you can, you will. Your mind is very much like a computer. Are you programming your mind with positive or negative thoughts?

Often I hear individuals make negative comments before going on an interview. You have probably heard them or made similar statements yourself. They sound something like this: "I really don't know why I'm going; they're probably going to hire someone else. It's a waste of my time to even go." Or "I'm really worried about this interview; there may be others more qualified than me," and the list goes on and on.

Essentially, whatever statements you put in your mind before and during an interview will determine its outcome. There is a computer term that illustrates this point: "G.I.G.O." or garbage in, garbage out! What are you programming your mind with before you go on an interview?

Successful self-selling means that you begin your interview at home, where you make positive statements to yourself as well as to family and friends. A winning, positive attitude will sound something like this: "I can do it. I just know I'm going to get this job." Or "I'm going to work hard and get ready for this interview. They're going to like me." You can literally think of hundreds more statements to assure yourself that you have the right attitude to sell yourself with enthusiasm.

DRESS LIKE A WINNER

To have a successful interview, you must not only think like a winner but also dress like one. The day before your interview, make sure your wardrobe is in order. Your clothes should be clean and pressed and your hair should be freshly washed. Project a professional image.

It has been said many times: "You never get a second chance to make a first impression." Research has shown that people make judgments about others in less than 60 seconds after meeting them. A first impression is comprised of your mannerisms, hair, clothes, jewelry, and perfume or aftershave, to mention a few. The best rule of thumb is to stay conservative in all of these areas. Save the trendy look for parties and weekends. In business, you want to draw attention to your skills, not your looks. When you leave an interview, you want the interviewer to remember you, not something you were wearing.

UPON ARRIVING AT THE INTERVIEW

A good candidate arrives at an interview at least 15 minutes early. When you arrive exactly on time, you are actually arriving late! Arriving early allows you plenty of time to fill out important pre-interview information such as an application.

Besides filling out pre-interview information, there are many other benefits to arriving early. First, you arrive relaxed and not preoccupied with traffic and other commuter worries. You are in a better frame of mind to focus on completing a winning interview. Second, you provide yourself time to observe the company, gather valuable information, and rehearse in your mind your exact interview performance—much like an actor who rehearses lines in his mind while waiting to go onstage. Often an interviewer may ask a receptionist or an employee who has observed you waiting for their opinion of you. For this reason, follow these guidelines when sitting in the waiting area:

- Sit professionally while waiting.
- Don't read magazines or newspapers to pass the time.
- Review your prepared questions and interview notes.
- Rehearse in your mind the five steps to a selling encounter.

An interviewer may or may not offer to shake hands when they approach you in the reception area. Follow their cue and only shake hands if they offer.

Also, an interviewer may offer you a cup of coffee or soda. This is a polite and cordial gesture on their part. It is best to refuse by simply stating: "No, thank you, I just had a cup before I arrived." I am aware of stories from recruiters who have actually had applicants spill the beverage all over themselves and the desk. More than likely, you may have some pre-interview jitters, so don't add more fuel to the fire! However, it is perfectly acceptable to take coffee at the final interview after an offer has been made and you're more relaxed.

LISTENING IS IMPORTANT

Good listening skills are a crucial factor in interviewing successfully. With good listening skills, you are able to gather a wealth of information that can give you power. Information always gives power, in any situation. Listen for a while before you start blurting out what you have and how it will help the company.

Good listening is demonstrated in a number of ways. Maintain good eye contact at all times. It is not necessary to stare the person down, but don't look at the floor, either. Take notes. Note-taking helps you to remember key bits of information that you will use later in the interview to sell yourself. Note-taking also makes you appear both reliable and professional. Correct body language will help you to listen. Nodding your head, leaning forward occasionally, and other gestures demonstrate that you are concentrating on what the interviewer is saying.

ASKING QUESTIONS IS IMPORTANT, TOO

Interviewers frequently pay as much attention to the questions that candidates ask as to the answers they give. The questions you ask will serve as an indication of how much of the interviewer's information you have understood, and will show your level of competence and sophistication. Listen carefully and ask intelligent questions about the company. Research the company well before the interview. Prepare some good questions based on your research and bring those to the interview as well. After all, you are also basing a decision about this job and this company on what you learn at the interview. Turn the interview into a true meeting of equals by politely, but firmly, asking the questions that are important to you.

Formulating good questions is not as easy as it sounds. Questions that gather information are called open-ended questions. An open-ended question is any question that cannot be answered with yes or no. This type of question demands information. It usually begins with who, what, where, when, how, or why. Some examples are: "What is the company's mission statement? How does the company handle employee evaluations? [or] Where are the company's other offices?"

The night before your interview, prepare a list of questions you will ask at the interview. A person who asks good questions is perceived as more intelligent than one who has no questions. Here are some sample questions to get you started. Add to the list those questions that obviously should be asked, based on the research you've done and what you learn from the interviewer.

Questions to Ask at the Interview

1. What are the strengths of the company and the department?
2. What are the career opportunities for someone entering this position?
3. What kind of orientation and training is available to new employees?
4. What other departments would the person who fills this position interact with?
5. To whom does this position report?
6. What are the growth plans for this company and department?
7. What are the prospects for future promotions?
8. What opportunities are there to transfer from one division to another?
9. How long was the predecessor in this position? Why did he/she leave?
10. What kind of support staff is available?
11. How often do employee evaluations occur?
12. What is the continuing education and tuition reimbursement policy?
13. How would you describe the company culture? Mission? Vision? Values?
14. What is the company's management philosophy?
15. What are the expectations of the person in this position?
16. How often is overtime expected?
17. What percent of the time will be devoted to various responsibilities?
18. What are the deadlines? Weekly? Monthly?
19. What venues do employees have to offer feedback and share creative ideas?
20. When would the position start?

Add additional questions of your own here. These questions should target the company and position precisely.

_____

_____

_____

_____

_____

QUESTIONS THEY WILL ASK YOU

Though every interview is different, all will include questions requiring more than a "yes" or "no" answer. The interviewer will be listening not only for content, but for sincerity, poise, judgment, and ability to think quickly.

Spend some time before the interview developing answers to questions that you think might give you trouble. The night prior to your interview is the time to role-play with a friend or spouse—or even a tape recorder—and go through each question. Going on an interview without some form of rehearsal is like an actor going onstage without practicing the script. Practiced simulation prepares you to demonstrate a confident and composed attitude at the interview. Prepare answers to give extemporaneously, remembering that there are no right or wrong answers. The purpose is to find out more about the subjective you. Aim for clarity, brevity, and, above all, honesty. Also, remember that the actual wording and substance of these questions will vary to reflect the circumstances of each particular interview.

Here is a list of questions frequently asked by interviewers:

1. What do you consider to be your strong points?
2. What do you consider to be your weak points?
3. What motivates you?
4. What is your definition of success?
5. What did you enjoy most about your last position?
6. What did you like least about your last position?
7. Where would you like your career to be in five years?
8. What are your short-term career goals?
9. Do you prefer to work alone, or as part of a team?
10. How do you get along with your peers?
11. How good are you at motivating people?
12. To what magazines do you subscribe?
13. What newspapers do you read?
14. What were the last three books you read?
15. What are your hobbies?
16. How do you spend your leisure time?
17. Are you active in community affairs? If so, describe.

18. Why do you want to change jobs?

19. Why are you unemployed?

20. Why do you think you would be an asset to the company?

21. How well do you work under pressure?

22. How do you feel about working overtime?

23. Would you be willing to relocate to one of our branch offices? Would you be willing to travel?

24. What did you learn in your last position?

25. How did you get along with your boss on your last job?

26. How did you get along with the staff in your last job?

27. Why do you want to work for this company?

28. What do you consider your outstanding achievements?

29. What kinds of problems do you enjoy solving?

30. How often have you been ill in the past five years?

31. Are you willing to take a physical exam?

32. Are you willing to take a series of personality tests?

33. Have you ever been fired? If yes, why?

34. Do you have management ability? Describe.

35. How ambitious are you?

36. What was your last salary? What is your minimum salary at this time?

DEVELOP A SIGHT-SELLER

For your interviews, begin now to develop a new lifelong companion called a sight-seller. Whether you are employed or unemployed, purchase a small black portfolio with approximately 8½ by 11-inch plastic protective sheets in the interior. Begin to make a scrapbook-type portfolio documenting work projects and successes that you can share with prospective employers at an interview. Your portfolio will be very similar to the ones that salespeople use on sales calls to tell prospective clients about their products and services.

To *say* what you have done is one thing, to show it and visually document it is highly effective and convincing to the listener. Here are just a few of the many visuals you could be collecting and inserting to build your sight-seller for your next self-selling situation:

- Letters of recognition from customers
- Letters of recognition from immediate managers and upper management
- Company awards
- Community service awards
- Product brochures you worked on, sold, or developed
- Task force documents that demonstrate your participation
- Published articles

- Work simplification ideas you implemented
- An outline of all projects you engaged in at your previous employer
- Photographs that document your work-related successes
- Current and past employers' marketing brochures

Now that you have a few ideas, take the initiative to be creative and start building your sight-seller. Once you've put it together, update it as frequently as necessary to reflect new accomplishments and achievements. You may even use it to present your case for an internal promotion or pay increase. It's a tool that will give you the edge over the competition when selling "Me, Inc." Above all, it will help you remember all the things you do that really make you valuable but are sometimes taken for granted and are even forgotten. Once you've built your sight-seller, bring it to your next internal promotion presentation or external job interview. You'll see the difference it will make.

SALARY NEGOTIATION

In most circumstances, you should not discuss salary at the first interview. The interviewer will make it a point to ask about your salary requirements. If it is the first interview, always respond "open." Countless individuals have lost job opportunities by answering this question with an exact amount. If you state a figure too high, you will appear demanding and overrated. Or, if you state a figure too low, you may be perceived as a poor-quality performer.

After you state that your salary requirements are open, explain to the interviewer that you have come to the interview with an open mind. Explain further that you believe that the right position with the right benefits would make your salary very negotiable.

It is assumed that you would not have gone to the interview if you did not feel the position would at least be in the ballpark of your compensation requirements. Discussion of salary and compensation requirements come at the final interview, after a job offer has been made. At this point, it has been determined that they want you. What a great feeling it is to be wanted! Now you are in a better position to negotiate.

In fact, always let the employer bring up the subject of salary, and try not to be engaged in salary negotiations until you are fairly certain that you have a job offer.

When asked about your present or last compensation package, answer concisely, including all bonuses and benefits. If you feel that you were underpaid, mention that as one of the reasons for wanting to change jobs.

If you were referred to the employer by an employment agency or headhunter, it's a good idea to let them do the negotiating for you. Because their fee is usually based on a percentage of your salary they will profit from your being hired. So rest assured that they will attack the question of compensation vigorously. Besides, as mentioned before, it's always helpful to have a third party negotiate for you.

If you are forced to do your own negotiating, stay flexible. If you know what salary range is being offered, put your salary expectations at the high end of the range. Remember, the interview is a screening process; if your requested minimum salary is considerably higher than the employer intends to pay, this could knock you out of the running.

Don't get boxed into a specific figure before you have to. Always talk in $5,000 to $10,000 ranges. If the interview has gone well and you are really interested in the company, aim high and then negotiate. Be sure to get all the relevant information concerning benefits: medical and dental insurance, profit-sharing plans, future salary increases, stock options, and so on. Consider all of the above as part of the total salary. If the subject of salary hasn't yet come up, and you are asked about your salary expectations, one approach is to answer the question with one of your own, "I'm glad you brought up the subject of compensation. What is the salary range for this job?" Let the employer give a figure, and then negotiate from there.

You should never decide *at* the interview whether or not to accept a job offer.

Instead, thank the employer for the offer and indicate that you will give it serious consideration. Ask for a few days to think it over and let them know when you will call back with your answer—remember, no longer than a few days or so. The company will continue interviewing until the job has been filled, so don't delay too long. Give yourself just enough time to weigh any other offers and reflect more thoroughly on this one.

9

Sample Resumes

On the following pages you'll see many sample resumes, one of which may appeal to you as an example to follow. Even though parts of the samples, especially the job descriptions, may resemble what you wish to express, never copy them verbatim. These samples are included only to give you ideas to use when writing your own resume.

Use your completed worksheets, along with the form of the resume you choose, and start writing. You will probably have to rewrite several times before you are completely satisfied with the results. Don't get discouraged!

Be sure to include all the pertinent information, and adhere to basic rules governing presentation and content. Here are some of those rules—the do's of writing a job-getting resume.

1. Do keep it brief; one page, or two at the most.

2. Do choose a chronological-style format; list your last or present job first, continuing in reverse chronological order.

3. Do place your name, address, and phone number in a conspicuous position on your resume.

4. Do make sure your career objective (should you decide to use one) gives your resume focus and is relevant to your experience and background.

5. Do list all dates of both employment and education history, leaving no unexplained gaps.

6. Do avoid long paragraphs; keep job descriptions under eight lines.

7. Do strengthen your resume by using implied pronouns and action verbs.

8. Do use 8½-by-11-inch paper, preferably white or light-colored (beige, cream, buff, gray).

9. Do use one side of the paper *only;* if two pages are used, be sure the sheets of paper are stapled together and your name is on each page.

10. Do make your resume visually attractive—use plenty of white space, wide, even-spaced margins, and clean, crisp type.

11. Do proofread your resume more than once. Make sure there are no misspellings, grammatical errors, or typos.

Sharon Cook Darrow
65 Elm Street
Kirkwood, Missouri 63122

Telephone: (314) 653-2244   Cell: (314) 555-4741   E-mail: sdarrow@aol.com

JOB OBJECTIVE: Accountant

EXPERIENCE:

1990–present   **Howell and Brooks,** St. Louis, Missouri
Accountant

Planned and organized own work under some supervision from the Group Manager. Assisted in determining the classifications, distribution, and recording of accounting data.

Reconciled discrepancies in subsidiary ledgers and made proper adjustments. Assisted in the preparation of standardized accounting reports and statements of limited scope. Analyzed and interpreted statements and reports.

1987–1990   **Koehler Manufacturing Company,** St. Louis, Missouri
Accounting Clerk

Handled basic accounting transactions, coded invoices for proper distribution, classified transactions, and processed warehouse invoices.

EDUCATION: B.S. degree—**Community College,** St. Louis, Missouri
1992

REFERENCES: On request

Dorothy Gilmore, CPA

312 W. 32nd Street
New York, NY 10031

Residence: (212) 814-2235   Cell: (212) 787-3400

WORK EXPERIENCE:

Barton, Klein & Dodd, CPAs
New York, NY 10007   June 1995–Present

Senior Accountant
- Preparation of income tax returns (Individual, Partnership, Corporation, etc.)
- Preparation of financial reports and statements
- Management advisory services for clients
- Review and Compilation Services
- Write-up and general ledger work
- Preparation of sales tax, commercial rent tax, and payroll tax returns
- Responsible for developing and maintaining accounting systems for clients
- Responsible for whole engagements with limited supervision

EDUCATIONAL AND PROFESSIONAL ACCREDITATION:
Certified Public Accountant, New York, 1995
Bachelor of Business Administration—Accounting
    Columbia University, 1994
Dean's List; elected to Beta Gamma Sigma
Graduated Summa Cum Laude

PROFESSIONAL AFFILIATIONS:
American Institute of Certified Public Accountants
New York State Society of Certified Public Accountants
Columbia University Alumni Association

REFERENCES:
Furnished upon request

Patrick J. O'Mara
45 Hunter Lane
Grand Rapids, Michigan 49505
(616) 432-0146   Cell: (616) 555-4218   E-mail: pjomara@aol.com

Job Objective: **Accountant**

Experience

1996–Present   <u>Millbank Furniture Company, *Grand Rapids, Michigan*</u>
Statistical Specialist—Prepared detailed financial records including status reports and current and historical reports. Prepared journal entries, maintained records for marketing expenditures and inventories. Processed warehouse invoices and prepared sales reports.

1991–1996   **Accounts Receivable Analysis Clerk**—Made nonstandardized journal entries, coded invoices for proper accounting routing. Analyzed details of regular accounts. Assisted and trained other accounting clerks.

1989–1991   <u>Walker Lumber Company, Inc., *Grand Rapids, Michigan*</u>
Cash Accounting Clerk—Performed various routine and nonroutine bookkeeping and basic accounting tasks including journal entries, verifying data and reconciling discrepancies, preparing detailed reports from raw data, and checking accounting documents for completeness, mathematical accuracy, and consistency.

1987–1989   **Accounting Clerk Trainee**—Prepared journal vouchers, entered postings, and filled in standard records and reports. Acquired a working knowledge of accounting office procedures such as posting and balancing, compiling data, preparing summaries, and verifying routine reports by checking against related details and previous data to reconcile irregularities.

Education   **Community College**—Currently enrolled in a statistics course and completed a two-semester course in mathematics.

Lakewood Business School—Completed courses in basic accounting principles, intermediate accounting, 1987.

References   On request.

1452 North Hill St.
Beechwood, Ohio 44416
(513) 621-4133

EDUCATION: Harvard University, Bachelor of Science in Economics
Major: Accounting. May 1993

Barnard College, 1989–1991
Course of study as above.

CAREER AFFILIATIONS:

Haskins & Sells, Certified Public Accountants, Beechwood, Ohio   9/01–Present
Senior Certified Public Accountant
Professional supervisory experience in oil and gas tax shelters, industrial
publishing, legal profession, retail, postproduction video services.
Primary responsibilities in planning, supervising, and reviewing audit
engagements through completion of engagement. Experienced in
corporate taxes, accounting systems analysis, internal control
evaluations, computer system controls, consolidations, financial
analysis, special projects in bankruptcy reporting as accountants for the
trustee, and overall investigations of client systems for the purpose of
improving operations and efficiency. Continuing professional education
courses in Accounting and Auditing I, II, and III, Bankruptcy, Taxes,
Written and Oral Communications, and Investment Analysis.

Deutch and Green, Certified Public Accountants, New York, NY   6/99–9/01
Staff Accountant
Staff accountant for audit of Shearson/American Express Company.
Audit responsibilities included footnote disclosure preparation, security
and exchange memberships, and cash.

Career Placement Service, Harvard University   9/97–6/99
Assistant to the Director of Student Career Planning and Corporate
Placement.

United States Navy Active Duty, Midshipman   6/95–9/97
Training in leadership, technical aspects of Surface Command,
Submarine, Flight, and Marine Operations.

(Continued)

<u>United States Navy Active Duty</u>, Midshipman   3/95–9/95
  Training at Naval Education Training Center, Newport, RI

<u>Information and Referral Service</u>, Cornell University   9/93–9/95
  Public Relations Service for dignitaries, corporate, and academic
  officials visiting Cornell.

<u>HONORS AND AWARDS</u>:

  <u>Dean's List</u>, Barnard College and Harvard University, 1989, 1990
  <u>College Scholar</u> Outstanding Academic Award, Barnard, 1989, 1990
  <u>Naval Reserve Officer Training Corps Scholarship</u>, 1988
    Fifty-five scholarships awarded to women on national basis.
  <u>National Sojourner's Award Outstanding Sophomore</u>, Barnard, 1990
  <u>Mobil Oil Corporation</u> Collegiate Competition Finalist, 1989

<u>PROFESSIONAL STATUS AND ASSOCIATIONS</u>:

  Certified Public Accountant, November 1998, New York State
  Harvard University Alumni Association

<u>REFERENCES</u>: Available upon request

Carla Johnson
124 White Drive
Sommers, NY 11416
Tel: (914) 968-3391
Cell: (914) 244-2000

WORK EXPERIENCE:

1995–Present   **Career Blazers Temporary Personnel,** White Plains, NY
Junior Accountant
Preparation of monthly sales analysis and incentive bonus
calculations using EXCEL. Analyze results to report directly
to the Chief Financial Officer. Responsible for account
analysis, carry forwards, bank reconciliations, and journal
entries necessary to close the month on a timely basis.

Accounts Payable Clerk
Reconciled vendor accounts whenever there was a
discrepancy. Supervised and trained new employees. Coded
incoming vendor invoices.

1994–1995   **ABC Corporation,** Harrison, NY
Accounts Receivable Clerk
Verified accuracy of the daily accounts receivable book.
Assisted Reporting Manager in preparation of monthly sales
analysis. Prepared accounts receivable checks for deposit.
Applied payments to receivable balances. Entered
adjustments to complete the breakdown of cash entries, as
well as to eliminate the uncleared charge-backs.

1986–1988   **Aetna Insurance Company,** Hempstead, NY
Office Manager
Managed divisional office in addition to handling customer
service for the area. Extensive supervision of trainees with
regard to phone sales, customer price quotes, and in-house
computer usage.

EDUCATION: **Nassau Community College**
Degree: Associate in Applied Science—1994
Major: Accounting

REFERENCES: Available upon request.

GREGORY T. PHILIPS

108-43 Homelawn Street
Jamaica, New York 11432
Tel: (212) 657-8843   Cell: (212) 441-7998   E-mail: greg@yahoo.com

Education:

1995–Present   Monroe College, *Yonkers, New York*

Currently enrolled in program leading to an M.B.A. Area of concentration is in financial management with special emphasis on the study of accounting for management control.

1991–1995   University of Fairfield, *Fairfield, Connecticut*

B.S. Major in Real Estate and Urban Economic Development. Extensive course work in real property appraisal and investment analysis.

Employment:

1/96–Present   Monroe College, *Yonkers, New York*

Assistant to the manager of analytical studies. (Six-week internship.) Collected and synthesized price data for college's annual inflation study. Project involved library research as well as telephone contact with college suppliers. Internship led to current part-time position of coordinating draft for final report.

9/95–12/95   Eaton Real Estate, *New Canaan, Connecticut*

Real estate salesperson. Employed part-time by Eaton for the purpose of buying and selling real property.

9/93–9/95   University of Fairfield, *Fairfield, Connecticut*

Head resident. Responsible for running all aspects of a college dormitory. Duties included supervising residents, kitchen, and maintenance staff and preparing all paperwork for Department of Student Affairs. Job was concurrent with full-time academic study to earn seventy percent of college expenses.

Summers: Monroe College, *Yonkers, New York*

Dispatcher: Employed by physical plant department with responsibility for keeping accurate records on thirty-vehicle motor pool.

Groundsperson: Responsible for maintenance of college buildings and grounds.

References: Available upon request.

Harvey Seller

Chicago, IL 61245

Tel: (213) 555-5218

Cell: (213) 769-4145

ACCOUNTANT/FINANCIAL MANAGER

with diversified public accounting, tax preparation, and financial management experience, seeks a position in financial management.

PROFESSIONAL EXPERIENCE

1995–
Present

A. H. Shapiro & Co., CPAs, Chicago, IL
Manager

Direct the activities of semisenior and staff accountants in the conduct of certified audits for a diverse clientele. Responsibilities include audit planning, supervision of the audit, and direct communication with top management of client companies.

- Participated in the conversion from a manual to a computerized billing system, resulting in a more efficient operation.
- Review audit results and confer with management of client companies regarding financial and operational weaknesses.
- Oversee the firm's tax planning activities.
- Assumed financial management responsibility for a client in the real estate construction business. Designed and implemented all internal systems, recruited, hired, and trained personnel and converted an existing manual system to an automated one. On a continuing basis, review company's financial results and make appropriate recommendations.
- Assisted a client in the publishing industry in the development of a budgeting and forecasting system. Subsequently, participated in negotiations to sell the company to a publicly held company.

(Continued)

- For another publisher, computerized all financial systems—accounts payable, receivable, general ledger, payroll, subscription fulfillment, and distribution. Concurrently, revamped systems resulting in increased cash flow and controls.

Joined company as a semisenior accountant. Participated in certified audits in the service and manufacturing industries. Responsibilities included the preparation of corporate, partnership, and individual taxes on the federal, state, and local levels.

1992– 1995	**Koltman, Portnoy & Cohen, CPAs,** Chicago, IL *Semisenior Accountant*

Joined this medium-size accounting firm as junior accountant. Promoted to Accountant and then Semisenior Accountant.

EDUCATION   M.S., Taxation—University of Chicago, Chicago, IL, 1992
B.S., Accounting—University of Chicago, Chicago, IL, 1990

REFERENCES   Personal and professional references available on request.

Edward T. Washington
48-01 129th Street
New York, New York 10021
(212) 794-2376

OBJECTIVE:	Junior Accountant/Auditor Trainee
EDUCATION:	Hunter College, B.B.A. 2002—Major: Public Accounting York Community College, A.A. 1994—Major: Business Administration
GENERAL BACKGROUND:	Five years' professional experience utilizing customer relations and general accounting principles with the following firms:

Adjustments Banker's Trust Co., New York, NY 2000–Present

Accounts Western Union Co., New York, NY 1997–1998

SPECIFIC EXPERIENCE:	Adjustments	Inscribing amounts on checks from different branches of banking established throughout United States; balancing customer accounts by keeping accurate records of payments and adjustments; exacting time-keeping records and forwarding to payroll division.
	Accounts	Processing and recording Western Union accounts including heavy customer contacts; keeping daily records of accounts receivable; acting as liaison between customer and accounting division; disseminating general information into specific codes for business purposes involving written correspondence and interpretative designs.
COLLATERAL COURSES:		Law, Management Science, Computer Information Science, Marketing, Business Management, Calculus, Statistics, Financial Analysis, Individual Taxation, Partnership Corporation Taxes, Estates and Trusts, Electronic Data Processing, and Advanced Professional Auditing (one year). Advanced Accounting practice. Seminar in Accounting, Specialized Accounting.
REFERENCES:		Available upon request.

SYLVIA SLATER
340 Slate Street
San Francisco, CA 81416
Tel: (219) 765-2448
Cell: (219) 899-6400

EMPLOYMENT HISTORY

7/95–Present

The Dalton School, San Francisco, CA
Admissions Representative

- Responsible for meeting weekly student application goal
- Had highest close ratio of applications to interviews
- Interviewed and followed up on over 250 students
- Dealt with guidance counselors to obtain transcripts for student evaluation
- Managed my enrollment of over 150 students
- Held financial plans for my student enrollment via computer analysis
- Maintained and monitored enrolled students' tuition payments

9/93–7/95

Hill & Rogers, Inc., San Francisco, CA
Executive Recruiter

- Counseled, interviewed, and qualified candidates
- Obtained candidates and clients via telephone solicitation and referrals
- Trained and supervised two recruiters
- Client contacts included: Banking, Brokerage, Marketing, and Financial Services Advertising

4/93–9/93

Stern & Stern, Inc., San Francisco, CA
Placement Counselor/Personnel Consultant

- Screened, interviewed, and advised candidates for clerical and/or nonexempt positions
- Assisted in resume writing
- Solicited new accounts
- Counseled applicants on interview techniques

8/91–4/93

Manning, Selvage & Lee Public Relations, San Jose, CA
Account Coordinator

- Executed special events
- Planned press conferences
- Obtained contacts in broadcast and print media
- Wrote press releases

EDUCATION

Ohio University
BA, Public Communications 5/91

REFERENCES

Available upon request

DIANE LEVITT
18 Anderson Ave.
Queens, NY 12416

Tel: (718) 889-9106
Cell: (212) 884-2240

EMPLOYMENT EXPERIENCE

October 1995–Present: **FRANK BRYOIER & SONS, INC.,** New York, NY
ADMINISTRATIVE ASSISTANT

Work for three principals, prepare confidential reports, compile agendas, schedule travel plans, screen correspondence, coordinate business appointments, maintain filing system, plan annual office parties, prioritize and distribute work, in charge of computerized accounts receivable for two companies, secretarial duties including word processing, billing and order entries, heavy phone contact with clients.

March 1993–August 1995:   **BAKER, TODD & BAKER, INC.,** New York, NY
EXECUTIVE SECRETARY/ADMINISTRATIVE ASSISTANT

Word processing, typing all specifications, correspondence, and expense reports as well as making all travel arrangements. In charge of job scheduling and directly involved in contract preparation. Secretary for fifty draftsmen along with three immediate supervisors and four department managers. Heavy phone and personal contact with clients.

July 1991–February 1993:   **HILL & BARRON'S,** New York, NY
SECRETARY

Secretary for three principals within three different high volume jewelry firms. Duties included typing bills and correspondence and having an operating knowledge of computerized accounts receivable. Heavy phone and personal contact with clients.

May 1989–July 1991:   **OTIS & MEYERS, INC.,** New York, NY
RECEPTIONIST

Receptionist for jewelry firm. Typed correspondence and assisted shipping department. Input all billing and shipping information.

EDUCATION

September 1990–June 1993.   **SIENA COLLEGE,** BRONX, NY

References furnished upon request.

ELLEN A. BRZOWSKI
81 St. Marks Place
New York, NY 10037
(212) 559-9630

VICTOR TEMPORARIES (1995–To Date)
New York, New York

Assistant to President
Interview applicants
Liaison with clients
Telephone sales
Bookkeeping

AMERICAN MOTORS CORPORATION (1992–1995)
White Plains Zone Office

Assistant Office Manager (Government Bonded)
Responsible for:
Expense accounts for—sales representatives, district managers, and all zone office personnel.
Travel letter authorizations.
Accident reports.
Accounts payable and receivable.
Zone sundry reports for car distribution.
"Parts" account for twenty-eight American Motors dealers.

REVLON (1988–1991)
New York Office

Supervisor of Order Department
Responsible for:
Liaison with cosmetic buyers of superior store chains.
Supervised eight members of staff.
Organized promotional material for new items.
In charge of setting up new accounts.

MARTIN CARPETS (1986–1988)
Brookfield, Connecticut

Assistant Manager
Customer relations
Sales representative
New accounts establishment

EDUCATION
Yorktown Teachers College (1984–1986)
A.S. Business Administration

References will be furnished on request.

DEAN ASHER

Address   49 W. Mangnot Lane
Easton, VT 05341

Telephone   Home: 919-619-0936
Service: 914-616-0319

Work Experience   1994–present: *Researcher/Technical Editor,* **Lipcot-Abbey-McLoyton-Thomas-McCarthy-Stratton (Engineers and Architects),** 345 Park Avenue, New York, Department of Environmental Planning and Socioeconomic Studies. Assembled information concerning complicated and sensitive subject matter through personal contacts; researched documents, statutes, and governmental procedures; set style and format; edited and proofread environmental impact statements and proposals.

1994: *Assistant Publicity Director,* **Mainman Ltd.,** 405 Park Avenue, New York. Assisted with ad campaigns, preparation of press kits, news releases, publicity events, and planning of Times Square spectacular billboard for RCA recording artists.

1993: *Reporter/Ad Salesman,* **The Lower Cape,** Provincetown, Massachusetts. Covered local news stories for shoppers' guide and local news weekly publication.

1992: *Customer Service,* **U.S. Committee for UNICEF,** 331 Easton Street, Easton, Vermont. Responsible for personal correspondence concerning customer complaints and orders in the greeting card program.

1988–1992: *Journalist,* **U.S. Navy.** Public Affairs Office, Third Naval District Headquarters, San Jose. Wrote news releases, photographed and organized mass media command presentations, press contact at official ceremonies, and admiral's aide at social engagements.

Education   Department of Defense
Information School (DINFOS)
Fort Harrison, Indiana

(Continued)

Northwestern University
National High School Institute
Evanston, Illinois

Graduate, 1988
Journalism/Public Relations

Graduate, 1986
Speech/Drama

Honors   Alternate Delegate to the World Youth Assembly, 1990.
                            United Nations, New York City

Organizations   Executive Secretary for the Neighbors of Teilson Park, YMCA.

Recommendations furnished upon request.

Rose J. Martinson
43 Racine Avenue
Skokie, Illinois 60076

(312) 546-7898

Job Objective:
Administrative Assistant

<u>Experience</u>
1995–present   **Howard T. Mack, Inc.,** *Skokie, Illinois*
Assistant to the president and owner of this firm dealing in rare coins and
stamps. The president, who travels extensively, is primarily concerned with
purchasing large collections and negotiating financial transactions
involving the expansion of company operations through new investments.

Responsible for employment, training, salary administration, and
terminations for 150 employees. Supervisor of four departments:
bookkeeping, shipping, direct mail sales, and customer relations.
Determine adjustments and credits on customer transactions. Responsible
for the monthly distribution of want lists to over 300 dealers. Determine
bid and purchase price on coins and stamps from private collections.

1991–1995   **The Field Foundation,** *Chicago, Illinois*
Assistant to Director of Office Services. Supervised office staff of thirty
clerical and machine operator personnel. Interviewed applicants, trained
new employees, scheduled work assignments, and made equipment
changes to improve efficiency.

1988–1991   **Northwestern University,** *Chicago, Illinois*
Assistant to Placement Director. Job searched and placed undergraduate
students in part-time jobs. Met with recruitment representatives from
industry and arranged interviews for them with students who were
completing graduate work. For the first two years in this capacity,
performed routine clerical and secretarial tasks.

<u>Education</u>

Northwestern University—A.B. degree, June 1988
History Major and Psychology Minor. Junior Class President.

<u>References</u>

On request.

ALVARO SUAREZ
40 West 72nd St.
New York, NY 10023
212-787-0871

EXPERIENCE

1996–2002 Personal Secretary to First Secretary of Dominican Republic to the United Nations, New York. Handled all personal correspondence, prepared all details for major international sports events in Dominican Republic, arranged housing and entertainment for dignitaries visiting Mission to the UN. Acted as interpreter.

1993–1996 Administrative Assistant and Secretary, ANCO International, New Jersey. Served in this capacity to President of this corporation. Assumed responsibility for office in his absence, including handling of all correspondence, translations in Spanish and Italian, transcribing of large volume of shorthand as well as dictaphone-typing; made arrangements for hotel accommodations and booked space for conferences, both domestic and overseas. Acted as interpreter for foreign company representatives visiting New York.

1990–1993 Executive Secretary to the Director of International Operations, Standard Tobacco International, New York. Handled all press contacts, translated foreign press releases, assumed all secretarial responsibilities, and assisted in all public relations activities.

1987–1990 Executive Secretary/Assistant Fashion Coordinator, Longine-Pioneer Corporation, New York. Translated fashion copy for magazines and newspapers, prepared press parties, fashion shows, performed secretarial duties.

EDUCATION
B.A. in Social Studies, 1987—University of Santo Domingo, Dominican Republic

LANGUAGES
Fluency in Spanish, Italian, and English

SECRETARIAL SKILLS
MS. Word, EXCEL, PowerPoint

REFERENCES
On request

NAME: David R. Chosack

ADDRESS: 987 Chicago Street
                  St. Louis, Missouri 63101
                  (314) 548-4375   E-mail: d.chosack@aol.com

EXPERIENCE:

<u>Kenyon and Eckhardt Inc.</u> *April 1993–June 2002.* Hired as Account Coordinator for Air France, Helena Rubinstein, and Foreign Vintage accounts. In addition to the regular duties, other responsibilities as coordinator were to check the monthly production invoices prior to their submission to the client and to insure that an ad was released to a publication for every insertion placed on a media estimate. The Anaconda, French West Indies Tourist Board, Royal Air Maroc, and Alfred Dunner accounts were added to the coordinating assignments.

    In March 1990, promoted to Account Executive on Air France account supervising all facets of the account. In detail, this included initiating and approving overall campaigns, writing copy, planning media, and complete supervision of print, radio, and TV production.

<u>Doyle Dane Bernbach, Inc.</u> *June 1990–April 1993.* Hired specifically to traffic portions of the Monsanto account in TV and print. Handled these portions until February 1986, then was transferred to the tire and corporate divisions of Uniroyal (TV and print). During this time, also assisted with traffic on Sony, portions of Burlington Industries, and other house accounts. Subsequently, the shoe and golf ball divisions of Uniroyal and American Tourister Luggage were added.

<u>McCall Corporation.</u> *December 1986–June 1990.* Position as Assistant Advertising Quality and Control Manager for production department of McCall's Magazine. Channeled flow of plates from various advertising agencies throughout the United States to our printing plant in time for each closing date of McCall's and Redbook magazines. Had gained experience in control of color quality as well as in the ordering of safety shells and electros.

    In January 1983, promoted to the position of Advertising Traffic Manager. In this capacity had complete charge over the responsibilities listed above, in addition to supervising a small staff.

<u>Kaiser, Sedlow & Temple.</u> *December 1984–December 1986.* Started with Burke, Charles and Guignon Advertising as Traffic Manager. When agency merged with Kaiser, Sedlow & Temple in June 1977, continued as Traffic Manager and Media Director on Twentieth Century Fox, Columbia Pictures, Embassy Pictures, and Arco Lighting.

(Continued)

<u>Comptom Advertising Agency</u>. *August 1983–October 1984.* Started as messenger in traffic department and gradually assisted traffic man with accounts such as Kelly-Springfield and some Procter & Gamble Company products.

EDUCATION: Queens and City Colleges 1984–1991

REFERENCES: On request.

Gregory L. Charleston
78 Oaktree Drive
Philadelphia, PA 19012
(215) 547-9834

PROFESSIONAL EXPERIENCE

LENOX CHINA/CRYSTAL   Trenton, NJ   8/93 to present
Coordinator of Advertising and Promotion

- Responsible for production and printing of all 4-color sales promotional materials, including catalogs.
- Write original copy, supervise others in copy writing, artwork, layouts, and production.
- Supervise production of dealer newspaper portfolio.
- Work on designs for p.o.p. materials and displays.
- P.R. release preparation and agency coordination.
- Supervise copy, preparation, and production of retail store envelope enclosure program.
- Budget work, have submitted several substantial cost reduction items.
- Trade show supervision and participation.
- Arrange and coordinate national press show.
- Sales meeting preparation and assistance.
- Experienced with photoshop and illustrator.

BUSINESS NEWS, INC.   Philadelphia, PA   1/92 to 7/93
Associate Advertising Sales Manager

- Account supervisor, sold and serviced over 500 accounts.
- Supervised in-house agency services for clients, including copy, ad design, production, and media planning.
- Wrote P.R. releases for clients.
- Did publication expansion research.
- Increased commission rate from $10 K/yr. to $17 K/yr. in eighteen-month period.

DUN & BRADSTREET, INC. Philadelphia, PA   8/91 to 1/92
Credit Services Salesman

MASSACHUSETTS MUTUAL LIFE INSURANCE COMPANY
Honolulu, HI; Allentown, PA   1/89 to 1/91
Life and Health Sales

(Continued)

EDUCATION   Muhlenberg College, Allentown, PA, B.A. in Psychology, 1989
                       U.S. Air Force Telecommunications-Electronics Management
                       School
                       Charles Morris Price School of Advertising
                       Sales and Marketing Schools

REFERENCES   Provided on request.

Maria Zawacki
68 Old Mill Road
Springfield, MI 48678
(313) 821-9641

Job Objective: To function as airline reservationist or reservations supervisor.

Experience

4/96–present   Reservationist, *Great North Airlines,* Detroit, MI. Make reservations for GN Airlines to all locations in United States and Canada; arrange connecting flights, teletype, and receive information.

7/87–4/96   Reservationist, *Trans-West Airlines,* Chicago, IL. Performed all reservation duties at O'Hare Airport; arranged connecting flights; type and teletype; operated all airline computers.

Education

June 1987   Graduated from Laverne Bell Modeling School, Chicago, IL.

June 1986   Commercial Diploma
Mother Seton High School, Chicago, IL.

References   Full references will be furnished on request.

20 Jerome Drive
Putnam Lake
Patterson, NY 12563

WILLIAM A. ELLIOTT

EDUCATION

1982–1985, School of Visual Arts, 209 E. 23rd Street, New York, New York. Graduated with Associate's Degree.

EMPLOYMENT

10/90–present—For the past thirteen years, worked for the New York Zoological Society as a Designer-Illustrator. During the last two years, held a supervisory position as the assistant Art Director. Duties included designing of all printed material used for the Zoo and Aquarium (annual reports, educational brochures, books, posters, letterheads, logos). Was also involved in the design and production of all the educational graphics that appear both outside and inside the buildings. All of the above mentioned work was designed and produced on the Zoo's property.

Additional experience—Three years' experience operating a 20 × 24 Chemco copy camera. Five years' experience silk screening multicolor back-lit graphics. Experienced with Quark, Photoshop, and Illustrator.

1/89–10/90—R. H. Macy's—Advertising. Worked freelance for Macy's designing all advertising for 22 departments such as Cosmetics, Jewelry, Children's Apparel, Sporting Goods, etc.

1986–1988—U.S. Army. Worked as Post Illustrator at Ft. Richardson, Alaska, during which time designed displays for A.U.S.A. Convention held in Washington, DC in September 1987. Also worked on the designing and construction of displays used in the commemoration of the Alaskan Centennial. Transferred to White Sands Missile Range, New Mexico, where worked on several Army promotional displays.

BILL ELLIOTT WILDLIFE ILLUSTRATOR
animal portraits • wildlife illustration • birds • fish • mammals 914-279-9338

CONSTANCE ANITA KRAVITZ

456 Philadelphia Road
Camden, NJ 08705
Phone: (609) 293-2423

BUSINESS EXPERIENCE

Electronics Age magazine
CHILTON PUBLISHING COMPANY, Princeton, NJ

1993 to present

Assistant Art Director—March 1993 to present
Report to Art Director and Managing Editor.
Responsibilities include art selection and preparation, illustrating, magazine layout, and some cover design. When necessary, act as a Chilton representative at our printers and serve in a supervisory capacity. Position involves heavy contact with artists, writers, editors, and suppliers and the ability to work under tight deadlines.

Production Editor—November 1991 to March 1993
Responsible for all copy flow on *Electronics Age.*
Programmed software for computer typesetting. Served as liaison between art and editorial departments and between the printer, various vendors, and the magazine. Completed an operations research study to determine more efficient production processes which resulted in a reallocation of personnel.

GREYSTONE PUBLISHING (Franson Corporation), Old Bridge, NJ

June 1991 to
November 1991

Production—Position included responsibility for the design and layout of decorating encyclopedias. Was working art director for a short time before leaving. Produced direct mail pieces using QuarkXpress.

DAN RIVER MILLS, Woodbridge, NJ

January 1991
to June 1991

Commercial Artist—Originated fabric design on hand loom.

(Continued)

THE TEXAS CATHOLIC NEWSPAPER Dallas, TX

January 1989   <u>Staff Artist</u>—Job entailed complete responsibility for all artwork
to January 1991   associated with the paper and its advertising. Also estimated
                      the amount of advertising and editorial copy per issue and
                      determined the forms accordingly. Designed cover and produced the
                      Diocesan Directory for 1991.

EDUCATION

September 1989   HUNTER COLLEGE, C.C.N.Y.   New York, NY
to August 1991   Studio and Art History major/English minor

September 1985   UNIVERSITY OF DALLAS   Irving, TX
to June 1987   Fine Arts Major

References available upon request

Morris Levine

21 East 50th Street
New York, New York 10017
(212) 966-0561

OBJECTIVE: Growth position that would effectively utilize my experience as commercial artist.

EXPERIENCE

1996–present   Art Director, *Schirmer Graphics Company.* Created original computer graphics for audiovisual shows and slide production, mechanicals for annual report production, and photography.

1991–1996   Assistant Art Director, *Berkley/Grosset/Putnum Publications, Inc.* Circulation Art Department. Created direct mail pieces, sales aids promotions, product ads, rate cards, logos, and letterheads, 4-color brochures, spot drawings and slides, from concept to completion.

1986–1991   Assistant Art Director, *Creative Arts Magazine Enterprises.* Created sales aids promotions, direct mail pieces, product ads, research studies, rate cards, brochures, logos, letterheads, and inserts.

1984–1986   Assistant Art Director, *Mechanical Designs* magazine. Emphasis on general boardwork, computerized layout and design.

1982–1984   Staff Artist, *Clint Crafts Publishers,* Art Department. General boardwork, layout, mechanicals, photo cropping, and scaling.

EDUCATION

Industrial Arts High School—Graduated June 1982, Commercial Arts Diploma.

REFERENCES

Furnished upon request.

JOYCE PETERS

14 State Street • Albany, NY 12415 • (313) 876-1266 • (313) 875-5000

CAREER OBJECTIVE   To secure a responsible position with a progressive firm that will utilize my skills and experience and provide growth opportunities.

BUSINESS EXPERIENCE

S<small>T</small>. M<small>ARTIN'S</small> P<small>RESS,</small> *Albany, NY*   Dec. 1995–Present

Jan. 1997–
Present

Position:	***Art Aide***
Responsibilities:	Responsible for trafficking illustrations, mechanicals, and electronic files between printers and production for new publications. Maintenance of departmental photo files. Also included in duties are phone work, filing, light typing of departmental correspondence, and maintaining freelance ledger. Input data to update inventory files. Create computer layouts and typesetting.

Dec. 1995–
Jan. 1997

Position:	***Illustration Expeditor***
Responsibilities:	Responsible for preparing, organizing, and expediting all material that flows between production department and printers. Record keeping in departmental log files.

A<small>LBANY</small> Y<small>OUTH</small> C<small>OUNCIL,</small> *Albany, NY*   Nov. 1994–Nov. 1995

Position:	***Clerical Office Assistant***
Responsibilities:	General office duties, including but not limited to filing, phone work, operation of all office equipment, including copiers and adding machines.

EDUCATION

Sept. 1987–June 1991   A<small>LBANY</small> H<small>IGH</small> S<small>CHOOL</small>

REFERENCES   ***Available upon request***

MARJORIE TARKINGTON

16 CALIFORNIA AVENUE

MIAMI, FL 33131

(305) 815-8334

PROFESSIONAL HISTORY

March 1997
to present

ART DIRECTOR

Marcia James Assoc., Miami, FL

Develop visual concepts for ads, brochures, press kits, direct mail packages, logos, and sales sheets. Direct studio and location photography. Commission and supervise illustrators. Interface with clients to obtain information and advance the creative process. Oversee print production including blueprint and 4-color film, and press approvals. Supervise graphic designer and freelance mechanical artists.

January 1996
to March 1997

ASSISTANT ART DIRECTOR

Stern's & Co., Miami, FL

Designed 4-color catalogs, weekly tabloids, ads, and store graphics for more than thirty major retail stores. Assisted Art Director with catalog production. Coordinated merchandise samples. Supervised fashion and product photography. Created corporate graphic materials.

January 1995
to January 1996

FREELANCE GRAPHIC DESIGNER

Designed ads, posters, brochures, and 4-color catalogs.

> Clients: *Deutch & Shea Advertising,* Miami, FL
>> *American Council on the Teaching of Foreign Languages,* Hastings-on-Hudson, NY

August 1993
to January 1995

GRAPHIC DESIGNER

The Daily Star, **Miami, FL**

Designed editorial pages. Created logos and computer layouts for special advertising sections. Created new advertising formats to attract new advertisers. Designed new publications: *New Men's News* and *The Women's Registry.*

September 1991
to July 1993

GRAPHIC DESIGNER

The Miami News, **Miami, FL**

Designed advertising, supplement covers, and photo pages. Edited photos. Photographed news events. Created and implemented weekly full-page photo essays. Introduced and managed in-house graphic design firm.

(Continued)

July 1989   FREELANCE FABRIC DESIGNER
to July 1991   Designed and printed fabrics using Japanese dyeing techniques. Created
                     "wearable art" costumes. Marketed garments through galleries and
                     participated in major wearable art exhibitions.

EDUCATION

September 1993   Graphic communications studies.
to 1995   School of Visual Arts and Pratt Institute, New York, NY

September 1990   Professional photography studies with Rae Russel, veteran magazine
to August 1991   photographer. Focus on photojournalism and portraiture.

September 1988   Master of Fine Arts Degree.
to June 1990   New York University

June 1978   Bachelor of Fine Arts Degree.
                     New York University

References available upon request.

LAURIE ADAMS

ADDRESS
24 Oak Park Road
Peekskill, NY 11304
(914) 341-4416

EDUCATION
1991–1995: Brown University, B.A. Studio Art.
Includes study at Sir John Cass School of Art, London,
England, and Rhode Island School of Design.

1990: Syracuse University, Photography and Art Workshop.

EMPLOYMENT
1995–Present: General boardwork, <u>Design Plus Inc.</u>, Yorktown
Heights, NY.

1995–Summer: General boardwork, <u>High Times Magazine</u>, New
York, NY.

1992–Summer: Mechanical, pasteup artist, <u>Lasky Company
Lithographers</u>, Millburn, NJ.

1990–Summer: Art Instructor, <u>Camp Rondack</u>, NY.

**HONORS AND
AWARDS**
Salutatorian, Morristown High School.
First Prize, Art Contest, City Federal Bank. Alumni Award,
Morristown High School. National Merit Scholarship Semifinalist.

REFERENCES
Available on request.

John Kassech
13-06 45th St.
Long Island City, New York 11106
(718) 929-1150

PROFESSIONAL EXPERIENCE:

1993–
present

Queens County District Attorney's Office
Flushing, New York

Assistant District Attorney
Trial litigation in major felony cases; extensive motion practice;
preparation and investigation of homicides, sex crimes, and
economic crimes; vehicular homicide supervisor.

1991–
1993

Silverman and Saltman
New York, New York

Associate Attorney
Civil trial litigations, contract negotiation; antitrust and corporate
law; Family Court and marital proceedings; and arbitration.

EDUCATION:

Loyola University School of Law
New Orleans, Louisiana
J.D., 1991

New York University
New York, New York
B.A., 1988; Major in Sociology

BAR ADMISSION:

New York Bar Association
Florida Bar Association
United States Supreme Court
United States District Court
    Southern District of New York
    Eastern District of New York
United States Court of Appeals
    Sixth Circuit

References furnished upon request.

ELIZABETH MORRIS
169 Ninth Street
Milford, PA 18428
Tel: (717) 296-6215   Cell: (717) 555-4414

BACKGROUND

Extensive experience in all legal aspects of real estate investments and corporate matters with management positions of increasing responsibility. In addition, eight years' prime responsibility for the risk management insurance programs of a national company.

EXPERIENCE

Private Practice   1998–2002

Associated with Harris, Newman & Miller, specializing in commercial, corporate, and real estate law.

State Farm Insurance Company   1988–1998
Vice President—Counsel and Assistant Secretary

Managed real estate investment division of Law Department, comprised of three attorneys and a paralegal assistant. Implemented and successfully completed fifteen real estate joint ventures in nine states within eighteen months. Completed negotiation and documentation for a unique joint venture condominium corporate headquarters. Consummated real estate investments on a national basis. Negotiated leases and brokerage agreements on owned properties and as tenant in national sales offices. Initiated and implemented errors and omissions insurance coverage for our national sales organization and the officers and directors of the company.

Associate Counsel

Conducted national corporate practice including real estate investments, litigation, construction contracts, leases, legislation, consumer protection, national marketing programs, and casualty insurance.

Esso Oil Company   1983–1988

Attorney (Law Department)

Maintained corporate practice including all phases of real estate. Responsible for antitrust, product contracts, landlord and tenant, asset and stock acquisitions.

EDUCATION

Columbia College: B.S., Recommended for Fulbright Scholarship.

Columbia Law School: Admitted New York State Bar.

AFFILIATIONS

Pennsylvania Country Lawyers Association: Secretary of Real
    Property Committee
American Bar Association
American Land Title Association
Association of Life Insurance Counsel

John Corwin
62 Pine Street
Scarsdale, New York 10583
(914) 823-1234

EXPERIENCE:

1/93–present

ASSOCIATE COUNSEL
Sklar Paints, Inc.
Yonkers, New York

RESPONSIBILITIES:
*Trade regulation/*restrictive business practices counseling. Monitor compliance with FTC Consent Decrees.

Draft and review *contracts,* including: distributorships; licenses (patent, know-how, trademark); import/export; purchase and sale of goods, services, businesses; joint ventures; leases, realty, secrecy, employment; secured transactions.

Negotiate warranty and product liability claims.

Review with management foreign legal requirements, and implement appropriate action.

Coordinate litigation in conjunction with local trial counsel.

Maintain corporate records for various subsidiaries.

EDUCATION:

New York University
Graduate School of Law
LL.M., January 1993
Class standing–Top Quarter

New York Law School
J.D., January 1992
Class standing–Top Quarter

Cornell University
B.A., June 1989
Class standing–Top Quarter

References available upon request.

RUTH LEVINE
412 E. 72nd Street
New York, NY 10313
(212) 412-3150
(212) 415-6800

EDUCATION:	M.B.A.—Financial Management, Fordham University, 1992
	B.B.A.—Accounting, Fordham University, 1982

EXPERIENCE:

Sept. 1994 to Present

Lord & Taylor, Inc. *Audit Manager*

Responsibilities include analytical review and verification of financial records and operating controls. Developed audit programs, established guidelines for physical distribution and warehousing of inventory. An integral part of the review was to evaluate the adequacy of internal controls and the extent of compliance with management policy. At audit completion, the exceptions were discussed and an objective opinion with remedial guidelines was submitted to management.

Jan. 1990 to Aug. 1994

Oxman Dry Cleaners, Inc.

Operated family dry cleaning establishment, engaged in all aspects of business activity necessary to its daily operation. Maintained financial records, performed purchasing and accounting functions.

Jan. 1985 to Dec. 1989

American Fabric, Inc. *Senior Auditor/EDP Auditor*

Conducted financial/operational audits of both domestic and international facilities. The review included an in-depth study of the manufacturing process, evaluated and recommended changes in policies concerning internal controls. Performed EDP audits, familiar with computer control applications on IBM Sys/37 DOS. Knowledge of COBOL and BASIC languages. Supervised and monitored performance of three staff auditors. The review provided management with assurance that effective controls and policies were being administered.

July 1982 to Dec. 1984

Haskins & Sells, CPA *Jr. Accountant/Auditor*

Participated in certified audits of clients in fields of banking, brokerage, hotels, construction, and insurance. The review included analysis, verification, and confirmation. Assisted in preparing financial statements, SEC reports, budgetary planning, and consolidations.

LANGUAGES: Fluent in Spanish and Italian

REFERENCES: Will be furnished upon request

DONALD PAIGE
75 Shore Road
Houston, Texas 75213
(415) 225-4889
(415) 765-6644

EXPERIENCE

SHAW AND SONS INC., *Houston, Texas*   June 1995–June 2002

   POSITION: *ACCOUNTS RECEIVABLE, BOOKKEEPER CREDIT & COLLECTION SUPERVISOR*

   DUTIES: Responsible for invoice processing daily and weekly. Checking service order changes and charge backs. In charge of cash receipts posting to computer, maintained customer billing files, supervised and trained collection and customer service representatives. Responsible for monthly closings, aging report generation. Credit investigations on all new clients and new client credit limits. Monitored Dun & Bradstreet reports for changing financial status on clients. Other duties: Payroll, Accounts Payable, Supervision.

BAYLOR INSTITUTE OF TECHNOLOGY   July 1992–June 1995
Department of Business and Finance, *Atlanta, Georgia*

   POSITION: *ACCOUNTING ASSISTANT*
   DEPARTMENTS: Payroll & Records/Grant & Contract Accounting

   DUTIES: Accounts payable, accounts receivable, budget forecasting and revision modification for direct and indirect cost for federal grants and contracts awarded to the institution. EDP Payroll biweekly processing for 54 different departments encompassing 700+ employees, via data entry to main computer.

**SOFTWARE/
HARDWARE**   IBM PC XT/IBM, LAN's/Data Media, EXCEL 42/Textronics/, MS Word

EDUCATION   Baylor University, 1990

REFERENCES   Available upon request.

Sample Resumes   **137**

Pablo Gonzalez
12 Prickly Pear Road
Santa Fe, New Mexico 87524
(505) 239-8765

POSITION OBJECTIVES

Desire to be Manager or Assistant Manager of a dynamic Accounting Department or Division with opportunities to be Assistant Controller.

WORK HISTORY

1991–present   Supervisor–Accounts Payable, *White's,* Santa Fe.
Supervise 5 people; process approximately 15 to 40 vendor adjustments and inquiries per day; handle accruals and reconciliations both quarterly and yearly.

1988–1991   Manager–Accounts Payable, *Quality Foods,* Santa Fe.
Supervised 25 people; processed approximately 600 invoices per day; audited vendor invoices for payment; handled vendor adjustments and inquiries.

1978–1988   Assistant Manager–Accounts Payable, *Pop-Rite Soda,* Los Angeles.
Supervised 17 people; processed approximately 500 invoices per day; balanced daily disbursements with computer printout.

1973–1978   Billing Supervisor, *Gardner Advertising,* Los Angeles.
Supervised 5 people; billed approximately 40 invoices per day; Accounts Receivable and Accounts Payable.

EDUCATION

Santa Fe Tech, Accounting Degree, 1973

REFERENCES SUPPLIED BY REQUEST.

MILLARD POLLOCK
1428 Cornelia Street
Brooklyn, NY 11227
(718) 384-3366

OBJECTIVE | To manage a general bookstore with large volume sales, and act as buyer for same. Particularly interested in rare editions and current literature.

EXPERIENCE

May 1996–
Present

Store Manager, R. Altman Bookseller,
Riverdale, New York.
Responsible for increase in sales of at least 25% since handling of inventory and selection of items for special sales. Present sales volume more than 20% above previous goal.

February 1995–
May 1996

Manager Trainee, R. Altman Bookseller,
Daytona Beach, Florida.
Trained in all phases of selling, customer relations, sales presentations, etc.

May 1994–
February 1995

Sales Clerk, Bainbridge Music Sales, Inc.
Springfield, Ohio.
Sold sheet music; recommended special pieces for chorale groups, instrumentalists.

EDUCATION

Attended University of Kansas September 1992 through June 1994.
Majored in Literature

PROFESSIONAL AFFILIATIONS

Member of NBS. Certified completion of NBS/FLS Booksellers Program.

REFERENCES

Complete references will be furnished upon request.

BUYER

JOHN SHORT

455 OAKS MANOR

Coconut Creek, Florida 33021

555-428-6124

BUYING • SALES • MANAGEMENT

Director of Footwear Buying for innovative chain of juvenile "mega" stores, as well as for one of the country's largest independent shoe retailers, with a broad-based background of more than 14 years of experience in every facet of the footwear industry.

Expertise in buying, sales, merchandising and marketing, as well as executive management, with planning, organization and implementation capabilities.

Proven track record of developing product lines, resulting in higher gross margins and profitability and meeting desirable inventory and turnover goals. Instrumental in setting up and developing shoe departments in three Florida stores from inception.

SUMMARY OF QUALIFICATIONS:

- Broad exposure and capabilities in a variety of related areas, including development of product lines, negotiating merchandise costs, pricing, and mark-up percent.
- Experienced planning advertising/marketing strategies.
- Strong communication and interpersonal skills.
- Excellent planning, organizational, implementation and supervisory ability.
- Expertise in staffing, training, and motivating personnel.

EXPERIENCE:

SHOES FOR YOUTH, INC., BOCA RATON, FL   **NOVEMBER 1993 TO PRESENT**
Buyer - Footwear
- Recruited by corporate management to provide footwear industry expertise in establishing chain of stores in South East Florida, which developed more than $24 million in annual sales from start-up.
- Developed store layouts and design, including display and fixturing.
- Complete responsibility for building lines of merchandise, formulating classification breakouts, and plan margin and generating over $3 million in sales for the shoe division.
- Successfully increased athletic shoe business by 20%.
- Developed strong working relationships with resources to insure style, quality, and assortment.
- Conduct market surveys to ascertain, interpret, and intensify key trends.
- Assist in developing sales/marketing strategies, plan advertising/promotion campaigns, and create ads.

PAYLESS SHOES, CHICAGO, IL   **MARCH 1987 TO OCTOBER 1993**
Buyer
- Total responsibility for developing and maintaining "women's athletic" and "children's shoe" assortments for 14-store retail shoe chain, generating in excess of $12 million annually, representing more than 12% of company's production.
- Conducted extensive research of manufacturers to determine latest styles and trends.
- Successfully negotiated and acquired Stride Rite merchandise line.
- Prepared sales analyses, planned marketing strategies, and merchandise distribution for the 14 stores.
- Developed specialized programs for sales associates, both new and existing personnel, as well as ongoing training programs.
- Maintained a 41% profit margin in children's, and 39% in athletics, through aggressive closeout and special purchases.

EXPERIENCE: (CONTINUED)

SAKS FIFTH AVENUE, SKOKIE, IL   MARCH 1986 TO MARCH 1987
Assistant Department Manager
- Supervised, trained, and motivated sales force to develop high degree of professionalism and sales closing ability.
- Maintained all commission and sales records, and assisted with preparation of department's budgets.
- Coordinated activities with buyers on a daily basis to advise them of proper assortments and fill-ins.

CHERNIN'S SHOES, CHICAGO, IL   AUGUST 1982 TO FEBRUARY 1986
General Manager
- Complete responsibility for all sales and in-store marketing activities for high volume Buffalo Grove and Morton Grove stores.
- Hired, trained, and supervised more than 80 employees, both staff and management.
- Prepared and maintained budgets; supervised inventory and cost control.
- Performed accounting functions, including reconciliations and P & L reports.
- Designed and implemented sales/merchandising programs to motivate staff and increase volume.
- Exceeded monthly sales plan by 10% through training and incentive programs.
- Initially employed as sales trainees and advanced to management after successful sales career.

EDUCATION:

WILLIAM RAINEY HARPER COLLEGE, PALATINE, IL
Business Management Courses

COMPUTER PROFICIENCY:

IBM PC and Compatibles • Spreadsheets • Word Processing

REFERENCES:

Furnished upon request

David Hershfield
166 Elm Street
Framingham, MA 02189
(617) 421-6822

Objective

To secure a position for the summer of 2003 as an athletic or senior counselor. Full Red Cross training and qualifications.

Experience

Summer 2002 *Athletic Counselor,* **Camp Wee-ta-kee,** Geneva, NY.
Responsible for all sports for the 14- to 16-year-old age group; sports included swimming, tennis, archery, and riding; supervised junior counselors.

Summer 2001 *Waterfront Counselor,* **Camp Endicott,** Turham, NH.
Supervised all lake sports, including canoeing, sailing, swimming, and water skiing.

Summer 2000 *Counselor,* **Camp Endicott**
Responsible for 65 boys; instructor in basketball.

Education

Junior at University of Pennsylvania, 2002.

References

References on request.

ROBERTA CALDWELL
35 Lyndon Way
Cromwell, NJ 07841

201-991-0328

OBJECTIVE   To be employed as cashier in large retail store in shopping center, preferably in Cromwell vicinity.

EXPERIENCE

1994–   Cashier, part-time, Bergen Supermarket, Bergen, NJ. Worked 20 hours a
2002   week as cashier at checkout counter.

1985–   Assistant Bookkeeper and Cashier, Howard's Retail Store. Collected and
1994   recorded mail-order payments as well as those made in person at credit office; prepared monthly statement; assisted bookkeeper in all record keeping.

1980–   Accounts Receivable Clerk, Homowak Mart, New Bergen, NJ. Received
1985   payments made in credit office and by mail, recorded cash, issued receipts. Prepared monthly statements to customers.

EDUCATION

1980   Completed six-month course in Business Computer Technology at Cromwell Business School.

REFERENCES

Furnished upon request.

Robert S. Showalter
135 Maine Avenue
Flushing, New York 11353
(718) 533-6857

SUMMARY:
Circulation management executive. Consumer, trade, business publishing fields.
Total expertise in all circulation areas, including subscription promotion, direct
response, graphics buying, agency sales, newsstand sales, fulfillment, computerized
systems, budgets, audit requirements.

EMPLOYMENT:

Mailis Publishing Co., Inc., New York, New York (9/97–present)
Circulation director and member of management planning board. Responsible for
the development and implementation of all circulation and related programs.
Initiated and implemented merchandise marketing program.

Reader's Digest, Inc., Mount Kisco, New York (1/94–8/97)
Assistant to vice president and circulation director. Involvement included all
circulation areas, subscription promotion, direct response programs, agency sales,
fulfillment, budgets.

Food Packaging, Inc., New York, New York (2/92–12/93)
Assistant to vice president and circulation director. Responsibilities included all
circulation areas, subscription promotion, direct response programs, agency sales,
newsstand, fulfillment, budget.

Computer/Data, Inc., New York, New York (6/85–1/92)
Operations manager for computerized magazine, book, direct mail, merchandise
fulfillment, and related services.

EDUCATION:

Queens College, Flushing, New York (1981–1985)
Hunter College's School of Advanced Business Administration (1980–1981)

REFERENCES:

Available on request.

Raymond J. Stetson
99 Perry Street
New York, New York 10014

212-924-8813 (home)
212-879-5500 (business)

Professional Experience:

1997–present
Clerk, The Metropolitan Museum of Art, New York, New York 10028.
Knowledge of all aspects in production and composition of internal museum publications. Responsibilities include photography, reduction, layout, sizing, and printing.

1996–1997
Clerk and Assistant Bookkeeper, Basic Books Co., New York, New York 10022.
Dealings in royalty allotments to educational publications' authors, including company as well as author dividends. Also, development of a computerization layout and feed-in to replace manual computations.

1994–1996
Intermediate Clerk, First Jersey National Bank, Jersey City, New Jersey 07302.
Solely responsible for computer feed-in of dealer commissions for mutual funds corporations. Control check of stock books and balancing.

1988–1994
Clerk, First Jersey National Bank, Jersey City, New Jersey 07302.
Accounts researcher, stock issuance, control of accounts receivable for mutual funds corporations. Daily use of telephone for communication of services to nationwide investors and their representatives.

Educational Background:

City College of NY, NYC 1988

References: Available on request.

CLERK—WORD PROCESSING

EVELYN PLUMER
259 Ridge Lane
Danbury, Connecticut 06810
203-742-3301

JOB OBJECTIVE: To provide top-quality, conscientious service as typist and
                 office clerk to industrial firm in New York City.

EXPERIENCE

1997– 20XX	<u>Typist, File Clerk</u>, Feinberg Associates, Danbury, Connecticut. Assemble data from legal reports, type revisions and legal contracts; serve as relief receptionist, maintain files, and provide general office assistance.
1994– 1997	<u>Typist-Receptionist</u>, Manzo Realtors, Forest Hills, New York. Served as receptionist to large Real Estate company; typed documents related to sale and purchase of property; filed records of clients and construction companies; maintained appointment schedules.

EDUCATION

Graduated with Commercial Diploma from Danbury High School,
June 1994.

OFFICE SKILLS

Type—95 wpm; MS Word, EXCEL, Internet Services, Fax and
Copiers.

REFERENCES

Will be provided upon request.

CLERK—DATA ENTRY

Chiala Dakazarom
465 West End Avenue
New York, NY 10023
(212) 622-4802

OBJECTIVE

Full-time employment as word processor or receptionist in New York firm.

EXPERIENCE

June 1996–
present

Data entry, Jorgensen International, Carteret, NJ.
Type data on office forms, file records, provide general office assistance.

EDUCATION

1994–1996

Attended Water Valley Junior College in Buffalo, NY.
Earned A.A. in English Composition, May 1996.

OFFICE SKILLS

Typing—110 wpm, Filing, Computers—hardware and software.

REFERENCES

Will be provided upon request.

DAVID STEIN
31 Oak Road
Sedona, Arizona 24156
(918) 883-4156

EDUCATION
Union College, Poughkeepsie, NY
Graduated June 2002
> Courses included: Marketing Research, Financial Management, Production Management, Introduction to Computer Systems, Accounting I and II.

EXPERIENCE
Summers 1999–'02

Allen Major Building, Inc.,
Rockville Centre, NY
Participated in inventory control, receiving and shipping, deliveries, advancing to counterperson.

Summers 1994–'99

Jordan Lobster Farms, Inc., and **North Shore Lobster Seafood Co.,**
Island Park, NY, and *Great Neck, NY*
Responsible for preparation of lobsters, sales, receiving and shipping, and general maintenance.

Summers 2001–'02
Part-time

Basic Needs, Inc.
Manhasset, NY
Assisted in running summer curb painting operation for various villages of Long Island.

ACTIVITIES
Member Union College Varsity Hockey 1995–'02
Participated in nationally recognized Marist College Institute for Public Opinion, Big Brother/Big Sister Program, Poughkeepsie, NY 2000

Intramural Sports Program 1999–'02

REFERENCES
Furnished upon request

PAUL RAYSON
(Confidential)
519 S. 4th Street
Edinburg, Texas 78539
Phone: Home: (512) 383-6655
Office: (512) 381-2515

OBJECTIVE   ADMINISTRATIVE STAFF

Research—Communication and Publications—Program Planning—Training

EXPERIENCE

<u>1994–present</u>. **Assistant Professor** in Department of History, **Pan American University,**
        Edinburg, Texas.
Conduct classroom lectures, discussions, examinations; lead and coordinate seminars.
Perform course design, involving research and organization. Serve on various
committees—e.g., honors council and self-study committee for University
reaccreditation—entailing research and writing activity. Handle diverse administrative
duties, including coordination of interdepartmental honors program, supervision of
research projects, student counseling, and recruitment.

Efforts have been instrumental in upgrading awareness of students in areas pertinent to
fields of study; in attracting new students to school and department; and in improving
personal skills in communication. Among accomplishments: Through course organization,
coordinated library of visuals, and revised and modernized reading list, succeeded in
revitalizing two honors courses that had suffered severe enrollment losses under
predecessor. Through extensive independent research, formulated and implemented
pioneering courses that have earned high standing among departmental offerings.

<u>1991–1994</u>.   **Assistant Professor** at **Falls View College,**
        Falls View, Mississippi.
Following brief fill-in assignment during emergency situation at West Chester College,
West Chester, Pennsylvania.
Performed teaching, research, administrative, and other functions similar to those above.

Previously, **Graduate & Undergraduate Student;** with concurrent employment
(1989–1991) as **Library Technician** in information services for **Free Library of New York,**
and as **Music Director** for church.

EDUCATION / PROFESSIONAL QUALIFICATIONS / LANGUAGES

Ph.D. and A.M. degrees in American Civilization, from University of Pennsylvania,
Philadelphia. Recipient of Woodrow Wilson, University and Harrison Fellowships, 1991.

(Continued)

B.A. (<u>with honors</u>) in American Studies, State University of New York at Buffalo. Elected to Phi Beta Kappa.

<u>Publications</u>: Author of Essay "Containing Communism: the Art of Getting Along" in *Reason;* and of book reviews in *American Quarterly.*

<u>Languages</u>: Essential fluency in French; also some Spanish.

REFERENCES

Will be furnished on request.

COMPUTER OPERATOR

DONNA ADAMS
477 Cypress Street
Plantation, Florida 33404
561-404-7712

COMPUTER DATA ENTRY • CUSTOMER SERVICE

More than 14 years of stable employment with international data vendor company, specializing in financial equity and commodity trading information. Experience includes marketing of services, as well as information research, computer data entry, verification, and file maintenance.

Known for skills and abilities to handle volume production with high accuracy rating on a time-urgent basis. Comprehensive knowledge of market reporting and data program, with strong ability to interface with prospective customers and deliver effective sales presentation. Capable of working independently or as part of a team effort.

SUMMARY OF QUALIFICATIONS:

- Diversified results-oriented experience in sales/marketing and customer service.
- Successfully maintained efficient data entry operation, requiring optimum accuracy under pressure of daily deadlines.
- Strong communication and interpersonal skills.
- Adept at planning, organizing, and implementing systems and procedures.
- Computer knowledgeable.
- Proven dependable and loyal with 14 years of stable work history.
- Ability to easily grasp new concepts and quickly benefit from a training situation.

WORK EXPERIENCE:

WALL STREET BROKERS, INC., BOCA RATON, FL   **7/84–PRESENT**
Marketing Representative   *(3/98–Present)*
- Respond to inbound telephone inquiries regarding various financial "end-of-day" market information services provided by this international data vendor.
- Conduct telephone sales presentation to sign up subscribers to software program which downloads info from the Internet.
- Act as consultant to prospective customers to assess their needs and propose the proper service to fulfill their needs.
- Ranked among the leading sales producers within the company.

Data Entry   *(7/84–3/98)*
- Responsible for researching and entering data information for the commodities market, including cash aspect and futures contract.
- Gathered information from news sources, such as Reuters, Bridge News, *Wall St. Journal, Barrons,* and *Financial Times,* as well as direct contact with Nasdaq and the various exchanges.
- Researched historical data from the microfilm archives, as well as newspapers and market reports.
- Checked and verified data for accuracy and amended errors and inconsistencies.

EDUCATION:

SPANISH RIVER H.S., BOCA RATON, FL

Continuing Education:
- Palm Beach Community College, Boca Raton, FL
  - Courses in the History of Art • Sketching Classes
- Adult Education Classes: Sign Language

COMMUNITY ACTIVITIES:
- Member: Greenpeace • International Fund for Animal Welfare • World Wildlife Fund

REFERENCES: Furnished upon request

HARRIET BACH
22 Windover Road
White Plains, NY 12148
(914) 948-7190

OBJECTIVE

A financial control or analysis position with management growth potential where knowledge of computers and finance can be combined.

EXPERIENCE

<u>Security National Bank</u>, White Plains, NY

1999 to 2002	—**Controller,** Shareholder Processing product line. Accountable officer for financial control, reporting and analysis, and contract compliance associated with the divestiture of Shareholder products. (a) Directed external cash exchanges of approximately $10 million annually under contractual terms. (b) Budgeted for operating expenses of about $8 million annually. (c) Problem resolution/negotiation with buyer's Controller. (d) Supervised staff of four.
1996 to 1999	Promoted four times from **Staff Assistant** to **Controller** while assigned to various Corporate Trust product lines: Bearer Bonds, Mortgage Backed Securities, and Information Services. Developed monthly product profitability and expense reports. Investigated expenses, allocated charges and business issues impacting product costs. Capital budgets for projects up to $20 million.

<u>Sears, Inc. International Headquarters</u>, White Plains, NY

1996	—**Systems Analyst Trainee.** Trained to write computer programs in structured COBOL, code own JCL, debug programs with Pro-test, use TSO and Pan-Velet, on an IBM 370.

<u>Ohio State University</u>, Columbus, Ohio

1990 to 1996	—**Administrative Assistant,** Clinical Science Program, College of Human Medicine. Managed staff support for six on-campus courses and one statewide clerkship. (a) Designed and implemented complex schedules for interviews, physical examinations, etc. (b) Secured physical facilities, hospital support, and equipment. (c) Supervised clerical and other employees.

(Continued)

1990   **—Administrative Assistant for Undergraduate Education,** Sociology
             Department. Found and recommended professors to teach extension
             courses. Academically advised undergraduates.

1984 to   **—Teaching Assistant,** Sociology Department. Half-time teaching or
1990   administrative positions for various faculty.

except   **—Clerk,** Libraries. Supervised student employees; maintained
1985 to   Reserve Room journal articles.
1987

EDUCATION
M.B.A. 1995. Finance. Ohio State University.
M.A. 1991. Sociology. Ohio State University.
B.A. 1984. Sociology. Ohio State University.

REFERENCES
Available upon request.

SUSAN EMORY
118 W. 79th St.
New York, NY 10023

Home: (212) 815-2324   Cell: (212) 718-3200

SUMMARY OF EXPERIENCE

Diversified accounting/auditing and management experience. Extensive background in financial analysis and accounting systems and controls. Currently as a working Controller responsible for timely financial reports.

6/97–Present	**David King Co., Inc., NY** **Controller:** Managing the financial, accounting and data processing functions. Supervising the maintenance of books and records, and the office staff. In charge of preparation of financial projections, budgets, analysis, statements, and tax reports. Advising management on opportunities and on actions to improve profitability.
6/91–5/97	**Paris Furniture Co., NY** **Accountant, Asst. Controller:** Responsible for the maintenance of company general ledger, preparation of financial reports, cash receivables, and inventory control.
6/83–5/91	**A. R. Sykes & Co., Harrison, NY** **Senior Accountant:** Supervised staff of seven accountants whose major tasks were the design and implementation of new integrated accounting systems for new and existing divisions and branches of the company. Conducted and performed field auditing, financial and operational.
9/82–5/83	**Otis Elevator Co., Yonkers, NY** **Accountant:** Performed diversified audit assignments.
EDUCATION	Fordham University, 1982, B.B.A. Major: Accounting Fordham University, 1989, Postgraduate Degree L.I.U., New York Master Degree Courses: Financial statements, analysis, quantitative analysis, and quantitative analysis for business research, 1994 Accounting Qualifying Certificate, State of New York, 1995 CPA Candidate
LANGUAGES	Fluent in French
REFERENCES	Furnished upon request.

Samuel J. Taylor
300 Riverside Drive
New York, New York 10025
212-797-3149

SUMMARY

Four years' experience as copywriter for leading publisher, as well as freelance writing of film reviews over the past five years.

EXPERIENCE:

May 1993– Present	Copywriter, Curtis-Hall, Inc., Publishers, Bergenville, New Jersey. Create and write advertising for direct-mail for premium sales and professional books; do layouts and graphic designs for cover material; train new copywriters; condense copy from full-size publications into "mini" books for premium sales.
September 1992– Present	Freelance Film Reviewer, for various news media. Write reviews on educational films for radio and newspaper presentation.

EDUCATION:

M.F.A., June 1991, New York University
B.A., June 1989, Cornell University

SPECIAL HONORS:

Phi Beta Kappa
Smithsonian Scholarship Award—1987 and 1988.

REFERENCES:

Will be furnished upon request.

CHRISTINA KAYE
40 Kalmbach Road
New City, New York 10956
(914) 222-3596

RESUME CAPSULE: Four years' experience as Copy Chief for leading sales agency, two years as Copy Chief and Senior Copywriter, as well as several years of freelance work for major producers of cosmetics, athletic organizations, and advertising firms.

EXPERIENCE:

October 1993–
April 2002

Copy Chief, *Martin Bruckner Agency,* New York City.
In charge of selection, execution, and all presentation of promotional sales material, for all accounts including leading cosmetic, lingerie, knitted garments, and linen manufacturers.

May 1991–
September 1993

Senior Copywriter, *Panels Unlimited,* New York City.
Sales promotion ads and literature to trade, consumer ads, and industrial copy.

June 1989–
April 1991

Assistant Copy Chief, *Allied Radio,* New York City.
Sales promotion, direct mail, trade and catalog copy, consumer ads for all departments. Responsible for special cooperative advertising with producers such as Goldenrod Ceramics, Cornucopia Stoneware, and Devon Cosmetics.

September 1987–
May 1989

Copy/Marketing Trainee, *McCabe Advertising, Inc.,* New York City.
Received training in all phases of copywriting/marketing.

EDUCATION:

B.B.A., June 1985, Pace Institute.

Graduate Work in Sociology, Advanced School of Social Research, Staten Island, New York, September 1985–1987

Executive Training Program, McCabe Advertising, September 1987–May 1989.

REFERENCES:

Will be furnished upon request.

CREDIT MANAGER

FRANCIS BELMONT

7212 River Edge Road
Miami Beach, Florida 33313
407-222-1212

SUMMARY OF QUALIFICATIONS:

- Strong management/administrative background, including hiring, training, customer relations, credit and collections, communications, and supervision.
- Practical business experience in dealing with financial institutions, retailers, chain stores, governments, contractors, hospitals, universities, and general industry.
- Completed Dun & Bradstreet Credit and Financial Analysis course and Dynamic Collection Techniques seminar.
- Personality and work habits characterized by perseverance, self-confidence, strong people skills, and desire to do the best job possible.
- Experience with Windows, Word, Excel, and Lotus 1-2-3.

WORK EXPERIENCE:

1999–2000 **Assisted family members in Ohio with care of elderly parents diagnosed with Alzheimers Disease. Mother has since passed away; Father has been placed in the care of Home for the Aged. Have returned to South Florida to continue with business career in Credit and Collections Management.**

1992–1998 **ALLENBY'S, INC**., Delray Beach, Florida
CREDIT MANAGER for furniture manufacturer
- Oversaw full-function Credit and Collection Department.
- Handled all credit and collection procedures, including credit analysis; approval of new accounts and maintenance of established accounts, utilizing Dun & Bradstreet Credit Reports; assigning of credit limits and full collection effort.
- Supervised staff of three management and clerical personnel.
- Provided credit and collection advice and assistance to other divisions of corporation.
- Worked with accounts in Latin American countries.
- Liaison with outside collection and attorney sources.
- Negotiated domestic and international letters of credit.
- Coordinated State sales tax audits.
- Maintenance of bad debt losses of less than .2% of gross sales.
- AS-400 on-line computer. CA-PRMS software package.

1981–1992 **BOTANY FLOWER,** Miami, Florida
CREDIT MANAGER for wholesale distributor of cut flowers with annual sales volume of more than $25 million
- Coordinated and supervised credit and collection activities of Miami Headquarters, a base of 1,200+ retail flower shop accounts in the South Florida area.
- Developed and implemented credit and collection policies and procedures and authored ***Credit Department Policies and Procedures Manual.***
- Supervision of personnel consisting of credit representatives and clerical assistants.
- Liaison with outside collection and attorney sources.

(WORK EXPERIENCE, cont.)

1970–1980   **FRIENDLY GREETINGS CORPORATION,** Cleveland, Ohio

REGIONAL ACCOUNT SUPERVISOR for major greeting card–novelty item manufacturer–distributor
- Responsible for all supervisory and administration functions of regional area in Corporate Credit/Customer Service Department.
- Accounts receivable, credit authorization and collections, utilizing Dun & Bradstreet for credit analysis and approval.
- Primary contact for accounts and fields sales representatives in handling of merchandise related problems and customer complaints.
- Managed staff of six, encompassing three account correspondents and three clerical assistants.

MILITARY:

1968–1970   **U.S. ARMY,** Honorable Discharge
- Military Police Detachment, Fort Sill, Oklahoma
- Transportation Movement Specialist, U.S. Army Headquarters, Long Binh, South Vietnam

EDUCATION:

KENT STATE UNIVERSITY, Kent, Ohio
Bachelor of Business Administration Degree, **1968**
Major: Marketing

ACTIVITIES:

America Legion Post No. 3221, Cooper City, Florida
Elks Lodge No. 2273, Plantation, Florida

Jerry Korban
345 Brighton Avenue
West New York, New Jersey 07093
Telephone: (201) 965-9845

Work Experience: Hazen and Sawyer, Engineers
360 Lexington Avenue, New York, New York 10017 (212) 986-0033

Work performed: trusted to solve unique problems throughout firm. Developed and negotiated with vendors of furniture, instruments (cameras, calculators, overhead projectors, etc.), stationery, and local and long-distance messenger services; supervised in-house mailroom and duplicating services. Designed covers; dealt with typographers, printers, and word processing suppliers; supervised production of reports and proposals. Responsible for office maintenance; dealt with building maintenance crew and outside firms; organized work parties for files reduction program; organized filing system; controlled 1100 drawings for a $43,000,000 project. Handled interviews for clerical staff; organized parties and seminars; performed library and media research as required.
November 1997 to present

Raventos International Corporation
150 Fifth Avenue, New York, New York 10011 (212) 924-2490

Work performed: marketed an architectural service that renovated, designed, and constructed church buildings; created copy and layout of brochures; wrote research reports on current developments in liturgy and architecture.
June 1995 to September 1997

Fort Worth Community Theatre, Fort Worth, Texas

Work performed: acting, stage managing, set building, lights, sound, and publicity.
September 1994 to May 1995

Education: Currently enrolled in Master of Urban Planning program at NYU.

State University of New York at Stony Brook
B.A. English
Graduated: 1997

ROSETTA DEL'ORIFICE
2109 Broadway
New York, New York 10023
212-787-3200

JOB OBJECTIVE   Position with food processor as staff specialist.

EXPERIENCE

1997–Present   <u>Assistant Dietitian (part-time)</u>, Food Services Department,
                     Masonic Temple, Detroit, Michigan. Helped plan menus and
                     supervised preparation of all meals.

Summers   <u>Assistant to Chief Dietitian</u>, Marlboro State Hospital,
1993–1997   Marlboro, Michigan. Helped translate convalescent diets into
                     actual meals, selected and delivered special meals to diet
                     patients.

EDUCATION

B.S. degree, Michigan State University 1997. Nutrition major. Graduate courses on
Environmental Effect on Man and His Menu, Special Food for the Elderly, and Food
Chemistry.

These courses provided an excellent background in elements of nutrition as related to
ecology, problems of the elderly, and commercial food processing.

HONORS

Dean's List throughout four years of college.

REFERENCES

Will be furnished upon request.

DOCTOR

CURRICULUM VITAE

John Aaron Scott, M.D., P.A.

---

444 Harrow Place • Boca Raton, Florida, 33433 • 561-555-3434

EDUCATION:
Downstate Medical Center, Brooklyn, NY 1985
M.D.

Emory University, Atlanta, GA 1981
Bachelor of Arts Degree, Major: Psychology Summa Cum Laude

Nova Southeastern University Graduate School 1/98–Present
Completing Executive MBA Program

POST GRADUATE TRAINING:
Montefiore Medical Center, The Bronx, NY 7/88–6/90
Cardiology Fellowship

Montefiore Medical Center, The Bronx, NY 7/85–6/88
Internal Medicine Residency

HONORS & AWARDS:
Graduate: Albert Einstein College of Medicine 1988
Davidoff Society Award for Outstanding Housestaff
Clinical Teaching

M. Curtis Langhorn Award for Most Outstanding 1981
Undergraduate Research for the Year

Undergraduate: Psi Chi National Honor Society
In Psychology

BOARD CERTIFICATION:
Cardiovascular Medicine 1992
American Board of Internal Medicine 1988
National Board of Medicine Examiners 1986

MEDICAL LICENSURE:
State of Florida, License #50027 1987
State of New York, License #168263 1986

CURRENT PRACTICE:	Cardiologist on staff: ■ Boca Raton Community Hospital ■ West Boca Medical Center ■ Delray Community Hospital ■ North Ridge Hospital

RESEARCH EXPERIENCE:

Transesophageal Echocardiography in the Assessment of Left Atrial Thrombosis and Embolic Risk

Effects of Kainic Acid Infusions into the Laternal   1980–1981
Hypothalamus on Behavioral Fragmentation (rat model)

PUBLICATIONS:

Corrected Junctional Recovery Time in Prognosis of Narrow Complex Complete Heart Block. Submitted for Publication, PACE 9/89

REFERENCES: Furnished upon request

ALBERTO ROSSI
One Top Stone Drive
Toledo, Ohio 43614
(419) 361-7444

OBJECTIVE

To serve as draftsman in supervisory capacity with manufacturer of mechanical or electrical products.

EXPERIENCE

1994–present	<u>Supervisory Draftsman</u>, Toledo Castings, Inc., Toledo, Ohio. Implement engineering designs of pipes and fittings into working plans. Work with both synthetic fiber and cast iron pipes and fittings. Examine and give recommendations on cost, durability, and feasibility of production designs.
1989–1994	<u>Senior Draftsman</u>, Fire Engine Division, Supreme Truck Manufacturers, Romulus, New York. Assisted Senior Draftsmen in designing basic parts of mountings placed on truck chassis in constructing fire engines. Position provided invaluable training in gross and detailed design and firsthand work with engineers and craftsmen.

EDUCATION

Certificate in Mechanical Drafting, Greenfield Trade School, Greenfield, New York—1989

REFERENCES

Will be furnished upon request.

NAME: Thomas Wolfson

BUSINESS ADDRESS: Coolidge Institution on War, Revolution and Peace,
                         Stanford University, Stanford, California 94305
                         PHONE: 617-734-2979

HOME ADDRESS: 209 Southside Street, Springton, California 90916

CAREER GOALS: Would like to work with a press interested in publishing scholarly books.
    Feel my broad liberal arts background provides a good frame of reference for reading and
    evaluating manuscripts submitted for publication. Having learned the basics of editing on
    the staff of a specialized quarterly, now desire to move to a position with a broader scope
    and more potential for development and advancement.

CURRENT POSITION: Information Editor, Hoover Institution, 1993–present.

RESPONSIBILITIES OF CURRENT POSITION: Primary responsibilities are those of
    Assistant Editor of the Russian Review, a scholarly journal sponsored by the Hoover
    Institution. Read and evaluate incoming manuscripts, edit accepted manuscripts (both
    for content and for style), correspond with authors, undertake basic bibliographic
    research related to accepted manuscripts, proofread at all stages of publication, assign
    new books to reviewers in appropriate fields, and secure necessary copyrights.

FIELDS OF SPECIALIZATION: History major (Russia since 1500, Eastern Europe since
    1453, and Western Europe since 1789); considerable study in political science (Soviet
    foreign policy, international Communism, and Marxist theory).

FOREIGN LANGUAGES: Active knowledge of Russian and French, passive knowledge of
    German.

FELLOWSHIPS: Teaching Assistantship, Indiana University, 1992–93, 1993–94
                Graduate Assistantship, Indiana University, 1994–95, 1995–96
                Doctoral Student Grant-in-Aid for Research, Indiana University, 1996–97

EDUCATION: Ph.D. (major: history), 1997 (expected), Indiana University
              M.A. (major: history), 1993, Indiana University, Bloomington, Indiana
              A.B. (major: history), 1991, Duke University, Durham, North Carolina

DISSERTATION: Rebuilding the Russian Army, 1909–14: A Study in the Formation of
    Policy under Nicholas II

REFERENCES: On request.

Gilbert G. Crossens
482 East 46th Street
New York, New York 10017

212-462-0934

OBJECTIVE   To apply background and interest in History to editing educational
                 books on Early American History.

EXPERIENCE

1996–2002   Instructor, Montveil Seminary, Montveil, Pennsylvania. Principles of
                 Economics, Early American History, History of Economic Thought.

1994–1996   Instructor, St. Agnes Convent, Convent Station, New Jersey.
                 Comparative Economic Systems, U.S. Government, U.S. History.

1992–1994   Instructor, Midvale College, Brooklyn. Economic Institutions,
                 American History.

1990–1992   Editor, The World Today, Historical Society of Philadelphia. Edited
                 encyclopedia commentaries on current events, particularly related
                 to American Politics and Historical Events.

EDUCATION
        Ph.D., Economics, Pennsylvania State University–1996
        M.A., History, Pennsylvania State University–1991
        B.A., Economics/History, Fordham College, New York–1990

REFERENCES
        Available on request.

Sample Resumes   **165**

JOHN W. BOSITINO
2109 Broadway
New York, NY 10023
212 SU 7-2200

OBJECTIVE   To obtain position as Senior Editor with publisher of high school/college texts, general trade.

EXPERIENCE

11/90–
present
     Editor, Brace Publishing Corporation, New York, NY. Assisted the editorial director in reviewing and selecting general trade and business education titles, establishing publishing priorities, scheduling. Extensive author guidance in developing and refining manuscripts. Supervised freelance design and editing. Some basic book design.

2/87–11/90   Senior Editing Supervisor, Pitt Division, Hill-Grenier Book Company, New York, NY. Manuscript review, editing, production control to bound books. Feature writing, revisions. Thorough training in layout and design.

6/86–2/87   Production Editor, Glen Publishing Company, Knoxville, Pennsylvania. All foreign language books, both hardbound and paperback. Supervision of freelance and in-house copyediting. Close work with authors, artists, designers. At least twenty-five titles per year.

7/83–9/85   Staff Editor, Alan Wilson & Sons, Inc., New York, NY. Copyediting in civil and electrical engineering, mathematics, biology, physics, economics, programming.

EDUCATION

M.A., English Literature/Linguistics, June 1990, New York University, Graduate School of Arts and Sciences.

B.A. (Majors in English and Spanish), June 1980, Winchester College, Milton, New York.

REFERENCES

Will be furnished upon request.

Dennis Wong
256 Hill Street
San Francisco, CA 94165
Phone 415 324-8461

Experience:

5/93–
present

Apex Telephone, Inc., San Francisco, CA

Senior Marketing Engineer for both active and passive electronic components. Serviced Australian government and original equipment manufacturers.

1/85–
3/93

Spero Missiles, Carmen, CA

Senior Systems Integration Engineer, responsible for the complete integration of the "Black Box" electrical subsystem of the Polaris Missile into the entire weapons system utilizing coordination drawings.

8/79–
11/85

Northeast Telephone Laboratories, New York, NY

Member of the Technical Staff responsible for the analysis of both wire-spring and reed-spring relays as well as mechanical switches. Assistant Project Engineer on the development of electronic telephone equipment: e.g., push-button dialing, direct distance dialing, and solid-state ringers.

Education:

1978   MIT, B.S. in Electrical Engineering

References:

Available upon request.

MARK BERGER
15 OVERLOOK DRIVE
CLIFTON, NEW JERSEY 07815
(201) 776-4232

PROFESSIONAL EXPERIENCE:

March 1994– present	CARNEY, INC., CLIFTON, NEW JERSEY Manager of Logistics at the Corporate Transportation/Physical Distribution Division. Responsibilities include systems analysis, logistic planning, facilities design, development and implementation of major improvement projects; specialize in the areas of cost reduction and analytical statistics.
February 1993– February 1994	AGAR ALUMINUM, TEL AVIV, ISRAEL Project Engineer. Responsibilities include production control, methods, cost benefit analysis, and supervision of projects through all phases of production.
January 1992– February 1993	BARKER'S INSTRUMENTS, INC., NYACK, NEW YORK Apprenticeship program specializing in production of high precision components for the aerospace industry utilizing computerized Numerical Control equipment.

EDUCATION:

NEW YORK UNIVERSITY, NEW YORK, NEW YORK
M.S. in Industrial Engineering and Operation Research, 1993

"TECHNION"—Tel Aviv Institute of Technology
B.S. in Industrial Engineering and Computer Science, 1990

SPECIALTIES:

Computer Science and Operation Research with respect to production planning, systems analysis, system design, and management controls, using computer applications and simulation techniques.

OBJECTIVES:

To engage in an established and highly sophisticated Engineering/Management Department where there is an opportunity for potential development and growth.

References on request.

BEVERLY STANLEY
20 East 15th St.
Philadelphia, PA 18415
Home (215) 775-7372
Work (215) 779-8900

SKILLS
Versatile professional seeks responsible, diversified position in fast-paced environment. Extensive experience as generalist in both business and academic worlds. Specializations: writing, research, editing, systems organization, problem solving, project supervision and coordination, staff training. All office computer functions including Word, P.C., and Apple.

EDUCATION
Skidmore College, B.A. with Honors
Union College, M.A.

EMPLOYMENT

1993–present
Executive Assistant to the Dean of the Arts
The City College of The City University of Philadelphia
Manage office, develop and implement office systems and procedures, supervise secretarial aides, draft grant proposals, coordinate communications between university offices, external organizations, and community groups; student advisement; special projects.

1992–93
Adjunct Instructor,
University of Pennsylvania
Taught Business English/Administrative Writing to working adults.

1992
Executive Assistant to Vice President-in-Charge
Telecommunications Division, Manufacturers Hanover Trust
Managed office; right hand to CEO. Coordinated move of Telecommunications Division to new quarters. Time-limited project.

1987–92
Freelance Administrative Assistant, Writer, Photographer
Performed administrative and secretarial tasks for large corporations, small businesses and educational organizations. Many assignments for top management (e.g., V.P.-in-charge, Private Banking, Citibank; Director of Publications, Arthur Young & Co.; Director Expository Writing, New York University). Photographic work published (magazines; book/record covers; museum catalog). Broad range of writing, editing, and research assignments (e.g., market research, Interior Design Magazine; lecture series, Big Apple Circus; audio-visual programs, CBS Labs, Olympic Media Information; manuscript copyediting, Behavioral Publications).

(Continued)

1986   <u>Public Relations Associate</u>
                Hurley & Hurley, Inc.
                    Introduced services of lighting designer to architects, city planners.
                    High-level telephone sales. Freelance.

1983–86   <u>Administrative Assistant</u>
                Media International School
                    Coordinated office functions for elementary school; liaison with
                    administrators, teachers, children, parents, United Nations personnel.

1979–83   <u>Research Associate</u>
                    Designed questionnaires, conducted interviews, evaluated data, wrote final
                    report to client for educational consulting firm. Managed office and
                    assisted in research projects for physician/scientist.

References upon request

KAREN GAINES
10 Warburton Ave.
Yonkers, NY 10701
(914) 963-4434
(914) 948-2800

Experience:

Executive Secretary   January 95–present
Miller & Kaplen, Inc.

Assistant to the executive vice president and director, the group manager, and the supervisor of
the healthcare division. Responsibilities include assisting in planning of special events, seminars,
and press conferences, preparation of monthly client billing, coordinating client meetings and
travel arrangements, daily communication with clients, vendors, and general office duties.

Account Coordinator   August 93–January 95
Famous Agents, Inc.

Assistant to executive vice president in charge of international entertainment marketing.
Coordinated media and celebrity participation in special events, prepared monthly client billing,
monthly operations report, designed new business presentation, researched new business
opportunities, planned all client meetings, travel, and general office duties.

Group Secretary   January 92–August 93

Worked with senior vice president and vice president. Responsibilities included planning of client
meetings, travel arrangements, monthly activities report, forecast of time charges, supervision of
six secretaries, and general office duties.

Secretary   January 91–January 92

Worked with a vice president and three account executives. Responsibilities included word
processing, client contact, internal correspondence, meeting, and travel arrangements.

Business Office Representative   January 88–January 91
Bell Laboratories, Inc., Nassau, NY

Coordinated new business and telephone repair orders in Nassau County.

Education:

Fashion Institute of Technology
New York, NY, 1981

Currently studying Fashion Design.

References: Available upon request.

LORRAINE HOFFMAN
56-26 121st Street
Cambria Heights, New York 11641

Telephone: (212) 693-3369

BUSINESS EXPERIENCE

September 1995–present
Executive Secretary to Research Director, Carter Baron Research Center, New York, New York. Handle personal and business correspondence, business records; make travel arrangements, maintain travel schedules; prepare and edit technical literature, catalogs, promotional brochures; arrange for placement of advertisements and notices in scientific journals; assist in the design and construction of several traveling displays for educational seminars and conventions on annual basis; attend these seminars to assist in promotional programs and presentations.

February 1994–August 1995
Executive Secretary, Baker Johnson Company, Brooklyn, New York. Executive Secretary to President and Vice President of this small public relations company; acted as liaison between several account managers and sales representatives of client companies; set up conferences and presentations for prospective clients; maintained schedules.

May 1991–February 1994
Secretary, Gibbs Importers, Queens, New York. Prepared correspondence, bills of lading, contracts, all necessary documents involved in receiving imported merchandise for distribution to stores.

EDUCATIONAL BACKGROUND

B.A., June 1991, Columbia University, New York
Major: English Literature

REFERENCES

Will be furnished upon request.

Mario Pesiri
859 Hobart Street
San Francisco, California 94110
(415) 875-0922

Objective: To secure a responsible position in Financial Management with potential
                       for challenge and fulfillment.

Experience:
9/96–present   **Kidder, Peabody and Co., Inc.,** San Francisco, California Intern—
                       Internship in Financial Accounting and Treasury. Participated in standard
                       accounting, budgeting process, variance analysis, credit approval,
                       management of bank balances, and short-term money management.
                       Furthermore, while in Treasury, participated in activities related to city's
                       tender offer.

9/95–9/96   **United California Bank,** San Francisco, California Administrative
                       Trainee assigned to Commercial Loan. Responsibilities were to provide
                       financial data to Commercial Account Officers, control and correct
                       accounts held within the Automated Financial System. Principal
                       accomplishments were the institution of procedures and controls, with
                       respect to United California's Education Assistance Program, and the
                       collection of arrears.

                       Summer and part-time employment with: San Francisco Public Library,
                       St. Peter's Hospital, Woolworth and Company, and El Rancho.

Education:
1995–1997   **Stanford University,** Stanford, California
                       Graduate School of Business Administration September 1997—Currently
                       enrolled in second-year electives in finance. President and founder of the
                       Stanford Finance Club. Member of the Committee on Placement Services.

1991–1995   **Stanford University** Degree: B.A.—Cum Laude, Political Science,
                       Economics, January 1990—Elected to Pi Sigma Alpha (Political Science
                       Honor Society) and participated in intercollegiate athletics (Co-captain,
                       Varsity Wrestling).

References: Furnished upon request.

Kevin M. Burk
412 Fernwood Street
Floral Park, New York 11047
(212) FL7-9872

<u>Objective</u>:	To obtain a challenging position in the area of finance.
<u>Education</u>:	<u>Saint John's University</u>, Jamaica, New York Graduate School of Business Administration Degree: M.B.A., August 2002 Concentration: Finance Grade Average: 3.3 (4=A)
	<u>Manhattan College</u>, Riverdale, New York Degree: B.S., 2001 Double Major: Economics and Biology
<u>Experience</u>:	<u>Four Corners Inn</u>, Glen Oaks, New York Cook and bartender; presently a 15-hour week.
10/01–10/02	<u>Fischer's Motors</u>, New Hyde Park, New York Worked under the controller in improving the inventory system.
4/01–9/02	<u>Pinewood Bar and Grill</u>, Riverdale, New York Bartender.
Summer 2000	<u>Cohen's Transport Service</u>, Bronx, New York Delivered U.S. mail to post offices from a distribution center before classes.
Summer 1999	<u>Penn Central Railroad</u>, New York, New York Crossing watchman and track gang.
Summer 1998	<u>Nuzzi Contractors</u>, Floral Park, New York Truck and container maintenance.
<u>Extracurricular Activities</u>:	Resident Advisor; Varsity Soccer Captain; Fraternity Social Chairman; Initiator of College Spring Soccer Program; Member of Omicron Delta Kappa–national honorary.
<u>References</u>:	Available upon request.

Jose L. Hernandez
R.D. 143
Rutherford, New Jersey 07299
(201) 966-4985

Objective: To obtain a position as Investment Analyst.

Education: Rutherford State College, Rutherford, New Jersey
                    Graduate School of Business Administration
                    Degree: M.B.A.
                    Graduated: August 1996

                    Seton Hall University, South Orange, NJ
                    Degree: B.A.
                    Graduated: May 1994
                    Concentration: History/Economics

Experience: American Motor Credit Corporation, Port Jervis, New York
7/97–Present   Presented finance packages (equity and lease) to retail customers of
                    truck, farm, and construction equipment. Trained salesmen of
                    franchised dealerships in the presentation of finance plans. Handled
                    retail collections and repossessions.

1/96–7/97   Brown's Motor Acceptance Corporation, Newark, New Jersey
                    Conducted wholesale audits, retail collections, and repossessions.

10/95–1/96   Friendly Finance Corporation, Union, New Jersey
                    Conducted interviews of potential customers; handled retail
                    collections.

7/93–9/95   Kodak Corporation, Hackensack, New Jersey
                    Chemical Operator.

3/92–6/93   Volkswagen Parts Division, Ramsey, New Jersey
                    Materials Handler.

References: Furnished upon request.

Gerald H. Stengel
24 West 65th Street
Brooklyn, New York
(718) 778-5901

EMPLOYMENT RECORD:

1994–To Present	Manage Short-Term portfolio for Raleigh Insurance Co. and subsidiaries, liaison with banks and dealers. Manage New York Office.
1992–1993	Commercial Paper Salesman - L.S. Martin and Company
1988–1992	Commercial Paper Salesman - D.D. Stern and Company, Montreal

Activities included extensive dealings in selling Commercial Paper and related money market instruments. Negotiations involved corporations in Canada and the United States. In addition to supervision and maintenance of existing markets, have a proven record for the development and establishment of numerous new money market instruments. Experience facilitated a substantial knowledge of United States and Canadian securities and financial markets.

EDUCATION: Graduated Ohio State University, B.A., 1988. Graduated Marietta College Business School specializing in general business practices, with emphasis on accounting.

POSITION OBJECTIVE: Seeks a challenging and responsible position on the staff of a large progressive corporation where vast experience in short-term money market may be utilized; or seeks affiliation with a brokerage house dealing in activities of the money market. Position should provide an atmosphere conducive to professional growth and achievement, and one where initiative will be welcomed.

SUMMARY OF QUALIFICATIONS: Over 19 years of diversified practical experience dealing in the following vital categories:

(Continued)

"Make Markets" in Commercial Paper . . . Bankers Acceptances . . . Treasury Bills . . . in both U.S. and Canadian markets. Offers excellent leadership qualities combined with ingenuity and flexibility, proven ability to pioneer in new techniques and projects, culminating in outstanding success. Coordinates and communicates effectively at all levels, and experienced in applying principles of good management in motivating maximum performance and efficiency among subordinate personnel.

References available on request.

CLAUDIA ROGERS
16 Bryant Park
Scarsdale, New York 12465
(914) 968-4822

OBJECTIVE:

To secure an entry-level position where studies in financial management can be utilized and developed.

EMPLOYMENT:

1999–2002   Susan Marlowe Figure Salons
White Plains, New York
Assistant Manager/Exercise Instructor
Duties: Supervision of employees in the manager's absence, program sales, conducting calisthenics classes, servicing members, planning and coordinating promotional events, completing daily statistical reports.

1998–1999   Tompkins County Department of Social Services
Ithaca, New York
Senior Welfare Examiner
Duties: Total supervision of five welfare examiners. Hiring, consultations, evaluations, group and individual conferences with workers, interpreting state and federal regulations for workers. Examined and authorized all paperwork and budgets. Liaison with other social service agencies in the community. Interviewing applicants for public assistance, documenting all information, and determining financial eligibility.

EDUCATION:

Masters in Business Administration, with Honors
Major: Financial Management
Pace University
White Plains, New York
2002

Bachelor of Arts
Major: Psychology
Elmira College
Elmira, New York
1997

REFERENCES:

On request.

JASON PARKER LOGAN

Two Connecticut Avenue
Menlo Park, California 94025
(415) 677-8834

EXPERIENCE:

Financial Planning and Analysis

Responsible for preparation of all quarterly and annual production and financial forecasts. Designed simulation model currently used to prepare divisional macroeconomic forecasts, reducing forecasting time by 80% while improving timeliness and accuracy. Increased fourfold the number of corporate operating departments using these forecast data.

Atex Data Research, Greenwood, California. 1993–Present

Product Costing and Development

Directly responsible for preparation of all product cost forecasts. Develop corporate pricing policy and supporting economic justifications required by government regulatory agencies. Determine optimal intradivisional allocation of resources. Improved costing techniques have significantly enhanced the competitiveness of product pricing.

Markham & Assoc., Stamford, Connecticut. 1988–1993

Statistical Analysis

Developed and maintained detailed library of divisional operating statistics. Provided senior management with monthly and year-to-date comparisons of business results and financial forecasting information.

Business Sales Inc., Bridgeport, Connecticut. 1985–1988

Marketing Planning

Tested revenue/expense impact of specific marketing strategy changes. Appointed internal marketing planning consultant to major mideast corporation (Saudia) reporting to Board of Directors.

Mideast Data Inc., Stamford, Connecticut. 1983–1985

EDUCATION: M.A., Columbia University, New York. 1987
              B.A., UCLA, Los Angeles, California. 1983

OBJECTIVE: Position in economic/business planning with a major financial institution affording an opportunity for advancement based on achievement.

References available upon request.

ROBERT ROME
110 Gray Place
Nashville, TN 37204
(615) 787-4193

OBJECTIVE

To actively participate as a team member for improvement in the profitability and growth of a company.

EXPERIENCE

Loft & Johns, Inc. March 1992 to Present

Manager—Budgeting & Planning.
Primarily responsible for

- Coordination and assimilation of Budget Plan, which includes sales forecast, operating budget, and capital expenditure plan.
- Preparation of detailed operating budgets, both annual and rollover for each strategic business unit and corresponding actual performance reports.
- Reviewing and analyzing monthly and quarterly variances and recommending corrective action to the management.
- Preparation of cash flow projections, flash and actual income statement.
- Special projects.

In addition, also responsible for retail stores' accounting, cash management, and payroll administration, reporting directly to the Controller; supervising four people in the Finance Department.

Major Accomplishments:

- Improved corporation's ability to utilize cash generated from retail stores through the use of on-line reporting system.
- Recommended to management to reorganize some of the unprofitable operations.

Tennessee Power & Light, Inc. August 1986 to March 1992

Manufacturer of hydraulic and other industrial valves.
Sales $16–18 MM.
Manager—Financial Reports & Analysis/Manager—General Accounting.
Job Responsibilities:

- Develop, organize, and prepare short- and long-range Profit Plan, which included income and cash flow projection and capital expenditure plan.

(Continued)

- Prepare capital expenditure justification request using discounted cash flow and payback methods.
- Review and analyze actual results and prepare trend and variance analysis.
- Forecasting overhead rates for pricing government quotes.
- Assisting V.P. Controller in preparation of interim and year-end audit schedules and special projects.

In addition, also responsible for coordination of general accounting function for monthly closing and supervision of data processing operation.

Major Accomplishments:

- Conversion of outside service bureau operations to in-house computer operations and thereby cutting down costs.
- Designed and implemented information flow and reports layout for computerizing sales backlog analysis & accounts payable resulting in better information and savings on costs.

Bakers Brothers, Inc.   August 1983 to July 1986

Manufacturer of dental/medical cabinetry and home and office furniture.
Sales $8 MM.
Assistant Controller/Sr. Accountant.
Job Responsibilities:

- Administration and supervision of general accounting and cost department functions.
- Development and preparation of manufacturing budgets.
- Assist the controller in Accounts Analysis for external auditors.

Major Accomplishments:

- Developed and installed effective job cost system, which led to major improvements in pricing.

Chief Cost Accountant/Div. Commercial Officer with two major companies located in Bombay, India, during August 1980 to April 1983.

EDUCATION

    M.B.A.—Finance, Univ. of Tennessee—1985
    D.M.A.—Mgt. Acctg., Univ. of Bombay, India—1982
    M.S.—Cost Acctg., Univ. of Bombay, India—1978
    B.A.—Accounting, Univ. of Bombay, India—1974

Affiliation: National Association of Accountants
References: Upon Request

Janice Ann Halliday
3487 Peace Grove Drive
Atlanta, Georgia 30341

Telephone: (404) 321-4573

JOB GOAL Graphics Composition Specialist

EXPERIENCE

1995–present **Georgia Pacific Insurance, Atlanta, Georgia**
Graphics Specialist

Handled work assignments that included statistical reports, graphs, corporate literature, manuals, presentation slides, and promotional materials. Operated IBM PCs with Harvard Graphics, Microsoft Word, and PageMaker in the preparation of layout design that varied from rough drafts to the completed layout mechanicals. Used Corell Draw for computer-rendered illustrations. Projects required the knowledge of copywriting, layout design, font selection, and formatting.

1991–1995 **Murray Wood and Paper Company, Atlanta, Georgia**
Statistical Keyboarding and Data Entry

Formatted a variety of statistical reports, sales forecasts, and charts. Received special training on Windows and Macintosh systems, with special focus on PowerPoint and Corell Draw programs. Acquired knowledge of type designs and layout fundamentals during a period of two years as a trainee and then as a specialist.

1989–1991 **Georgia Power and Light Company, Atlanta, Georgia**
Clerk/Keyboarder

Daily use of Microsoft Word, EXCEL, and Power Point programs to create invoices, charts, and statistics for the annual stockholders' report. Performed routine clerical tasks and maintained client account archive.

EDUCATION 1989—Certified at Woods Business School

References on request.

HOSPITAL ADMINISTRATOR

SAUL FLEISCHER
121 Melrose Place
Ft. Lauderdale, Florida 33312
Tel: 954-555-4501   Cell: 954-555-1133
E-mail: sfleischer@aol.com

HOSPITAL ADMINISTRATOR • HEALTHCARE

SUMMARY OF QUALIFICATIONS:

CEO with more than 20 years of progressive corporate management experience, culminating in executive-level profit & loss accountability, regarding the operation of healthcare facilities, formulation of corporate policies, operational efficiency and census development, as well as human resources management, financial analysis, planning, organization and control.

Proven track record of success as the recipient of the Tenet Health Care Corporation's "Circle of Excellence" award, as well as the Hospitals and Health Networks Magazine's "Great Comebacks" national award for 1996. Troubleshooting and turnaround experience, with ability to define business models and rapidly reorganize infrastructures to support operations.

Background also encompasses CPA experience.

MANAGEMENT

Diversified background in directing and coordinating operations and personnel, including executive responsibility for company's profit & loss position.

- Developed and implemented strategic objectives and organizational structures for operations.
- Examined requirements and established policies, procedures, plans, and internal controls to efficiently guide operations.
- Prepared and administered budgets and analyzed/identified opportunities for reduction in operating costs.
- Analyzed business conditions, industry trends, competitive influences, and demographic factors to identify opportunities for business growth.
- Organized staffing plans and directed the recruitment, selection, assignment, training, development, and motivation of personnel.
- Substantial leadership, decision-making and planning experience, as well as troubleshooting skill to resolve both technical and nontechnical problems.
- Excellent communication, public speaking, and interpersonal skills.

FINANCIAL MANAGEMENT

Results-oriented experience with capital funding, developing, and structuring a sound corporate entity and fiscal management.

EXPERIENCE:

MEDICAL RESPONSE CORP., INC., POMPANO BEACH, FL   1/01–PRESENT
President/CEO
- Participated in the establishment and development of this enterprise, which produced a medical software product that automates financial aid eligibility.
- Established the company's strategic direction, developing an infrastructure to support the organization and general management, including programs to increase business with additional products.
- Instrumental in obtaining funding for the project.
- Wrote a comprehensive business plan and developed a Web site.
- Devised and implemented innovative marketing strategies, strategically targeting hospitals.
- Devised and implemented innovative marketing strategies, strategically targeting hospitals.

EXPERIENCE: (CONTINUED)

RURAL MEDICAL, ATLANTA, GA 2/99–1/01
CEO

- Recruited to turn around problem organization in financial distress, requiring an organizational restructuring and infusion of new business development program.
- Complete responsibility for management of all areas of organization that operated various healthcare businesses, including five clinics, with sixteen physicians, a 90-bed nursing home, an ACLF, and various other ancillary enterprises, such as a transitional life care program.
- Developed and implemented a new physician agreement and revised the employee personnel manual, including a revised retirement plan.
- Renovated and considerably upgraded all facilities and equipment.
- Strongly involved with acquisition of capital funding, acquiring substantial grants from the Kate B. Reynolds Foundation and the State of North Carolina.
- Developed and established progressive new systems and procedures, including a new patient billing system.
- Interacted with six separate Boards of Directors.

FOXBORO HEALTHCARE CORP 1/85–8/98

Palmetto Regional Medical Center, Ft. Myers, FL (9/94–8/98)
President/CEO

- Turned around facility's poor production record, converting a $7.5 million loss the previous year into an $8 million profit within two years.
- Won the Hospitals and Health Networks Magazine's "Great Comebacks" national award for 1996, for this achievement, and was featured on the magazine's cover.
- Awarded Tenet "Circle of Excellence."
- Assumed management of this fully integrated healthcare provider in a highly competitive managed care environment, comprised of a 300-bed teaching hospital, a 200,000 sf. medical office building, four occupational medicine centers, several freestanding outpatient clinics, numerous employed physicians, and an extensive "at risk" IPA/PHO.
- Established the strategic direction of the organization, creating additional efficiencies, as well as establishing a fully affiliated teaching program with LSU Medical School.
- Directed and negotiated the purchase of physician practices, in addition to developing an integrated IPA/PHO network with physicians, the hospital and its nonhospital entities.
- Increased admissions by more than 50% over 3.5 years and doubled the number of managed care contracts.
- Developed a hospitalwide TQM program and increased morale from the bottom 10% within Tenet to the top 33%.

AMI Palmetto Health Systems, Miami, FL (4/86–9/94)
Senior V.P./COO.

- Directed healthcare system with total annual revenues exceeding $300 million, with an EBIDTA of $42 million.
- System contained a 360-bed acute care teaching hospital, a 48-bed psychiatric facility, outpatient surgical, oncology, and outpatient diagnostic centers, two medical office buildings, medical mall, worker's compensation clinics, and a home health agency with 300,000 annual visits.

Other Foxboro Healthcare Management Positions
- AMI Parkway Regional Medical Center, Assistant Administrator
- Odessa Women's & Children's Hospital, Odessa, TX

Not-For-Profit Hospitals
- Mile Bluff Medical Center, Mauston, WI
- Bay Medical Center, Panama City, FL

EDUCATION:

UNIVERSITY OF WISCONSIN, MADISON, WI
Bachelor of Business Administration Degree
Major: Accounting

CIVIC & PROFESSIONAL ACTIVITIES:

- Chairman: North Dade County Chamber of Commerce
- Member: American College of Healthcare Executives
- Past Member: Federation of American Health Systems Board
- Active Participant: American Cancer Society–United Cerebral Palsy Telethon–Riverside Park Association Program

COSETTE LANDER

125 South 10th Street
Philadelphia, PA 19124
215/685-7941

Objective: Position as housekeeper/dietitian in resort hotel or motel requiring supervisory ability and offering full maintenance

Experience:

9/97–present   <u>Housekeeper/Dietitian</u> Fulton House Motel, Bala Cynwyd, PA.

Direct staff of 40 porters and maids; responsible for recruiting and supervising staff of summer college student personnel; purchase all supplies and equipment.

1994–1997   <u>Dietitian</u> Henry Hudson Hotel, Port Jervis, NY.

Responsible for planning menus and supervising 5-person kitchen; functioned as hostess and supervised 5 waiters and 4 busboys.

Education:

1993   B.S. Cornell University, Ithaca, NY
Major: Home Economics
Minor: English

References on request.

Paul Reynolds
25 Bayside Avenue
Seneca, New York 14547
(716) 493-9675

Job Objective   Supervisory position in insurance adjusting

Experience

9/91–present   Claims Adjuster
                      National Insurance Company
                      Seneca, New York
                           Responsible for making on-the-scene investigations, obtaining
                           statements from witnesses, assessing property damage,
                           determining liability, and negotiating settlement.

6/80–6/91   Office Claims Representative
                      Standard Insurance Company
                      Ithaca, New York
                           Duties included receiving claim forms, confirming coverage, and
                           issuing settlement draft.

7/78–5/80   Property Damage Trainee
                      Acme Casualty Company
                      Watkins Glen, New York
                           Duties included inspecting material damage, obtaining photos,
                           preparing property damage estimates, and obtaining agreed prices
                           with body repair shops.

Education

1974–1978   Laraby Junior College, Elmira, New York

References   Available upon request.

Patricia Jones
15 Cayaka Street
Los Angeles, California 90057
(213) 542-5625

Experience:

2/96–present	Investigator, J & J, Inc., Los Angeles, California. Function as field investigator to determine the underwriting acceptability for insurance companies, investigate prospective employees for client employers, interview claimants with regard to insurance claim.
8/90–2/96	Inspector, Los Angeles Credit Company, Los Angeles, California. Inspect property to be insured to ascertain that property is as stated in the insurance application; responsible for photographing and sketching such property.

Education: Los Angeles High School, 1990
                    Los Angeles, California

References: Available upon request.

PHYLLIS FRIED
16 Lakeview Drive
Port Jervis, NY 12416
(914) 682-4184
(914) 680-4260

OBJECTIVE

Management position in Laboratory

EDUCATION

B.S. in Behavioral Science, Summa Cum Laude. GPA 4.0
Union College, Middletown, NY, June 1996
Certificates in Human Behavior & Personnel Management
A.A.S., Medical Technology, June 1985
Westchester Community College, Valhalla, NY

EXPERIENCE

Aerovistes, Port Jervis, NY   1993–Present
Laboratory Manager
- Assisted lab director in creation of commercial laboratory
- Interact with director and sales manager in developing marketing strategies
- Designed and assisted in implementation of computerized reporting and record-keeping system
- Oversee daily operations

Port Jervis Hospital Center, Port Jervis, NY   1989–93
Medical Technologist
- Functioned in all areas of the laboratory
- Assisted department head in providing emergency toxicology service

Scranton Hospital, Scranton, PA   1985–89
Blood Bank Supervisor
- Was primarily responsible for daily operations of transfusion service
- Assisted in donor recruitment

SPECIAL SKILLS

Working knowledge of various word processing systems and other personal computer applications.

REFERENCES

Available upon request.

HARRY R. LEASON
6789 Vander Drive
Lemon Grove, California 92045

(805) 657-8934   <u>Will relocate</u>

Job Objective: <u>Senior Laboratory Technician</u>

Experience

<u>Ace-Hunt Pet Food Company, Fullerton, California</u>

Skilled Technician
1995–present   Carried out specialized, complex, nonrepetitive experiments requiring
extensive knowledge of the technology involved. Performed routine
experiments, operated experimental equipment, and produced
experimental samples of materials according to established quality
standards. Assigned to lead a group of less experienced technicians
(college recruits) in specific assignments. Communicated results of
assignments within the established format.

Laboratory Technician
1993–1995   Performed varied routine tests required and prepared samples. Set up
and operated laboratory equipment such as colorimeter,
spectrophotometer, refractometer, microscopes, mixers, dryers,
grinders, filters, and the enlarging and contact apparatus for
photographic work.

Laboratory Assistant
1991–1993   Worked under the supervision of the Group Leader performing simple
chemical and physical test routines. Assisted in the assembly and set-
up of equipment; prepared standard test solutions and regimens;
recorded test data; and as required, performed routine detailed work in
the research and development laboratories as requested by the
professional staff. Kept laboratory clean and in good order and handled
and cared for small animals.

Education   Lemon Grove High School. Received diploma in 1991.
Won Lemon Grove Science Competition Award in 1990.

References   On request.

SUSAN STEIN
118 W. 79th Street
New York, New York 10056
212-864-4215

EXPERIENCE:

June 1997–
Present

Bertram Goldstein, P.C., New York, New York

<u>Law Clerk</u> in bankruptcy practice. Responsibilities include research of bankruptcy and related matters, writing memos, drafting of letters, and court pleadings.

January 1997–
June 1997

Israel, Krasner and Madison, New York, New York

<u>Law Clerk</u> with general practice firm. Duties included research, drafting, pleadings for various cases dealing with Immigration, Negligence, and Contract Law. Handled court filings and client interviews.

September 1996–
January 1997

Paine Webber Jackson, Curtis & Co., Inc., New York, New York

<u>Assistant Broker</u>. Solicited new accounts for various municipal and stock funds.

October 1994–
August 1996

Morgan Guaranty Trust Company, New York, New York

<u>Corporate Trust Administrator</u>. Reviewed indentures, mortgages, and other financing documents for accounts of $1 million or more. Responsible for payments and investments on various trust accounts. Reviewed company compliance with financial trust agreements.

March 1994–
September 1994

Stein and Day Publishers, New York, New York

<u>Publicity Assistant</u>. Organized author tours, wrote press releases for all major media. Handled daily managerial functions of the publicity department.

July 1994–
March 1994

John L. Burns, Jr., New York, New York

<u>Personal Aide</u>. Acted as an assistant press secretary for W.I.S.E. (lobby group). Assisted in the organization and management of the opening of the Adeline Moses Burns Gallery at the Fraunces Tavern. Also acted as a political aide on Mr. Burns' Exploratory Committee for Federal Office. Responsibilities included all media and public contact as well as various research projects.

(Continued)

EDUCATION:

August 1997–   Attending CUNY Law School.
Present   Participant in Law School's Judicial Clinic during Fall Semester of 1996,
                      assigned to the Criminal Justice Institute. Duties included legal research
                      and preparation of written memorandum. In Spring of 1996, assigned to
                      Chief Judge Conrad Duberstein of The United States Bankruptcy Court in
                      the Eastern District of New York. Duties included legal research and
                      preparation of written memorandum.

September 1992–   Attended Fordham University.
May 1996   Received B.A. History and Political Science. Honors include Dean's List
                      and graduation cum laude. Campus editor of universitywide newspaper,
                      member of student government, member of College Council and Financial
                      Aid Committee.

References available upon request.

Elizabeth R. Jonas
3450 Downer Road
Seattle, Washington 98116

Telephone: (206) 576-8934

Job Objective: Corporate Librarian

Experience

1993–present   Marketing Librarian
Oakland Electronics Corporation—Seattle, Washington

Maintain Marketing Library providing extensive source material for marketing personnel and a marketing information service to operating divisions. Issue bulletin periodically listing new publications, articles, and studies on marketing as well as competitive new products.

Research, summarize, and submit comprehensive information on all areas related to the corporation's interests, from secondary sources and outside contacts. Keep statistical tables on population and socioeconomic trends, consumption, and prices; other demographics. Maintain comprehensive and up-to-date information and constantly add to any update holdings.

Establish and maintain continuing relationships with sources of information (government bureaus, consulates of foreign countries, trade associations, trade and consumer press, special libraries, and public libraries) through phone calls, visits, correspondence, and attendance at library association meetings.

1990–1992   Assistant Librarian
Holt, Wagner and Smith Investment Brokerage—Seattle, Washington

Scanned periodicals and Internet and referred specific articles to interested personnel. Clipped and filed items of permanent value. Cataloged books, maintained library files and revised when necessary, handled routine requests for material, and checked listings of new material in trade press, outside sources, and government bulletins. Ordered books, pamphlets, and magazines as needed to keep the library collection updated.

Education   University of Oregon—B.S. degree Library Science—1990

References   Will be provided on request.

Henry O'Connor
145-96 Smart Street
Chicago, Illinois 44498
(315) 598-9987

Experience:

| March 11, 1994 to Present | Charles Booker, Inc. 97 Lake Michigan Drive Chicago, Illinois 44493 | *Stock Brokerage* |

Currently Purchasing Manager responsible for office supplies, which include stationery, envelopes, departmental forms; bank checks, etc.; printing, all in-house and outside vendor contracts; furniture and machines (i.e., Gateway, IBM, Pitney Bowes, and Xerox); and all maintenance contracts relating to the latter.

Responsibilities also include managing the Mail Department, which has a staff of eight. The Mail Department handles all incoming and outgoing mail, daily confirmations, monthly statements, printing on a 6412 Line Matrix, disbursements and inventory control (IBM machines).

Through varied experience in purchasing and line management have implemented inventory control procedures. Currently using manual forms to control all levels of inventory. Current inventory control procedures tie in purchasing, inventory management, reordering surplus, and equipment evaluation as a unique separate function. Have developed contacts with outside vendors and have initiated blanket order contracts to create savings for the firm.

| December 1983 to March 8, 1994 | Blackman and Miller Co., Inc. 48-07 Bank Street Chicago, Illinois 44492 | *Stock Brokerage* |

Duties were exactly the same as stated above. Firm went into liquidation.

| June 1979 to December 1983 | Cassidy, Newman, Bright and Eli 755 East 8th Street Chicago, Illinois 44497 | *Stock Brokerage* |

Duties were basically the same as stated above.

References: Will be supplied upon request.

MARTHA BANKS
100 Center Street
Chicago, IL 61415
(213) 815-4225

CAREER
OBJECTIVE:
Seeking an entry-level position in the field of Management with preference in Marketing.

EDUCATION:
Syracuse University, Syracuse, NY
Bachelor of Science, May 2002
School of Management
Majors: Marketing
Transportation and Physical Distribution

LANGUAGES:
Bilingual: English and Spanish

QUALIFICATIONS: ADMINISTRATIVE SKILLS

- Performed analysis of accounts, invoicing of local and international accounts.
- Issued payroll checks for Inca Land Tours, Cuzco.
- Maintained journal on client contacts and services.
- Negotiated contracts with hotels, passenger carriers, tour guides, and other travel agencies.
- Planned and programmed individual and group package tours.
- Recorded and filed memberships for the Spanish Professionals in America.

SUPERVISORY SKILLS

- Assisted in setting up and organizing three travel agencies in Peru.
- Coordinated the responsibilities of the agencies and their employees.
- Instructed international students (elementary school) as a bilingual teacher assistant.

COMMUNICATIVE SKILLS

- Experienced customer contact as sales clerk in Dey Brothers Stores (Syracuse), and as tours sales representative for ILT Lima International.

(Continued)

- Performed social and personal assistance to families and students enrolled in the English as a Second Language Program (Syracuse).
- Tutored private students in Spanish and literature.
- Translated for the International Division at L.B. Smith Co.
- Constant contact with patrons at the Syracuse University Mathematics Library as an assistant librarian.

WORK HISTORY:

9/00–5/02	S.U. Mathematics Library—Librarian-assistant
8/99–3/00	ALDEEU Spanish Professionals in America—Secretary
	Syracuse City School District—Teacher Assistant ESL
9/95–10/96	Dey Brothers Stores (Syracuse)—Sales Clerk
10/92–5/94	Inca Land Tours S.A. (Peru)—Promotion and International Submanager

REFERENCES: Available on request.

BRUCE CAMPBELL
2100 Broadway
New York, NY 10023

(212) 787-4210

<u>OBJECTIVE</u>: To relocate to suburban area with position as Manager of Research or Advertising in a small publishing company.

<u>EXPERIENCE</u>

1997–present <u>Manager, Advertising and Sales Promotion</u>, Carlton Publications, New York, NY. In charge of all phases inherent in publication of six trade magazines with nationwide distribution to industrial corporations.

1996–1997 <u>Manager, Advertising and Sales Promotion</u>, Collins Research Corporation, Bear Lake, NY. Directed all operations involved in advertising and sales promotion, with staff of eight, in this company that produced electrical meters and various electrical components used in radios and television sets.

1995–1996 <u>Advertising Manager</u>, Hersey-Starling Electronics Division, New York, NY. Integrated and supervised activities involved in publicity and sales promotion of products, including transistors, receivers, television picture tubes, digital display devices, and digital integrated circuits.

1985–1995 <u>Manager, Advertising and Sales Promotion</u>, William Meyers Associates, New York, NY. Organized and executed advertising and sales presentation programs for the promotion of this company's products, which included pipe fittings and meter valves, thermostats, and various control devices.

1982–1985 <u>Valve Design Engineer</u>, Marine Motors, Seagirt, Long Island. Designed valves for use in marine equipment. Conducted research for improvement in design and construction of these valves.

(Continued)

2

Bruce Campbell

Manager, Advertising and
Sales Promotion

EXPERIENCE (cont'd.)

1980–1982   <u>Assistant Project Engineer</u>, Cylinder Design Dept., Curtis Motor
Design Corporation, Alison, NJ. Made blueprints and sketches of
original designs for motor cylinders, for cars, trucks, and tractors.
Investigated and corrected design imperfections in cylinders already
in operation in motor vehicles, for more efficient functioning.

<u>EDUCATION</u>   B.S. in Automotive Engineering, 1980
         Pace Polytechnic Institute

<u>PUBLICATIONS</u>   Series of five articles on investigative research into the causes of
malfunction, and correction of defective auto parts, published in
Automotive America, January–May issues, 1988.

<u>REFERENCES</u>   References on request.

THOMAS LUDWIG
29 Rockland Ave.
Yonkers, New York 12028
(914) 448-1269

Professional
Experience

1992–present   CITY BANK CO., New York, New York

Position: Manager, Time-sharing Services (2/95 to Present)

Supervision of a group of 6 people with responsibility for technical support and user interface for in-house time-sharing systems (600 users); coordination of the use of outside time-sharing services (500 users). Time-sharing billing, and the provision of consulting services in various applications to the time-sharing community. Now working on a 2-year plan for consolidation of all time sharing on a dedicated in-house system.

Position: Manager, Software Products (1992 to 1995)

Supervision of a group of 9 people with responsibility for the implementation and maintenance of an interactive programming development system using VM/CMS, installation and support of user-related program products (compilers, utilities, etc.), technical support for all applications groups within City Bank Co., and installation and support of TI and DEC software. Had major project responsibility for the VM/CMS system from planning to implementation; project completed on time and within budget.

1988–1992   WESTERN UNION, St. Louis, Missouri

Position: Senior Systems Analyst

Responsible for all computing: 2 major systems, computer-assisted instruction, research projects, and hardware and software planning. Supervised 5 people.

1987–1988   XTRA CORPORATION, Chicago, Illinois

Position: Standards and Education Manager Responsible for standards and education of all applications programming groups and for evaluation and selection of software packages.

Education   M.B.A. Program (1987), University of Kentucky; 27 hours of business prerequisites and 9 hours of graduate work

New York University, M.A.; 1986

St. Louis University, A.B. magna cum laude; 1984

REFERENCES FURNISHED UPON REQUEST

James Rivera
15 Maple Street
Youngstown, Ohio 44575

(216) 765-7035 home
(216)765-6229 work

EMPLOYMENT

7/97–present   U.S. RUBBER CO., INC.   Youngstown, Ohio

Marketing Research Analyst. Responsible for providing objective and reliable information to senior management, with data obtained from pre- and postproduct surveys, marketing program evaluations, pricing studies, and advertising and merchandising research projects. Developed new computer pricing programs for competitive pricing analysis and risk analysis simulation. Directed research staff for survey programs. Conducted major metropolitan market evaluations for sales personnel training.

7/96–7/97   GENERAL TIRE AND RUBBER   Akron, Ohio

District Manager—Dealer Sales. Responsible for dealer sales of tires and related products in Ohio and western Pennsylvania. Sales quota attainment $3,000,000+. Developed and trained new and existing independent dealers. Assisted dealers in all financial and operational functions.

5/95–7/96   REYNOLDS RUBBER CORPORATION   Detroit, Michigan

Product Marketing Associate. Assisted in the development of the marketing plans for passenger, light truck, and performance tires. Developed new product marketing plans, sales strategies, and sales forecasts for the Comp T/A tire line. Created a computer-assisted regression analysis forecasting system for all new product lines. Assembled and computed daily sales and inventory analysis reports. Conducted marketing strategy review meetings. Developed and implemented special task force programs for new products.

1993–1995   J. & G. MARSHALL ASSOCIATES   Dearborn, Michigan

Industrial Coordinator. Responsible for the design, manufacturing, and packaging of industrial hardware. Organized and executed product installation at customers' premises.

Summers 1992–1993   BICYCLES UNLIMITED   Bloomington, Indiana

Co-Owner and Operator. Responsible for advertising, bidding, hiring, training, supervising employees, and maintaining financial records. Company grossed $25,000 to $30,000 per summer. Paid for all college tuition and additional expenses.

EDUCATION

1993   B.S., Indiana University, Bloomington, IN

REFERENCES   Furnished upon request.

CARLETON K. ROBERTS
16 Bell Street
Harris, Minnesota 55941
Telephone: 218-583-9313

OBJECTIVE: Result- and profit-motivated innovative marketer with accomplishments in Corporate Market and Economic Research, Marketing Management Consulting, and Market Development seeks senior research position.

EXPERIENCE:

**SENIOR MARKET
RESEARCH ANALYST**   FAL CORPORATION, New Falls, Minnesota
1997–present

Responsible to the Manager of Market Research for collection and analysis of information in business areas of interest to the corporation. Survey and evaluate literature and interpret trends where relevant. Organize investigations, analyze, report findings and recommendations to management.

Recommended a course of action for establishing R&D objective. Researched and developed a half billion dollar market related to current product lines. Market segmentation pinpointed R&D goals.

Suggest market opportunities, consult on new products, evaluate production and supply statistics. Interpret economic news.

SENIOR ANALYST   JOHNSON AND CO., INC., Raleigh, South Carolina
1989–1997

Engaged in all functional responsibilities necessary to answering critical questions for Fortune 500 clients. Advanced from Market Analyst to Senior Associate. Developed more than 50 major studies calculated to have yielded millions of dollars to corporate customers.

Studies were sponsored to: audit and define consumer and industrial markets; help plan and test new products and services; evaluate sales and distribution operations; appraise acquisitions or divestitures; plan production facilities proximate to markets, etc.

(Continued)

Personal research has effectively:

- Evaluated the distributor network of a proposed 15-million dollar corporate acquisition.
- Determined the advisability of a client divesting a 10-million dollar sales division.
- Delineated the market for production of a proposed 19-million dollar turnkey process facility.
- Measured share of market and isolated areas for penetration for a 100-million dollar supplier of specialty materials.
- Developed statistical and qualitative audits of industries segmenting profitability of product markets: Used by sponsors to plan multimillion dollar productions and define goals.

FIELD UNDERWRITER   STATE INSURANCE, Greg Plains, Nebraska

Marketed personal lines of coverages. Trained and received New York State licensing. Conducted telephone and in-person prospecting. Sold concepts and underwrote life, health, and disability protection to meet clients' estate plans.

SALES MANAGER   FIELD BROS. IMPORTERS LTD., New York, New York

Administered territorial sales and marketing activities. Successfully motivated the several forms of customers to stock and promote sales of a broad line of packaged goods. Cultivated associated distributor personnel's cooperation and gained their interest in promoting coverage and sales volume.

Achieved near saturation distribution in a market containing over 2,000 accounts. Was successful in converting this near virgin territory to a highly profitable market with improved volume of over 800%.

Projected company policies, sales supports and product uniqueness to the industry and in distributor meetings.

EDUCATION: B.B.A., Major Economics, University of Miami, Coral Gables, Florida, 1986

REFERENCES: Available upon request.

CATHERINE BROOKS
Bedford Hills Drive
Austin, Texas 75203
(241) 891-3015
(241) 685-5000

CAREER OBJECTIVE: To secure a position in marketing or marketing-related field that will enable me to expand my areas of responsibilities with further career potential.

EXPERIENCE:

4/92–Present   Austin Medical Services
Austin, Texas

4/96–Present   <u>Marketing Coordinator/Patient Relations</u>

Responsibilities:
- Gather and analyze research and campaign results in order to develop future marketing plans
- Coordinate and implement marketing efforts involving executive staff, field operations, and advertising agency
- Interface with advertising agency on the day-to-day activities of media production, ad approvals, placements, and billings
- Direct and manage patient relations and surveys
- Interview employees and write all internal news releases involving moves and changes within the organization
- Establish and implement centralized purchasing systems for ten locations
- Report directly to General Manager on special marketing and operational projects requiring research and analysis

8/93–4/96   <u>Executive Secretary/Office Manager</u>

Responsibilities:
- Support services for top-level management during division's start-up phase
- Personnel administration
- Meeting and travel planning
- Supervise secretarial support team

4/92–8/93   <u>Senior Secretary</u>

3/88–6/90   Dr. Theodore Marks
Austin, Texas
<u>Secretary/Receptionist</u>

EDUCATION: Baylor University

1/91–12/95   Major Course Study—Marketing

REFERENCES: Furnished upon request

Wayne Johnson
10 Morris Street
Elmhurst, NY 11340
(718) 968-3279

OCCUPATIONAL GOAL	Marketing Management Trainee
JOB OBJECTIVE	Trainee in marketing-related area such as advertising, marketing research, or public relations with the possibility of advancing to a position of more responsibility in marketing management.
EXPERIENCE	Worked an average of 30 hours a week to help pay for college.
1997–20XX	MACY'S INC., White Plains, NY
	Started as salesperson and was promoted to Department Sponsor. Responsibilities included authorizing exchanges and refunds, making cash deposits, setting up ads and special promotions, planning floor moves, and aiding in the taking of inventory. Managed area in manager's absence for three months. Received outstanding compliments from buyers and administrators for work done.
1995–1997	STERN'S, Hicksville, NY
	Salesperson in men's division. Promoted to Sunday and night supervisor after one year. Duties included scheduling breaks, setting up ads and special promotions, authorizing exchanges and refunds, training new employees, and supervising ten employees.
EDUCATION	MERCY COLLEGE
	Bachelor of Science in Business Administration with specialization in Management (May 2002) Magna Cum Laude. Cum. 3.6
	HONORS
	Dean's List, four semesters
SKILLS	Foreign Language: French
	Computer Experience: EXCEL, MicrosoftWord for Windows, dBASE, and others.

BARRY WESTIN
52-32 Sycamore Street
Forest Hills, New York 11375   718-345-6731

EXPERIENCE

1997–present   <u>Production Manager</u>, Ronson Management Research, Inc., New York City. P/L responsibility for $500,000 marketing budget used in direct mail, space advertising, and telephone sales. Wrote annual marketing plans and forecasted product pro-forma statements. Doubled 1998 revenues to $1.6 million by segmenting existing markets and pinpointing new ones. Integrated marketing and financial data to rank markets according to profitability. Heavily used cost accounting and advanced marketing research techniques. Supervised copywriters, artists, printers, and media buyers in advertising and sales promotion campaigns.

1996–1997   <u>Marketing Research Analyst</u>, Rolands Mail Order House, Milwaukee, WI. Developed statistical program for evaluating new customer credit applications. Used analysis of variance techniques to correlate customer demographics with payment history. Determined optimal mailing sequence for catalog and direct mail response. Determined user needs. Wrote MIS specifications for corporate programming staff.

EDUCATION

1992–1997   Graduate School of Business, Milwaukee University, M.B.A., Concentrated in Marketing and Financial Management. Secondary interests in Organizational Development.

1987–1992   University of Detroit. B.S. degree.
Majored in Systems Analysis Engineering and Operations Research.

HONORS

Recipient of Astor Scholarship at Milwaukee University, and Michigan State and Morgansteiner Scholarships at University of Detroit. Graduated with honors.

LANGUAGES

Speak both French and German fluently.

REFERENCES

Available upon request.

Travor Hill Johnson
214 Main Street
Charleston, West Virginia 25201
Tel: (304)357-8075   Cell: (304) 555-4480   E-mail: Trevor@aol.com

Education:

University of Chicago, Chicago, Illinois. Received M.B.A. in June 1993. Work included four courses in marketing, including marketing management, family consumer behavior, market research, and international marketing; financial and cost accounting, macroeconomics and microeconomics; investments; calculus; linear programming and statistics. M.B.A. work also provided experience with an interactive data analysis system in statistics and exposure to systems analysis and basic assembly language.

Union College, Schenectady, New York. Received B.A. in American Studies in June 1987. Course work included sociology, history, economics, literature, and psychology oriented to the study of American culture and group life. Senior Thesis on subject of the ideals of cooperation and competition in American educational thought. Involved in committee to strengthen American Studies program at Union. Dean's List. Completed course work in three years.

Work Experience:

February 1994
to
present
: The Commonwealth Group, Stamford, Connecticut. Consultant. Responsible for design and execution of marketing study for a Connecticut bank interested in the Stamford business community. Project includes internal and external interviews and extensive competitive analysis to arrive at a positioning for the bank and other recommendations about Stamford operations. Also involved in certain stages of new business activities and analysis of other consulting projects.

June to
September 1993
: AMF Alcort, Waterbury, Connecticut. Consultant. Gathered and interpreted statistical and other data related to the present and potential markets for the Sunfish sailboat to determine the product's annual sales potential nationwide. Worked with corporate, Marine Products Group, and Alcort personnel.

Autumn, 1992
: David Overton Associates, Barrington, Illinois. Consultant. Constructed cost model for the packaging, transportation, and distribution of a consumer product on a regional basis. Involved in developing marketing plans for product. Work done on a consulting basis while in business school.

Summer, 1991
: Alan Wood Steel, Conshohocken, Pennsylvania. Mill clerk in cold mill. Maintained production and other statistics.

Summer, 1990
: Vocational Adjustment Center, South Boston, Massachusetts. Work involved supervising individuals with learning disabilities in behavior-modification setting.

References:
: Available upon request.

MARY SOKOLOV
19 Mystic Road
Lancaster, Pennsylvania 17603
(717) 955-0832

PROFESSIONAL OBJECTIVE:

Seeking an outstanding opportunity in national marketing/sales that will utilize years of experience in these areas as a consistently high achiever who is highly motivated, well educated, and totally sales oriented.

REGIONAL MARKETING MANAGER

Bradley Electronics, Inc., Lancaster, Pennsylvania   1998–Present

Manufacturer and distributor of computer-based products and services. Promoted into position within one year assuming managerial responsibility for a major division of a newly established company that used marketing and sales skills.

- Increased sales volume more than 49% each consecutive year in a highly competitive market.
- Responsible for a sales division that has generated a tripling of sales and profits for a three-year period.
  —Staffed and trained outside sales force
  —Became a resource person, troubleshooter, and closer for sales staff
  —Initiated telemarketing program including staffing and training personnel setting up successful incentive plan
  —Created and wrote individualized proposals

- Developed sales and marketing strategies
  —Designed brochures, demonstration kits, advertising, direct mailings
  —Input into product design

MARKETING REPRESENTATIVE

Lancaster Laboratories, Philadelphia, Pennsylvania   1993–1998

Sold mechanical equipment, supplies, drugs, and medicines to physicians. In conjunction with attending school in order to finance my education. Worked part-time until graduation and then assumed the position full-time.

- Enlarged markets for established and new products, which resulted in a substantial increase in new accounts.

(Continued)

OTHER:

INDEPENDENT CONSULTANT of computer systems and peripherals utilizing background in developing accounting and marketing systems for the business client. 1993 to Present.

EDUCATION:

B.S. ACCOUNTING/MARKETING, Scranton University, Scranton, Pennsylvania, 1993

WILLING TO RELOCATE

REFERENCES WILL BE FURNISHED UPON REQUEST

MARKETING TRAINEE

JOHN APPLEBY
4482 Congress Avenue
Ft. Lauderdale, Florida 33055
Tel: 954-555-4545   Email: Appleby 305@yahoo.com

SALES/MARKETING TRAINEE

Entry-level candidate for starting opportunity in sales/marketing or management training program, with exposure and proven capabilities in developing account relationships, providing sales support, and quality customer service for major international manufacturing corporation.

Demonstrated ability to handle challenging and diversified duties of ever increasing responsibility, as key link in order processing chain with foreign clients. Provided expertise, regarding product knowledge and system procedures for processing multimillion dollar sales orders. Prior experience encompasses inside and outside sales of various products and services.

SUMMARY OF QUALIFICATIONS:
- Diversified results-oriented experience in sales processing and customer service.
- Demonstrated ability in planning, developing, and implementing operational programs.
- Strong communication and interpersonal skills.
- Extensive contact with both domestic and international clients, responding to inquiries and resolving problems.
- Skilled and adept with time management and territory development.
- Capable of working independently or as part of a team effort.
- Computer proficient.

EDUCATION:
PALM BEACH COMMUNITY COLLEGE BOCA RATON, FL   (Anticipated completion 12/03)
Associate of Business Administration Degree
Major: International Business

EXPERIENCE:
MOTOROLA CORP., BOCA RATON, FL   **10/99–PRESENT**
International Liaison
- Coordinate all aspects of order processing for Motorola's "Source Tagging" (UPP), program for foreign corporations and major domestic customers, including Black & Decker, Delta Faucet, Energizer, Campbell Hausfeld & Emerson.
- Assisted Sales Reps and new customers with source tagging information and account set-up with label procedure, as well as provide documentation for customs clearance and shipping orders.
- Review orders for accuracy and completeness and check for product availability.
- Provide general support for Sensormatic centers in Europe, Canada, and the Pacific Rim area.
- Achieved company recognition with invitation to Alaskan trip, for assisting the sales team reach its financial targets.

Temp Associate
- Initial employment as a temporary.
- Received recognition as "Associate-of-the-Month," for conscientious efforts to maintain high standards for reliability, flexibility, and work performance.

MELROSE OFFICE SOLUTIONS TECHNOLOGY SERVICES, PEMBROKE PINES, FL   **9/96–1/97**
National Wholesale Representative
- Established and maintained strong working relationships with dealers in IL, WI, KY, and TN, selling office machines and all OEM supplies, with accountability for negotiating sales margins.

FIBER INTERACTIVE ASSOCIATES, FT. LAUDERDALE, FL   **3/96–9/96**
Account Executive
- Successfully sold general partnership opportunities in new business investment through cold calling and personal networking.

REFERENCES: Furnished upon request

Anthony T. Faulk
569 59th Avenue
Tulsa, Oklahoma 74105   Telephone: (918) 529-3309

Job Objective: <u>Marketing/Sales Director</u>

Experience
1995–present   King Regan Corp., Tulsa, Oklahoma
                      Assistant to President
                      _____

                      Directed the marketing for new products in the freeze-dried field.
                      Researched the market and competition, test-marketed products,
                      and trained sales force for national distribution. Followed the
                      successful distribution of products on consumer level with the
                      training of institutional sales staff to open key institutional accounts.

                      Found new markets for established products and opened European
                      distribution for U.S. products. Developed sales and marketing
                      strategy, searched for and identified specific markets, and
                      developed methods of penetrating those markets.

                      Responsibility for advertising, packaging, promotions, and product
                      development.

1993–1995   Crowley Industrial Bag Inc., Cleveland, Ohio
                      Marketing Director
                      _____

                      Responsibility for diversification to consumer products, opening key
                      accounts, directing new technology. Utilized market research
                      methods, impact point of purchase pieces, and both product and
                      corporate advertising to launch the consumer products. Worked
                      closely with package designers to develop unified packaging with a
                      hard-sell profile. Supervised training of a special sales force.

1990–1993   Ace Marine Supplies and Boats, Chicago, Illinois
                      Product Manager
                      _____

                      Created new markets for established products and recommended
                      product improvements. To capitalize on the growing demand for
                      fiberglass boats, worked with designers to make changes in our 40-
                      foot yacht to create a 40-foot motor sailboat. The market followed
                      our trend and sales more than doubled over sales on the original
                      yacht in the line in previous years.

                                                                (Continued)

1988–1990	Chicago Sun Times, Chicago, Illinois
	Salesman

Sold classified and display advertising in local market.

Education   1988 M.B.A. degree from University of Chicago.

Graduated 1985 from Xavier University with B.S. and B.A. degrees in Economics and Accounting.

References   On request.

George Adams
10 Waters Road
Santa Fe, NM 87121
(505) 371-0200

OBJECTIVE   Senior sales or marketing position with major software vendor.

EDUCATION   North Texas State University, B.A. Mathematics; 1981

EMPLOYMENT HISTORY

1995–
present

Software Systems of North America
Santa Fe, NM

As Account Manager, responsibilities include marketing DATABASE II and associated products in North Texas and Oklahoma and establishing a Dallas office. Attained quota of $1.1M, finishing 101% of quota for 1996.

1987–1995

Forum Corporation
Phoenix, AZ

As Marketing Representative from February 1989–January 1990, responsibilities included marketing the entire product line, territory planning and management, and revenue forecasting and budget control. Ranked Number 2 in the United States at 216% of quota ($547,000 in booked business and 7 new systems installed).

Promoted to Senior Marketing Representative. Finished 9-month sales period of 1990 with $220,000 in business while developing a new territory.

Was Marketing Representative of the Month in July and September, 1989. Other positions held were Systems Programmer, Systems Engineer, Senior Systems Engineer, District Support Manager.

1981–1987

Information Leaders
El Paso, TX

As Systems Engineer in Life Insurance Industry Group was responsible for entire Letters and Notices Systems for three life insurance accounts; for defining, implementing, and coding new letters for existing systems; for maintaining and improving existing systems; and for supporting application programmers.

References: Available upon request

ANDREW EASTON
10 Tyrolia Avenue
Lawrence, NY 11559

Home Phone: (516) 513-0791
Business: (516) 886-1169

BUSINESS HISTORY

TYLO AND TYLO, INC.

1993–present   Associate Media Director

Prepared media plans for Lenox China, International Silver, Binney and Smith (Crayola), Loctite, Connecticut Bank and Trust Co., Julius Wile.

CONEDIA AND EVVON, INC.

1987–1993   Prepared media plans and supervised media research. Handled buying on such accounts as Dutch Boy Paint, Hartford Insurance, Genesee Beer, Snow Crop, and Chun King.

ESTHERSON ASSOCIATES

1981–1987   Print Media Buyer and Media Specialist (Business Papers)

Prepared media plans and recommendations on magazines, newspapers, and business papers for specific accounts including Continental Can, Armstrong Cork, U.S. Steel, and DuPont.

Served as a member of the Media Plans Board, which reviewed and made basic recommendations for all accounts. Acted as consultant on business media to many accounts that were basically assigned to other buyers. This included both New York and out-of-town offices, with some contact with virtually every Estherson Associates account.

Served for four years as a member of the Business Paper Committee of the American Association of Advertising Agencies.

1978–1981   Print Buyer

Wrote media recommendations on specific problems and handled print buying and estimating for DuPont, TWA, and others.

EDUCATION   Haverford College, B.A., 1978

REFERENCES   Available upon request.

R. S. WATSON
270 Runnymede Street
Lipton, Arkansas 19701

EMPLOYMENT

1993–Present   Jessica Blaine, Inc.—St. Augustine, Florida

President: activities consisted of planning, account acquisition, creative direction, copy, media selection, and related functions.

1991–1993   T. Teaks, Inc.—Reno, Nevada

Account Executive: complete responsibility for all agency activity on Harcourt Brace Jovanovich, Inc., Subaru Automobiles. Assisted as Account Executive on Singer Fabrics and Notions, plus related agency operations, new business, and special projects.

1989–1991   Field and Spring International, Inc.—Chicago, Illinois

Assistant Account Executive: Eastern Airlines (Broadcast and Print), functioned under the Y and R training program on the following accounts: Dash, Salvo, Gainesburger, Top Choice, Marshall Cavendish Ltd., Travelers Insurance, Liggett & Myers, General Cigar, Pepsico International, British Rail.

1986–1989   Uni Med, Inc.—Chicago, Illinois

Division Chief: responsible for the supervision and coordination of activities of 27 employees in the Group Contracts Division of the Correspondence Department.

EDUCATION

Hofstra University, Hempstead, L.I., New York
B.S., Business Administration, 1986.

REFERENCES

Will be furnished upon request.

MEDIA SALES

ALICIA WILLOUGHBY
4455 Anderson Avenue
Hollywood, Florida 33032
Tel: 954-555-4568   Cell: 561-555-4104

• MEDIA SALES • ADVERTISING • GRAPHIC DESIGN •

Sales and Marketing Professional, as well as award-winning graphic artist and designer, with more than 20 years of multifaceted background developing and exploiting markets for diversified products and services. Successful track record of expanding client base, organizing and developing territory and increasing sales and market share. Consistently rated among top producers in advertising space sales, was responsible for generating more than $1.8 million in annual revenues.

Extensive experience in space sales and developing effective advertising programs, as well as executing all creative elements of production. Expertise in graphic design, worked as animator/action artist for Hanna-Barbera Studios in California, in addition to designing and creating advertising campaigns. Winner of five "Addy Awards" and listed in "Who's Who in America."

SUMMARY OF QUALIFICATIONS:

- Diversified results-oriented experience in sales/marketing, business growth, and customer service.
- Skills and expertise in market strategy, planning, implementation, and administration of marketing programs.
- Experienced and adept with Time management, Needs Assessment, Client Profile Evaluation, and Commitment Strategies.
- Strong aptitude for cold canvassing, strategic targeting, and closing sales.
- Excellent communication, sales presentation, and interpersonal skills.
- Strong advertising production experience and creative talent.
- Capable of working individually or as part of a team effort.
- Computer proficient.

EXPERIENCE:

BELL SOUTH ADVERTISING & PUBLISHING, WEST PALM BEACH/DEERFIELD BEACH, FL 6/99–3/02
Senior Advertising Consultant
- Complete responsibility for planning, developing, and marketing "Yellow Page" advertising within territory, from Jupiter to Miami, FL.
- Established consultative relationships with accounts to assess needs and produce solutions to their advertising requirements.
- Educated clients in media planning and budgeting to produce the most cost-effective marketing strategies.
- Assisted with creation of initial advertising layouts.
- Consistently increased ad revenues and exceeded projected sales goals.
- Recipient of many sales prizes and bonuses, was top rated producer in last campaign, with revenues exceeding $90,000 per month.
- Successfully completed comprehensive sales training program.

YELLOW BOOK USA, BOYNTON BEACH, FL   4/98–6/99
Account Executive
- Expanded client base of advertisers, selling ad space for 20 separate directories from Miami to Jupiter, FL.
- Provided expertise for production values, including layouts and computer graphics.
- Established strong working relationships with accounts and provided ongoing customer service.
- Contacted local merchants through qualified leads and cold-calling.
- Achieved ranking in top 10% of Account Executives.

SOUTH FLORIDA NEWSPAPER NETWORK, CORAL SPRINGS, FL   7/97–4/98
Advertising Consultant
- Sold advertising for 34 weekly community newspapers, including *The Boca, Delray* and *Boynton Times, The Boca Business Journal, The Coral Springs, Margate* and *Tamarac Forums, The Sunrise Times,* and the *Jewish Journal.*
- Worked with advertisers to coordinate all elements of newspaper ads, both display and classified, including concept, design, and production.
- Successfully performed time-sensitive tasks under pressure of daily deadlines.

EXPERIENCE: (CONTINUED)

SHENANDOAH PODIATRY, MARTINSBURG, WV   1/96–7/97
Public Relations
- Directed all aspects of P.R., for this new physician's practice, including advertising, radio-TV, direct mail, community events and participation in health fairs, generating annual billings of more than $2 million.
- Coordinated efficient flow of patients for examination and consultation, in addition to setting up new patient files, maintaining and updating existing files.
- Oversaw patient billing and insurance coverage verification.
- Acquired comprehensive knowledge of medical practice procedures and medical terminology.

GRAPHICS FROM THE WILDSIDE, VIRGINIA, MARYLAND, WASHINGTON, D.C.   2/92–1/96
President/Manager
- Developed extensive client base for this advertising agency, which included *National Geographic* Magazine, *World* Magazine, Smithsonian Institute, Sports Authority, World Cup Soccer, and Eckerd Drugs.
- Consulted with clients to plan and execute advertising and promotional campaigns, including retail store grand openings.
- Designed and produced brochures, catalogs, logos, and direct mail pieces.
- Outsourced printing requirements.

TENBY CORPORATION, POMPANO BEACH, FL   3/90–2/92
Art Director
- Created silkscreen designs for a line of sportswear merchandise, including shorts, T-shirts, tanks, sweat shirts, pants, and hats for a list of major retail department store chains, such as Walmart, Target, Zayres, and Bradley's.
- Designed logos and graphics for 50 college teams, as well as the NFL, NBA, and NASL.
- In addition to design and illustration, separated colors and shot film positives, stats, burned screens, and set type and graphics on the computer.

WILLOUGHBY MARKETING AND DESIGN, CLEARWATER, FL   4/85–3/90
President
- Established business to provide graphic designs for client's advertising and marketing programs.
- Major clients included: Mutual Media, Inc., Eckerd Drugs, Pioneer Savings Bank, Jeep Eagle, Home Shopping Network, Union Carbide, Ramada Inn, Columbia Equities, Inc., and People Express Airlines.

UNIVERSITY OF KENTUCKY, LEXINGTON, KY   1983–1985
Teacher–Graphic Design

HANNA-BARBERA STUDIOS, LOS ANGELES, CA   1981–1983
Animator/Action Artist
- Worked on various cartoon series, including Skoobie Doo, Yogi Bear, Flintstones, and the Harlem Globetrotters.

EDUCATION:

NEW SCHOOL FOR SOCIAL RESEARCH, NEW YORK, NY
Master of Fine Arts Degree
Painting and Sculpture

PARSONS SCHOOL OF DESIGN, NEW YORK, NY
Bachelor of Fine Arts Degree

SKILLS:

Computer Proficient: Macintosh G-4 OS • Typestyler • MS Word • Painter • Quark Express • Illustrator • Photoshop
Welding and Plaster casting • Various stat cameras • plate burners

AWARDS & ACHIEVEMENTS:
- Five "Addy Awards"
- "Who's Who in America"

ALICE RAND
180 Pine St.
Bronxville, New York 12415
(914) 949-4077

OBJECTIVE	Challenging position as a media trainee.
EDUCATION 9/97–present	MONROE COLLEGE, Yonkers, New York Currently enrolled in program leading to an M.B.A. Concentration in financial management with special emphasis on the study of accounting for management control.
9/95–6/97	UNIVERSITY OF FAIRFIELD, Fairfield, Connecticut B.S. Major in Real Estate and Urban Economic Development. Extensive course work in real property appraisal and investment analysis.
EMPLOYMENT 9/97–present	MONROE COLLEGE, Yonkers, New York Assistant to the manager of analytical studies Collect synthesized price data for college's annual inflation study. Project involves library research as well as telephone contact with college suppliers.
9/95–6/97	UNIVERSITY OF FAIRFIELD, Fairfield, Connecticut Head resident. Responsible for running all aspects of a college dormitory. Duties included supervising residents, kitchen and maintenance staff, and preparing all paperwork for Department of Student Affairs. Job was concurrent with full-time academic study to earn seventy percent of college expenses.
SUMMERS	
1996	EATON REAL ESTATE, New Canaan, Connecticut Real estate salesperson. Employed part-time by Eaton for buying and selling real property.
1995	MONROE COLLEGE, Yonkers, New York Dispatcher. Employed by physical plant department with responsibility for keeping accurate records on thirty-vehicle motor pool.
1994	Groundsperson. Responsible for maintenance of college buildings and grounds.
REFERENCES	Available on request.

MEDICAL TECHNOLOGIST

DONALD BROOM
4401 Oak Tree Lane
Tampa Bay, Florida 34414
Tel: 561-555-0101 Cell: 561-555-6789

• RADIOLOGIC TECHNOLOGIST •

Experienced Radiologic Technologist seeks employment opportunity to advance a career in medical diagnostic technology. Three years postgraduate experience in all medical diagnostic procedures involving the use of general radiographic techniques. Extensive Operating and Emergency Room experience.

Background also encompasses work experience in various business enterprises, including positions with managerial responsibility and interfacing with people on all levels, providing quality customer service.

SUMMARY OF QUALIFICATIONS:
- Five years "hands-on" experience and capabilities with x-ray modality.
- Excellent communication and interpersonal skills.
- Demonstrated planning, organizational, and implementation ability.
- Diversified business experience, including sales and customer service, as well as personnel supervisory responsibilities.
- Capable of working independently or as part of a team effort.
- Computer knowledgeable.

EDUCATION:
WEST BOCA MEDICAL CENTER   10/96–10/98
School of Radiologic Technology
Registered Radiologic Technologist

Rotated training at the following medical facilities:
- Delray Medical Center, Delray Beach, FL
  - Acquired experience in the medical trauma unit.
- Delray Medical Center Outpatient Facility, Delray Beach, FL
- Cleveland Clinic, Ft. Lauderdale, FL
- West Boca Medical Center, Boca Raton, FL
- Hollywood Medical Center, Hollywood, FL

Broward Community College, Ft. Lauderdale, FL
Associate of Science Degree Candidate

WORK EXPERIENCE:

MEMORIAL HOSPITAL WEST, PEMBROKE PINES, FL   4/99–7/02
Radiologic Technologist
- Acquired in-depth x-ray experience at this 184 bed metropolitan general hospital.
- Extensive experience in the OR and ER.

NATIONAL TIRE & BATTERY, DAVIE, FL   6/96–8/97
Customer Service Adviser
- Assisted customers with merchandise selection and resolving problems and complaints.

DISCOUNT AUTO PARTS, TAMARAC, FL   11/93–6/96
Parts Specialist/Team Leader
- Supervised daily store operations in absence of store manager.
- Responsible for maintenance of extensive parts inventory, supervising shipping and receiving from company warehouse and entering data into computer program.

REFERENCES: Furnished upon request

MARGIE A. THOMPSON
89 WOODRIDGE ROAD
APARTMENT # 123
COLUMBUS, OHIO 43212
(614) 443-7785

EXPERIENCE:

August 1995–
Present

CERO'S AND KLINE'S
Canton, Ohio

Assistant to the Store Manager/Merchandising Hardlines

Redesigned departments including: redefining of classifications, merchandise, and fixture presentations resulting in sales increases of 10–20%. Coordinated the efforts of buyers and display department personnel to achieve aesthetically pleasing, cohesive vignettes representing market trends and store direction. Created more awareness of merchandise presentation and coordination throughout the home furnishings divisions.

June 1993–
July 1995

HOUSE FURNISHINGS, INC.
Cleveland, Ohio

Buyer/Merchandiser/Coordinator: Accessories

Reduced the resource selection by 60 and increased volume by 15% while opening 50% fewer stores. Raised the net profitability of department by 35%. Raised the turnover rate of merchandise in stores from 1.5 to 2.5 times per year via tighter selections, controls, and the implementation of an inventory control system. Within capacity of merchandising consultant to over 250 stores in the area of gifts and accessories, have shopped all major national accessory markets and researched, coordinated, and published 5 service manuals that are utilized for resources, merchandise, and display techniques. Directed dealers with designing, merchandising, and displaying their in-store gift shops.

(Continued)

January 1990– June 1993	<u>SUNSHINE DEPARTMENT STORE</u> 224 West Market Street Cleveland, Ohio

<u>Department Manager: Men's Accessories, Candy, and Smoke Shop</u>

Reduced personnel budget by 30-man-hours per week through more efficient use of personnel. Supervised 25 employees. Reordered all merchandise sold in departments. Responsible for all department areas including personnel, housekeeping, displays, merchandising.

<u>EDUCATION:</u>   B.S. Business Management
Bowling Green University

References on request.

GEORGE W. WILLIAMS
244 Washington Boulevard
Flushing, NY 11304

718-492-6490

OBJECTIVE   To obtain position in supervisory capacity with Metallurgical
Laboratory.

EXPERIENCE
1/95–Present   <u>Technical Advisor and Editor</u>, Scientific Journal of America, New York,
NY. Write and edit articles on latest developments and innovations in
ferrous industries; conduct in-field research for collection of data for
feature articles; public relations responsibilities with domestic industries
related to metallurgical processes.

5/92–1/95   <u>Production Supervisor, Metallurgical Division</u>, CITOR Chemical
Laboratories, White Plains, NY. Conducted quality control checks on
Chemical, Physical Metallurgy, Metallography regarding future
production requirements; handled customer complaints with respect to
both metallurgical and nonmetallurgical process deviations; ordered all
supplies necessary to heat treating; supervised and scheduled
assignments of laboratory technicians and production workers.

8/87–5/90   <u>Metallurgical Trainee</u>, Allison Steel Works, Pittsburgh, PA. Trained in
metallurgical aspects of metal defect reduction, nondestructive testing,
chemical analysis development, and implementation of processes
involving physical testing, cost reduction; gained experience in Quality
Control, including statistics control charts, and developed skills in both
metallurgical and nonmetallurgical process deviations. Assisted in
supervision of eight laboratory technicians.

EDUCATION
B.S. in Metallurgical Engineering, June 1987, Wheeling University, Pennsylvania.

PROFESSIONAL SOCIETIES
Member of American Society of Mining Engineers, American Metallurgist Society, Institute
of Metallurgical Engineering.

REFERENCES
Furnished on request.

NIKITA WYCKOFF
2011 Connecticut Road
Island Park, NY 11558
516-889-0448

SUMMARY: Worked as Mutual Fund Accountant for twenty years in variety of corporations, also included thirteen years' experience in bookkeeping.

EXPERIENCE

1993–present	Mutual Fund Accountant, Capital Advisory Service, Inc., New York City. Prepared monthly financial statements; calculated net asset value of Fund's capital stock; maintained full set of books, including general ledger; recorded daily transactions and assigned data for computer processing, calculated interest on bonds and short-term paper.
1992–1993	Mutual Fund Accountant, Walker's Management, Inc., New York City. Responsibilities same as above.
1989–1993	Mutual Fund Accountant, J.R. Stern Advisors and Distributors, New York. Worked on financial statements, general ledger, S.E.C. reports (N-IR and N-IQ), taxes.
1975–1989	Mutual Fund Accountant and Bookkeeper, Brewster Management Corporation, Long Island. Complete responsibility for maintaining Fund's books, including general ledger, pricing of Fund's shares, supervision of clerical staff of four, liaison with Custodian and Transfer Agent, general correspondence, and all duties connected with conducting the Fund's business transactions.

EDUCATION

LL.B. of the University of Riga, Latvia, Faculty of Law and Economics, 1975.

Certificate in Investment Analysis, 1980, Finance Institute of New York.

LANGUAGES

Fluency in Russian, French, German, and Latvian.

REFERENCES   On request.

NURSE

PEGGY FINCH
2234 Oriole Parkway
Plantation, Florida 33345
561-555-4809   E-mail: pfinch@hotmail.com

• **REGISTERED NURSE** • **HEALTHCARE ADMINISTRATION** •

More than 15 years of multifaceted nursing experience as a staff nurse in large metropolitan and teaching hospitals. Comprehensive experience and ability in emergency services, as well as responsibility for managing nursing staff and services as resource and charge nurse at a community hospital.

Strong clinical skills, with extensive experience in organizing and implementing policies, procedures, and controls to efficiently guide unit activities. Responsibilities included preceptoring new hires, in addition to direct patient care.

SUMMARY OF QUALIFICATIONS:

- Skilled and adept in all aspects of administration of nursing care and duties.
- Certifications: CPAN • ACLS • PALS.
- Excellent communication and interpersonal skills.
- Strong patient assessment skills.
- Demonstrated leadership ability with excellent planning, organizational, implementation, and developmental skills.
- Supervisory experience, with demonstrated resourcefulness in resolving problems.
- Computer proficient: MS word • Internet.

EXPERIENCE:

BOCA COMMUNITY HOSPITAL, BOCA RATON, FL   **10/87–PRESENT**
Staff Nurse—PACU
- Responsible for direct patient care, in this Perianesthesia Care Unit, including all basic nursing duties, such as patient assessment and vital signs, administration of medications, charting, documentation, IVs, and venipuncture.
- Serve as resource nurse, filling in for supervising nurse, when necessary, as well as Preceptor for new hires.
- Follow physicians' orders from patient charts, with accuracy and completeness.
- Prepare ambulatory and nonambulatory patients for surgery pre-op., as well as postoperative nursing, including intensive care.
- Experienced and thoroughly familiar with intensive care duties.
- Responsible for discharge planning and instruction of patients, regarding home care and use of medical devices and equipment.
- Ongoing involvement in unit-based quality assurance.

BRIGHAM & WOMEN'S HOSPITAL, BOSTON, MA   **6/77–7/87**
Staff Nurse—PACU
- Diversified experience in Cardiac Surgical ICU and ER units in the Harvard University teaching hospital.
- Duties included basic nursing functions, including starting IVs, drawing blood, EKGs, medications and checking vital signs.

EDUCATION:

SEWICKLEY VALLEY HOSPITAL, SEWICKLEY, PA
School of Nursing

<u>Continuing Education:</u>
Florida Risk Management Institute
- Legal Nurse Consultant
- Case Management Course

MARTIN MILTON
24 Woodbine Drive
Cherry Hill, NJ 08003
(609) 685-4039

EXPERIENCE

1991–present Customer Relations Manager, Premium Publishing Company, Morris Hills, NJ. Manage Customer Relations Dept., with staff of 13 full-time employees. Maintain effective and efficient customer relations, maintain and control procedure of work flow, act as liaison between sales, operations, and customers. Analyze and make decisions for adjustments, credits, and debits. Involved in all phases including processing of orders, shipping, returns, sales, credits. Prepare reports (weekly and monthly) on statistics, problems, and make recommendations when needed. Handle all problems related to personnel, vacations, time cards, interviewing, hiring, and training.

1985–1991 Administrator-Office Manager, Civic Center, Plainfield, NJ. Maintained and supervised bookkeeping and accounting records according to established practice. A/P, A/R, payroll, purchasing, check reconciliation, general ledger. Prepared periodic financial statements, reviewed budget, maintained accurate membership records; handled enrollment of new members; prepared calendar of events for all affiliated groups, coordinated the use of facilities; supervised building and maintenance staff. Administered and executed all policies made by executive board.

1980–1985 Field Sales Representative, Martin's Gift Shop, Avenue of the Americas, New York City, NY. Called on wholesalers, chain, and retail stores as representative of manufacturer and importer of novelties, souvenirs, costume jewelry, etc. Involved extensive travel throughout Midwest states. Set up and exhibited at numerous trade shows.

EDUCATION

1980 Dearborn Jr. College, Ridgelake, CO
Two-year certificate, Business Administration.

1985–1987 Bradley Business School, Rutherford, NJ
Night courses in Business Administration.

REFERENCES Available upon request.

Martha Bender
1600 Nevada Street, N.W.
Washington, DC 20006
(202) 929-3006
(202) 787-3400

GOAL:
Seeking a challenging position as a Senior-Level Legal Assistant which provides an opportunity for both greater responsibilities and future advancement.

EXPERIENCE:
October 1994 to Present

Morris, Banker, & Rand
Washington, DC

CORPORATE PARALEGAL: Responsibilities include training and supervising Unit Trust Department Legal Assistants in the preparation of materials for the issuance and sale of Fortune 100 Corporate and Municipal Bond Funds, compliance with relevant SEC and NASD fund regulations (including 1933 and 1940 Act requirements), direction of financial printing, and coordination of closings with key sponsors (Smith Barney, Kidder Peabody, Drexel Burnham) and evaluation services (Moody's, Standard and Poors). Also assist in preparation of other corporate closings including mergers, debt restructuring, reorganization of Limited Partnerships, and stock offerings.

January 1993 to October 1994

Estate of Harris Co., Bankruptcy
New York, NY

Responsibilities included reconciliation of Real Estate Claims against the Estate, recording monthly progress of claims processing, and discounting leases to determine fair rental value of breach of lease claims. Developed and maintained a series of indexed systems for internal and court-ordered changes and final disposition of these claims. Also assisted in the development and implementation of EDP System to record this information for all claims against the Estate.

EDUCATION:
New York University, New York, NY
Took several graduate-level courses in psychology.

Skidmore College, Saratoga, NY
B.A. English, Minor: Fine Arts
HONORS: Dean's List, 1990–92
ACTIVITIES: Publicity Director for Student Program Board, Activities Coordinator for Seminar in Communications, Student Council, Editor of Literary Magazine.

REFERENCES:
Furnished upon request.

ADAM STERN

100 Sycamore Lane
Nashville, TN 37204
(615) 595-1309 (home)   (615) 587-1300 (work)

OBJECTIVE:

Experienced holder of ABA-approved trusts and estates paralegal certificate seeks challenging position.

EXPERIENCE:

1996–Present Elliot, Elliot & Farber, Nashville, TN
Trusts and Estates Settlement Assistant.
Prepare, analyze, and compile data of new estates; transfer securities, brokerage, custody, and check accounts for estates and trusts; terminate and distribute assets of accounts; compile and prepare financial statements, fiduciary, and personal tax returns; pay estate and trust expenses for new and ongoing accounts; research and interpret pertinent information concerning estates and trusts, court experience.

1995 Burton Advertising Associates, Inc., Nashville, TN
Assistant to Bookkeeper.
Fast-paced environment, involving deadlines, heavy workload, computing payroll for 250 workers weekly from 3 offices, billing and checking balance sheet for taxes paid by employees.

1994 Carnegie Records, Nashville, TN
Administrative Assistant in the Public Relations Department.
Worked with confidential material and gained familiarity with office procedures.

1990–92 Acme's Emporium, Nashville, TN
Clerk.
Worked to finance education while attending classes on a full-time basis. Successfully assumed the responsibilities of cashier, sales, and opening and closing of department.

1988–90 IBM, Endicott, TN
Co-op Assistant.
Duties included terminal work, typing, filing, and heavy phone contact.

EDUCATION:

University of Tennessee, Nashville, TN
Lawyers Assistant Program.
Specialization in Trusts and Estates. (ABA approved) December 1993.

Richmond College, Richmond, VA
Bachelor of Arts, Sociology, May 1995
Pertinent Course Work: Accounting 1, Statistics
Computer Experience: IBM, Macintosh, MS Word, EXCEL, PowerPoint, and others

REFERENCES:

Furnished upon request.

JAMES MICHAEL SOLOMON

1619 Lexington Avenue, Apt. 19B
New York, New York 10128
Home: (212) 369-2751
Work: (212) 940-7721

JOB OBJECTIVE:

A supervisory position offering increasing responsibility in the area of law firm administration.

RELEVANT WORK EXPERIENCE:

January 1994 to Present	Paralegal/Case Supervisor. Smith, Collins, Frederick, Clarkson & Cohen, New York, NY. Handle administrative responsibilities including hiring permanent and temporary paralegals, distributing and supervising work, and working in conjunction with other departments such as word processing; prepare billing to clients, communicate with clients, digest depositions, legal research, create trial exhibits, and organize antitrust litigation files specifically organizing, categorizing, and cataloging large document productions.
Summers 1989–1993	Work experience includes clerking at various retail establishments (including Montgomery Ward) and a bank; responsibilities included sales, administrative, and office work and collections.
EDUCATION:	New York University, New York, NY School of Continuing Education. Courses completed include Practical Account Management (emphasis on planning, workflow, research, presentations, and client relations); Filmmaking: Techniques and Technology; and Film Production I. Adelphi University, Garden City, NY Completed lawyer's assistant program (ABA-approved) in winter of 1993; instruction included drafting and communicative legal techniques and legal research. Boston University, Boston, MA Graduated June 1992, with Bachelor of Arts Degree; Major—English; Minor—Psychology. Courses include Public Speaking, Techniques of Debating, Newswriting and Reporting, and Photography (journalism). Extracurricular Activities: Program director and disk jockey at WTBU (university radio station); administration, organization, and planning in connection with presidential election campaign; and personal solicitation of funds for various charities.
REFERENCES:	Furnished upon request.

Stanley Y. Gerbreem
12 Central Street, South
Omaha, Nebraska 68114
(402) 456-0976

Job Goal:	Payroll Supervisor

Experience:

1991–present	Vanderbilt, Lowe and Thomas, Inc., Omaha, Nebraska Payroll Clerk

While in training, became familiar with corporate personnel and payroll policies, various unit payroll practices, benefit plan program, and appropriate tax manuals.

Examine and process changes to the basic computerized payroll file for approximately 500 employees. Maintain control totals for different types of changes by unit (increases, new hires, terminations). Examine time sheets and other records to apply overtime and exception pay practices, processing special payments (sales bonus, incentive awards); and prepare manual checks for emergency situations.

Maintain employee absence and vacation records. Compose routine correspondence. Solve discrepancy problems.

1989–1991	Meyers & Harris Distribution Center, Omaha, Nebraska Clerk in Marketing Research Department

Performed standardized clerical tasks following company procedures. Maintained salary ledger for department, assembled and classified vouchers, entered postings for the department budgets.

Education:	Portland District High School, Portland, Oregon Diploma of Business Studies, 1987
Military:	Served a two-year term in the Coast Guard.
References:	Available on request.

HUMAN RESOURCES MANAGEMENT

Barbara Winters
1645 West Brook Drive
Passaic, New Jersey 07056
(201) 455-6767

EMPLOYMENT HISTORY:

WAVERLY CORPORATION (PULP AND PAPER COMPANY), New Rochelle, New York

7/2/93– Present

Administer Corporate Savings and Investment Plan, Retirement Plan, and Long-Term Disability Plan.

SAVINGS AND INVESTMENT PLAN

Maintain all records of activity. Review and approve new enrollments and terminations. Calculate and process monthly cash transactions connected with transfer of company and employee funds to the Trustee. Prepare information to Corporate Tax Department in connection with various S.E.C. reports. Assist and advise local Benefits Representatives with administration of the Plan.

RETIREMENT PLAN

Calculate and file with actuaries refunds of contributions on all salaried nonvested terminations. Deposit and refund cash contributions received from foreign and domestic subsidiaries. Act as troubleshooter between hourly locations and actuaries.

DISABILITY PLAN
Calculate monthly Long-Term Disability premiums. Coordinate and process salaried Long-Term Disability and New York State Disability claims. Maintain all records and correspondence.

11/27/92– 6/29/93

TRENTON MEMORIAL HOSPITAL, Trenton, New Jersey (Unemployment Insurance Clerk)
Administered unemployment insurance claims.

(Continued)

4/8/88– 11/22/92	CLAYTON INDUSTRIES, Trenton, New Jersey (Personnel Assistant) Recruited and oriented clerical, production, and some technical personnel. Processed merit and cost-of-living increases. Administered Blue Cross, Major Medical, Life Insurance, Workers' Compensation, New York State Disability, Unemployment Insurance, etc.
2/14/83– 4/5/88	WESTBURY INC., New York, New York (Assistant Personnel Supervisor) Recruited, oriented clerical employees. Processed performance appraisals and merit increases. Maintained employee records.
EDUCATION:	Villanova University, B.B.A., 1983.

References available on request.

JEANETTE ELWELL
32-22 224th Street
Brooklyn, New York 11263
718-962-2668

JOB OBJECTIVE   To apply experience, mature insight, and education to position in
                     personnel administration where effective personnel management can be
                     promoted.

EXPERIENCE PERTINENT TO OBJECTIVE

1991–present   Personnel Manager, Hart and Dunlap Co., Inc., New York City. Reported
                     to Vice President of Personnel in this major publishing firm in fulfilling
                     responsibilities as supervisor of personnel services for New York office.
                     Conducted salary surveys, established salary ranges and progression
                     rates for each level. Installed and maintained job evaluation plans,
                     questionnaires, application forms, etc. Revised and formulated training
                     programs, designed progress reports, and initiated appraisal procedures
                     for employee performance. Ran successful recruiting campaigns for new
                     employees for reference book subsidiary. Initiated and implemented
                     programs to improve and utilize potential of staff members. Represented
                     company at hearings with City and State Boards. Was involved in
                     development of company policies with responsibility for interpretation
                     and implementation in everyday practice. Consulted with managers on
                     numerous problems such as manpower planning, upgrading, performance
                     evaluation.

EDUCATION

M.B.A., Management—Graduate School of Business Administration, New York University, New
York, New York, June 1991.

B.A., History, University of Rochester, New York, February 1989.

Personnel Management Course, National Conference Board of Industrial Management, 1990.
Techniques and planning for effective personnel programs were developed with the use of group
case histories and lectures.

REFERENCES

Upon request.

Stella Davidoff
165 Williams Street
Dallas, Texas 75213
(818) 929-3456
(816) 921-4000

OBJECTIVE

To obtain a position within an organization that will provide continued growth, learning, and opportunity to contribute as a Human Resource Professional.

RELATED EXPERIENCE

4/92–Present *Client/Personal Representative,*
Career Blazers, Dallas, Texas

- National temporary placement service.
- Enhance delivery of service to established accounts; prospect and develop new accounts. Cater to the individual needs of client companies.
- Ensure customer satisfaction by backing promises with strict attention to administrative details. Match temporary employee to the job requirements.
- Recruit temporary managers, accountants, secretaries, word processing specialists, and other clerical personnel at college campuses, professional organizations, etc., for client corporations.
- Conduct 30 to 50 exempt/nonexempt applicant screenings and interviews weekly.
- Follow-up sales staff contacts of new and established clients.

1983–1991 *Assistant to Director/Head Music Counselor*
Moore County Day School, Dallas, Texas

- Conducted informational tours for prospective campers and their families.
- Projected and promoted Hillel School's image; set a high performance pace.
- Supervised team responsible for preparing camp for openings/closings each year.
- Planned and prepared schedule of activities for each group and counselor.
- Supervised all music and music-related activities.
- Produced and directed several large scale performances throughout the season.

(Continued)

1985–1991 *Vocal Music Teacher,*
Public Schools, Dallas, Texas

- Taught vocal music to individuals and groups of students; emphasized musical, social, and scholastic development.
- Planned curriculum to enhance students' learning, growth, and self-esteem.
- Took into account students' abilities and potentials.
- Achieved excellent results with "reluctant and eager" learners.

EDUCATION

June 1993, M.B.A. Degree in Industrial/Organizational Psychology University of Texas

1989 B.A. Degree in Psychology, Minor in Human Resources Management Baylor University

BARBARA JO BERNSTEIN
307 East 78th St.
New York, NY 10021
(212) 429-4678

OBJECTIVE   A position in personnel with a salary commensurate with the
                 opportunities afforded.

WORK EXPERIENCE
6/97 to present   Hapcourt Research Company. Inc., 789 Park Avenue, New York, NY

                  Personnel Interviewer
                  Responsible for all nonexempt and some exempt recruitment for the
                  parent company and several subsidiaries (approximately 1,800
                  employees).

                  Counseling duties included employee-subsidiary relations and formal
                  exit interviews.

                  Involved in special reports dealing with EEO, Affirmative Action
                  programs, Wage and Salary surveys, and employee computerized
                  programs.

                  Responsible for handling medical and dental benefits for The
                  Psychological Corporation, a subsidiary of 250 employees.

                  Administrative Assistant
                  Primary responsibility was to obtain permission to reprint material in
                  our school textbooks; also responsible for some secretarial work.

9/96 to 4/97   E.F. Hutton, 280 Park Avenue, New York, NY
                  Secretary
                  Responsible for all secretarial duties for an account executive.

EDUCATION   Muhlenberg College, B.A. History, June 1996. Penn State.
                  Instructor's Level I certification in secondary history education.
                  Graduated with a cumulative average of 3.15.

                  Katherine Gibbs, Certificate of Completion ENTREE program,
                  August 1996.

                  New York University Graduate School of Business Administration,
                  Currently attending evenings, January 1996 to present.

REFERENCES   On request.

Dorothy Rogers
145 Pacific Drive, Apt. 2C
Marina Del Ray, CA 90087
(213) 346-6144

Experience

1990–present
<u>Photographer</u>, Wilson Studio, Malibu, CA.
Chief photographer in still life, high fashion studio. Directing models, booking locations. Black and white and four-color photographs.

1980–1990
<u>Beauty Fashion Photographer</u>, *Trend* Magazine, New York, NY.
Developed analytical themes for feature articles, news stories, and photo essays. Hired and booked models, responsible for stylists.

1978–1981
Freelance Photographer

Exhibits

1991
Famous Women, Fine Arts Center, Los Angeles, CA
1986
In Black and White, Beveridge Bldg., Chicago, IL

Education

Ellison School of Photography, Ellison, CA, 1980
High School of Music and Art, New York, NY, 1978

References on request

C. KIMBALL PRETTSON

14 Panther Place
Stamford, Connecticut 06814

Telephone
Days—(203) 674-0867
Eves.—(203) 976-3457

Present Employment:

1996–Present:

Production Manager for Meridian Studios
Port Chester, New York

Meridian is a full-service house specializing in large format photography for advertising, slide production, and artwork. Meridian services many of the major corporations and agencies in Westchester and Fairfield Counties.

Responsibilities:

- Head up and oversee all in-house production.
- Control job flow and client specifics.

Prior Experience:

1993–1996

Chief Assistant to George Taubert, Taubert Studios, Mount Vernon, New York

1991–1993

Co-owned and managed commercial studio with partner.

1990–1991

Head of black and white commercial lab.

Professional Education:

Germain School of Photography 1988–1990.

Familiar Formats:

Five years' extensive 4 × 5, 2¼, 8 × 10, and standard 35mm formats.

Job Assignments:

- Table-top product photography
- Set styling and lighting
- Portraiture and glamour photography
- Artwork archival shoots
- Slide mounting and chrome retouching
- Overlay preparation and mounting
- Packaging comps

Darkroom Experience:

Complete black and white capabilities

References:

Available upon request.

PHYSICAL THERAPIST

ELLEN WEINSTEIN
4400 Military Trail #304
Boca Raton, Florida 33433
561-555-5698   E-mail: ellen7@aol.com

• PHYSICAL THERAPIST •

Physical Therapist with broad-based education and training, as well as clinical experience in various therapeutic approaches and treatment programs. Masters Degree in Physical Therapy and a B.S. in Physical Education and Fitness Management.

Demonstrated ability in organizing and implementing health & wellness programs, incorporating all aspects of patient care from initial assessment, testing and treatment regimens.

SUMMARY OF QUALIFICATIONS:

- Excellent training and experience in all aspects of physical therapy.
- Rapid mastery of new skills and responsibilities.
- Strong communication and interpersonal skills.
- Excellent organizational and implementation know-how.
- Proven ability to handle projects independently or as part of a team effort.

PROFESSIONAL EXPERIENCE:

JOHNSON PHYSICAL THERAPY, DELRAY BEACH, FL   10/00–12/00
Physical Therapist
- Worked with all types of physically impaired patients in a clinical environment employing a "hands-on" technique, including Myofascial Release.
- Organized new fitness center, with responsibility for administrative functions, as well as assessment of clientele, instruction, and supervision of exercise programs.

DR. ARTHUR PAUL F.A.A.O.S., TAMARAC, FL   8/00–10/00
Physical Therapist
- Performed part-time therapeutic services for general orthopedic patients.
- As the office's sole therapist, conducted evaluations and developed treatment plans utilizing joint mobilizations, exercise, modalities, as well as educating patients regarding disability and self-treatment care.

MEDICAL PROGRAMS, INC., DAVIE, FL   8/00–10/00
Physical Therapist
- Provided physical therapy evaluation and treatment as part of team approach in this "Comprehensive Outpatient Rehabilitation Facility" (CORF), in conjunction with occupational and speech therapists, as well as social and psychological services.
- Administered individual patient treatment, one-on-one, 3 to 5 times a week.
- Established treatment plan after evaluation, subject to physician's approval.

EDUCATION:

UNIVERSITY OF ST. AUGUSTINE FOR HEALTH SCIENCES   5/00
Master's of Physical Therapy

Relevant Courses: Equivalent to Continuing Education credit:
PNF 1: Proprioceptive Neuromuscular Facilitation   Instructor: Vicki Johnson
S-1:   Introduction to Spinal Evaluation & Manipulation   Instructor: Stanley Paris/Jim Viti/Jeff Rot
E-1:   Extremity Evaluation & Manipulation   Instructor: Catherine Patla

EDUCATION: (CONTINUED)

UNIVERSITY OF DELAWARE, NEWARK, DE 8/96
Bachelor of Science Degree
Major: Physical Education Studies–Fitness Management

INTERNSHIPS:

HOLY CROSS HOSPITAL, FT. LAUDERDALE, FL 2/00–4/00
Inpatient Rehab
- Evaluated and implemented rehabilitation programs for orthopedic, functional decline, and neurological patients.
- Participated in conferences with physicians, patient/family, and health care team.
- Performed research project: "Therapeutic approaches for Parkinson's Disease."

HEALTH SOUTH, SEVERNA PARK, MD 1/00–2/00 and 8/99–10/99
Outpatient Affiliation
- Evaluated, assessed, and treated sports medicine and orthopedic injuries.
- Supervised and collaborated with ATC and PTA.
- Inservice presented–Swiss Ball.

MEMORIAL REGIONAL MEDICAL CENTER, HOLLYWOOD, FL 1/99–2/99
Acute Care
- Evaluated and treated acute patients with trauma, cardiac, and orthopedic diagnoses.
- Performed co-treatments with OT and ST.
- Participated in hospital's annual health fair, educating employees on proper body mechanics.
- Case study presented–"Traumatic Brain Injury."

VOLUNTEER EXPERIENCE:

PALM BEACH INSTITUTE OF SPORTS MEDICINE, BOCA RATON, FL 6/96–8/96
Therapeutic Exercise Intern
- Supervised patients through therapeutic exercise & functional testing.
- Reviewed and updated patient exercise programs.
- Performed isokinetic testing, as well as bioprompt feedback on patients.

MEDICAL CENTER OF DELAWARE, STANTON, DE—Acute Care 6/94–3/96
UNIVERSITY OF DELAWARE STUDENT FITNESS CENTER, NEWARK, DE 2/95–5/95
UNIVERSITY OF DELAWARE PHYSICAL THERAPY CLINIC, NEWARK, DE 4/94–5/95
- Clinical volunteer experience in a dynamic outpatient setting.
MEDICAL CENTER OF DELAWARE, WILMINGTON, DE—Inpatient Rehab 1/94–8/94

ACHIEVEMENT/SKILLS:
- Dean's List, University of Delaware
- National Sorority: Active Member, University of Delaware (1992–1996)
- Figure Skating: Competitive figure skater for 10 years, training with World & Olympic coaches.
- HIV/AIDS, CRP & FIRST AID CERTIFIED

PROFESSIONAL AFFILIATIONS:
- APTA/FPTA: Orthopedic section member since 1998
- ACSM member (1996–1998)

REFERENCES: Furnished upon request

ERNEST COHEN

16 Denver Lane

Denver, CO 80202

(725) 842-9860

(725) 644-7600

SUMMARY

Production Manager with creative abilities in concept design, client relations, operations and logistics planning, financial and inventory control, and promotion.

ADMINISTRATIVE ACCOMPLISHMENTS

- Established accounts payable/accounts receivable systems to meet the needs of three different businesses, including the calculation and distribution of commission checks.

- Reviewed and evaluated prices for office equipment and supplies, interviewing and developing relationships with wholesalers and retailers to reduce purchasing costs.

- Coordinated and controlled the transportation of hundreds of props varying in size and value, arranging for safe delivery and insurance coverage.

- Improved distribution of promotional material to over 500 clients monthly, utilizing a computerized mailing list and supervisory skills to simplify the process.

- Arranged for catering of meals for production staffs of up to 50 people, evaluating menu preferences, checking visual attractiveness, and supervising delivery of services in a variety of indoor and outdoor locations.

CREATIVE/CONSULTING SKILLS

- Develop rapport with clients, utilizing active listening skills to ensure a mutual understanding of the desired concept for development.

- Offer clients several options for achieving the style they seek, combining my ability to think creatively and apply the perspective of my professional experience.

WORK HISTORY

10/96–Present   *Freelance Photo Stylist*

Major clients: Black & Decker, Lorus, Ralph Lauren, Revlon, Robert Peritz Designer, Timex, John Wiley, and Warner Bros.

(Continued)

10/94–10/96   *Central Office Manager/Production Coordinator/Full Charge Bookkeeper*

                     Paul Christensen Photography Studio, Ted Morrison Photography Studio, New York City.

9/93–10/94   *Purchasing Agent*

                     Yonkers General Hospital

SPECIAL SKILLS

Windows for PC programs: EXCEL, Power Point, WordPerfect, and MS Word

EDUCATION

—Boulder College, Denver, CO
  B.A., Psychology, Awarded June 1983
  Dean's List

—Assisted Fulbright Scholar in the production of a documentary aired on cable television: "Out of the Double Bind: A View of Bilingual Education."

Business and personal references upon request.

PROGRAMMER/ANALYST

CHARLES WATSON
4450 N.E. 67th Terrace
Lake Worth, Florida 33445
Tel: 561-555-1001   Cell: 561-555-4302
E-mail: Watson@aol.com

• SYSTEM DESIGN/ANALYSIS • PROGRAMMING •

Senior Systems Analyst and Database Management Professional with more than 23 years of broad-based experience designing, developing, and implementing software systems. Special expertise with PeopleSoft program, as well as mainframe/UNIX and Client Server areas.

Comprehensive knowledge and understanding of business procedures and practices, with demonstrated ability to design and write reports with SQR, Crystal, and Cobol. Substantial experience in supervision and training of personnel, and resourceful resolution of both technical and nontechnical problems.

SUMMARY OF QUALIFICATIONS:
- Extensive and diversified Information Technology experience.
- In-depth knowledge of database design concepts, as they relate to PeopleSoft, data organization, and storage.
- Substantial experience composing functional and technical documents, as well as testing specifications.
- Strong communication and interpersonal skills.
- Capable of working independently or as part of a team effort.

I.T. SKILLS:
PeopleSoft: Tools 8.0 & 7.5 • Financials (A/P, A/R/Billing • GL • AM • Project Cost • Budget) • HR • Payroll • Process Scheduler • Application Engine • PeopleCode • Object Security • Message Agent • Database Agent • EDI Manager • Data Migration • Upgrade Tool • Tree Manager • Query • SQR • Crystal

Database: Oracle 7, 8, 8i • Informix • SQL • DB2

Mainframe: (OS MVS): COBOL • COBOL II • CICS • SAS • REXX • MVS JCL • IBM Utilities • TSO • ISPF • CLIST • Panvalet • Changeman • VSAM • CA7

UNIX: Sun Solaris • HP • Unix Shell Scripting

Testing Tools: Xpediter • Intertest • TPNS • CEDF • SPUFI • QMF • Fileaid

PC Tools: MS Word • Excel • Power Point • Visio • Lotus • FTP • C/C++ • Java • SQLBASE UltraEdit • SQLLoader • SQLPlus • SQR • PeopleSoft (Financials, HRMS, Payroll) PeopleTools 6.0, 7.5, 8, 12 • Rational ClearQuest • DB2 Connect • Citrix Metaframe Windows 95/98/NT, 2000

EXPERIENCE:

FREELANCE, VARIOUS LOCATIONS   **2000–2001**
IT Consultant
Capital One, Richmond, Va
- Full life-cycle implementation of Peoplesoft version 8—HR, Payroll and Benefits that included analysis, design, code, test, and implementation. Modified pages and records, and customized processes by making peoplecode changes.
- Prepared detail design documents for the Employer Burden and American Express outbound interface files, including creation of new PeopleSoft records, pages, and process definitions and SQRs.
- Coded and tested the interface SQR and on-line programs, utilizing Oracle 8I and Unix Platform.
- Participated in functional and technical peer reviews, regarding performance enhancements.
- Designed and coded payroll, HR, Benefits, and Security SQL, providing a wide variety of information for end-users.
- Created templates to run Import Manager Scripts, updating Oracle/People Soft custom tables.
- Migrated projects from across platforms.

EXPERIENCE: (CONTINUED)

Hammond Corporation, St. Louis, MO

- Served as troubleshooter to resolve AR Customer Conversation panel problems running in a Unix, Informix Client Server environment.
- Wrote SQRs to resolve production conversion data issues and created new reports.
- Analyzed and identified AR/Billing production problems, involving panels, subpanels, Peoplecode, SQR, and Application Engine programs.
- Identified and corrected Billing Account Entry Table tax related problems.
- Modified various Crystal reports to enhance features.
- Resolved process malfunction issues by accessing PeopleSoft Customer Connection, where issues were identified, downloaded, and used for applying patches.
- Wrote test case scenarios and created test scripts for System Testing Group.
- Performed program peer reviews, technical reviews, and project presentations.
- Updated change request database to reflect problems and resolutions and documented system changes.

Aetna Insurance Company, Hartford, CT

- Translated functional specifications into technical specs in a Unix, Oracle8, Client/Server environment.
- Participated in a PeopleSoft HR, Benefits and Payroll conversion project to upgrade PeopleSoft to version 8.
- Coded and tested Cobol conversion programs, running on an IBM mainframe.
- Wrote SQR interface programs to run on a Sun/Unix, Oracle 8.0 platform.
- Created and executed SQL load scripts to load HR, Benefits and Payroll Tables on Unix.
- Analyzed, identified, and made modifications to various HRMS and Payroll panels and subpanels.
- Made Peoplecode changes allowing new employees integration into the TAFW (Time Away from Work) system.
- Coded SQRs to support retroactive pay.
- Wrote JCL and PROCS to facilitate execution of Cobol conversion programs on the mainframe and SQRs on a Unix platform.
- Wrote Unix Shell scripts for executing SQR interface processes on the UNIX platform.

WINN-DIXIE STORES, INC., JACKSONVILLE, FL   1999–2000
Senior Programmer Analyst

- Analyzed, designed, developed, and implemented enhancements and upgrades for PeopleSoft AP module, running in an MVS DB2 environment.
- Analyzed, identified, and debugged production problems in Asset Management and A/P systems.
- Modified run control tables, added batch jobs to process scheduler, and created new table and views.
- Performed system maintenance, as well as system regression testing.
- Mapped EDI transactions used EDI Manager to monitor inbound and outbound agent processes.
- Provided primary support for AP (Lights Out Pay Cycle, using Database Agent and Message Agent), AR and GL.
- Modified and debugged Peoplecode and Application Engine programs.
- Conducted fact-finding workshops with clients to determine business needs.
- Composed functional/technical documents, as well as testing specifications and performance-tuning enhancements.

MANVILLE CORPORATION, PENSACOLA, FL   1988–1999
Senior Software Engineer

- Created and modified Panels, Xiat Table vanables, Prompt Tales and various Queries in a Unix, oracle7, Client Server environment.
- Coded and tested interface processes, customizations, and SQR reports.
- Provided after-hour production support for PeopleSoft Financial Systems (AP, AM, GL, AR, Project Cost, Budget).
- Wrote SQR/FTP interface to keep PeopleSoft and Legacy data in sync during conversion.
- Performed system testing and integration for the FBI's National Crime Information Center project.
- Attended programmer peer-reviews to examine COBOL/CICS programs for accuracy and attention to detail.
- Wrote and used TPNS scripts to repetitively test COBOL/CICS programs and validate output against test scenarios provided by the user requirement.
- Acted as a System Analyst and liaison between the FBI and Harris Corp. to ensure requirements for all on-line systems were implemented as stated by the client.
- Documented test results and presented them to the FBI reviewing committee.
- Prepared test plans and evaluated test results to determine compliance with system specifications.

POLICE OFFICER

JOHN JAMESON
4414 Ostrow Lane
Delray Beach, Florida 33484
Tel: 561-555-6676   Cell: 561-555-4415

• SECURITY MANAGEMENT • LAW ENFORCEMENT •

More than 19 years of multifaceted background in the criminal justice system, encompassing administrative functions, as well as uniformed patrol and detective work with the Fairfield County Sheriff's Office, culminating in the rank of Sergeant in the Community Policing Unit.

Experienced in all areas of criminal investigations, including narcotics, juvenile crimes, gang activities, and prostitution. Skills and expertise in state-of-the-art investigative procedures and techniques, with broad-based background and knowledge of criminal law and judicial procedures. Currently engaged in programs to establish enhanced community relations and to develop better law enforcement solutions to areas of community crime problems. Developed and implemented various innovative programs to enhance police image and create favorable public relations.

Received numerous citations for superior performance, as well as certifications in various areas. Background also encompasses security management and the protection and safety of commercial facilities.

SUMMARY OF QUALIFICATIONS:
- Diversified results-oriented experience in law enforcement, investigations, evidence analysis, and apprehension of felons.
- Broad exposure and capabilities in a variety of related areas, including planning and executing surveillance operations, as well as administrative responsibilities, developing and implementing procedures, personnel training, and motivation.
- Strong planning and organizational skills, with demonstrated ability to work effectively with fellow officers, as well as community leaders and private citizens.
- Strong communication and interpersonal skills.
- Substantial supervisory experience and the resolution of both technical and nontechnical problems.
- Capable of working independently or as part of a team effort.

EXPERIENCE:
FAIRFIELD COUNTY SHERIFF'S OFFICE, FAIRFIELD, VA   1985–PRESENT
Sergeant—Community Policing Unit
- Supervisory responsibilities for unit charged with securing peace and security of the community and enhancing "quality of life."
- Work with community leaders to formulate policies to proactively resolve criminal activities in the area, including special projects related to drugs and gang activities.
- Unit specifically responsible for service of court orders and arrest warrants.
- Command Deputy Sheriff's, preparing work schedules and overseeing daily assignments, including criminal investigations, surveillances, and traffic control.
- Supervised upwards of 140 personnel, while serving as Acting Lieutenant.
- Investigate internal disciplinary issues, evaluating and recommending appropriate disciplinary action.
- Organize and implement training programs for new Deputies.
- Prepare and administer budgets.

Detective
- Served in various units investigating different criminal activities, including gangs, property-related crime, and special investigations, regarding sex crimes and crimes against children and the elderly.
- Extensive experience in the investigation of law violations and the apprehension of criminals.
- Developed action plans, utilizing sophisticated investigative and enforcement techniques, including electronic surveillance and evidence data processing and analysis.
- Gathered and maintained intelligence data and identification of individuals involved in criminal activities.
- Interviewed and obtained statements from victims, witnesses, and suspects in preparation for trial proceedings.

Deputy Sheriff
- Investigated violations of county ordinances, motor vehicle, and state laws.

EXPERIENCE: (CONTINUED)

SUNRISE POLICE DEPARTMENT, SUNRISE, FL   1983–1985
Police Officer
- Performed street patrols to ensure a maximum police presence as a deterrence to crime-related activities.
- Enforced local ordinances, motor vehicle, and state laws.
- Interviewed witnesses and suspects and apprehended offenders.

K-MART CORPORATION, BOCA RATON, FL   1980–1983
Security Manager
- Supervised store security programs designed to overcome merchandise theft losses, from both internal and external sources, as well as credit card frauds.
- Trained and supervised security staff to conduct surveillance, investigation, and apprehension of perpetrators.
- Implemented corporate policies, plans, systems & procedures, and internal controls.
- Interviewed suspects and prepared investigative reports.
- Conducted in-store meetings to educate employees.

EDUCATION:
    PALM BEACH ATLANTIC COLLEGE, WEST PALM BEACH, FL   5/00
    Bachelor of Science Degree
    Major: Organizational Management

    <u>**Continuing Education:**</u>
    State of Florida Law Enforcement Academy
    • Radar Operator • Sex Crimes Investigation • Stakeout and Surveillance • Organized Crime and Juvenile Delinquency • Homicide Investigation • Field Training Officer • Narcotics Investigation • Credit Card Fraud • Environmental Crimes Investigations

COMMUNITY ACTIVITIES:

- Member: **Youth Advisory Council–Boca Raton's Promise** (Affiliated with America's Promise, devoted to providing safe places, mentoring, and marketable skills for youth).

REFERENCES: Available upon request

ELLA TURNER
4820 Bronx Road
Bronx, New York 10467   212-822-9416

EXPERIENCE

July 1993–Present Production Manager, Publications, Inc., New York City. Serve as liaison between the Editorial and Sales Departments. Responsibilities include the overall preparation and layout of two major trade publications, including annual directories. Design and makeup of ads and reprints, complete follow-through of advertising materials, insertion orders, and advertisement schedules. Direct contact and working knowledge of printing schedules and full responsibility for printing/production costs.

December 1992– Assistant to the Coordinator, United Society of Magazine
November 1993 Photographers, New York City. Entire processing of applicants and potential members; presenting their work to Board of Trustees for final acceptance to the Society.

July 1991– Sales Secretary, Media Management, New York City. Handled
November 1992 secretarial duties and expansion into overall participation in circulation and production responsibilities. Varied functions in this position included proofreading; handling of insertion orders, contracts, advertising material; and billing.

EDUCATION

Academic Degree from St. Anthony High School—June 1991.

REFERENCES

Will be furnished upon request.

PROGRAMMER TRAINEE

PATRICIA SMITH
4430 N.E. 66th Way
Dania Beach, Florida 33062
954-555-4828   E-Mail: psmith@aol.com

• IT SYSTEMS • INTERNET/WEB TECHNOLOGIES •

Information Technology candidate for starting opportunity in the MIS field, with a B.S. Degree and high academic achievement. Multifaceted experience with financial analysis, database development and intranet application programming. Exposure and capabilities with interactive multimedia applications and Web site technology. Created and updated software and assisted with development of Web sites.

Background encompasses accounting services with CPA firm, as auditor and financial analyst, as well as preparation of monthly financial statements and tax forms, for a business management consulting company. Hired by Arthur Andersen LLP, after intensive interviewing and screening process.

SUMMARY OF QUALIFICATIONS:

- Training, exposure and demonstrated capabilities in a variety of related areas, including computer operating systems, languages, computer networking, and database management.
- Strong communication and interpersonal skills.
- Excellent scholastic record, with demonstrated ability to quickly learn and grasp new concepts.
- Capable of working independently or as part of a team effort.
- Strong organizational, research, and analytical ability.
- Demonstrated resourcefulness and ability to resolve both technical and nontechnical problems.

EDUCATION:

FLORIDA STATE UNIVERSITY, TALLAHASSEE, FL   5/01
Bachelor of Science Degree
Major: Management Information Systems
GPA: 3.5   Cum Laude   Golden Key Honor Society   National Collegiate Scholarship

<u>School Activities:</u>

- MIS Association • National Society of Collegiate Scholars • Lady Renegades (Founded off-campus service organization. Fundraisers for March of Dimes, Muscular Dystrophy, etc.)

SKILLS PROFILE:

Software: Office 97/2000, Quickbooks, Outlook
Languages: C, C++, Cobol, Visual Basic
Internet: Frontpage, Dreamweaver, ColdFusion, HTML, Workshop
Operating Systems: Windows 9X, NT 4.0, MS/DOS
Databases: Oracle, SQL, Access

WORK EXPERIENCE:

CHARLES, EDWARDS & MELVILLE, FT. LAUDERDALE, FL   11/01–PRESENT
Auditor
- Conducted field audits to review and analyze corporate ledgers.
- Met with commercial clients to prepare analysis of financial statements, balance sheets, and P & L position.
- Utilized Quickbooks, Quicken, E-Pace, and Creative Solutions programs in auditing process.

HARRIS CONSULTING, TALLAHASSEE, FL   3/00–3/01
Executive Assistant/Associate Consultant
- Developed and updated Help File for the Florida Emergency Reimbursement System.
- Participated with team developing intranet application for Dept. of Revenue enabling employees to track career progress.
- Participated with team to develop "The Wanderings" Web site, utilizing FrontPage.
- Prepared monthly financial statements and tax forms for a $500,000 company.

FRANK BEATTY
50 Union Boulevard
Union City, NJ 07087
201-864-4239

OBJECTIVE   Position with State agency of investigative and correctional nature on larger scale than that of previous experience.

EXPERIENCE

1991–present   <u>Caseworker-Investigator</u>, Union City Dept. of Social Services. Investigate eligibility and maintain clients on public welfare.

1986–1991   <u>Parole Officer</u>, Narcotics Division, New Jersey Narcotic Addiction Control Center. Conducted investigations, supervised narcotic addicts, apprehended violators.

EDUCATION

M.B.A., Public Administration, February 1990, Fairleigh School of Business Administration, Upton University, NJ.

B.B.A., February 1986, Fairleigh School of Business Administration, Upton University, NJ.

HONORS

William Bucknell Scholarship Award
John Fairleigh Scholarship Award
Psi Chi Honorary Professional Psychology Fraternity

REFERENCES

Suitable personal references furnished upon request.

Claudia Johnson
16 Quincy Court
Silver Springs, MD 72415
(208) 541-2246

OBJECTIVE: A public relations position managing publications, publicity, and special events.

PROFESSIONAL EXPERIENCE:

5/98–12/02   **SILVER SPRINGS CENTER**
Communications Consultant: created new logo; restructured format and focus of monthly publication; wrote and edited first issue of revised publication; negotiated with and coordinated printers, typesetters, and graphic artists, and redesigned stationery and monthly direct mail item.

8/96–10/98   **MARYLAND COLLEGE OF OPTOMETRY**
Public Relations Associate: edited and produced three quarterly newsletters; wrote and placed news releases; arranged television and radio interviews; conducted bimonthly continuing education seminars; interfaced with the media during press conferences and special events; and created visual information displays.

3/96–5/96   **WASHINGTON STAR**
Reporter: researched and interviewed for information and wrote news and feature articles.

5/95–9/96   *Freelance Writer:* wrote feature articles for health organization and product publicity for advertising agency.

1/92–8/94   **REGENT INTERNATIONAL SCHOOL**
Teacher: taught third- and fourth-grade classes in multilingual school; supervised five aides as student-teacher; designed specialized programs and record-keeping systems; and produced and co-directed musical that involved more than sixty children.

EDUCATION:

5/95–5/96   **NEW YORK SCHOOL OF ADVERTISING AND JOURNALISM**
Diploma in Advertising and Certificate of Journalism.

9/86–5/91   **VASSAR COLLEGE,** Poughkeepsie, NY. Bachelor of Arts-English.

9/85–5/89   **PACE UNIVERSITY,** Briarcliffe, NY. Junior Year Exchange Program.

HONORS:

5/96   **THE SULLIVAN MEMORIAL AWARD:** for student work in writing and preparation of company publications, presented by the International Association of Business Communicators.

References and portfolio available on request.

HELEN C. CHESTERFIELD
43 Crescent Lane
Port Washington, NY 11050
(516) 384-9227

SUMMARY: Seventeen years' public relations and advertising experience in multidivision corporation and public relations firms. Direct experience included financial and product publicity; business and technical articles and speeches; institutional and product public relations and advertising; shareholder and employee relations. Supervised department and directed successful efforts of public relations and advertising agencies.

EXPERIENCE:

Nov. 1993
to present

Director of Communications
GAF, Inc., Woodside, NY

Advertising, public relations, shareholder relations for this American Stock Exchange company.

March 1992
to Sept. 1993

Account Executive
Howard P. Schmidt Associates, New York, NY

Corporate, financial, and product public relations for industrial, consumer, and financial services companies. Corporate planning, executive speeches, annual reports, brochures, feature articles, news releases, and scripts. Also analyst meetings, press conferences, marketing seminars, broadcast interviews, corporate advertising. Good relations with all segments of financial community, and trade, general, and business media.

April 1989
to Feb. 1992

Account Executive
Spahr, Smith and Associates, New York, NY

Supervised corporate and financial public relations activities for client firms (construction, medical products, leisure time, electronics). Wrote and placed news releases, speeches, feature articles, annual reports, brochures, and leaflets. Arranged for press conferences, analyst meetings, and personal interviews.

(Continued)

HELEN C. CHESTERFIELD

May 1980 to March 1989	**Advertising and Public Relations Manager** **Page Co., Inc., New York, NY**

Coordinated all internal and external (agency) advertising and public relations activities, scheduled space advertising and product publicity, prepared advertising budgets and analyses. Also originated sales literature, directed mail, organized trade shows, edited sales newsletter and house organ, prepared annual reports, and supervised staff of four.

EDUCATION: B.S., New York University (1979)
Undergraduate, University of Chicago

MEMBERSHIP: American Public Relations Society
New York Public Relations Association

REFERENCES: Available upon request.

Joanna Curtis
29 East 12th Street
New York, New York 10003
212-669-7839

JOB OBJECTIVE   Seeking position in public relations as a staff assistant, or in a secretarial or administrative capacity.

EXPERIENCE

1991–present   Legal Secretary, S. Jerome Berg Associates, Bronx, New York. Handle legal correspondence, great deal of technical, legal details requiring knowledge of legal terms and format, much telephone contact with clients, appointment scheduling, often working under pressure to meet court dates, etc., so that necessary documents are completed on time.

1988–1991   French Teacher, Brookville High School, New York.

1987–1988   French Translator, Markum Engineering Corp., New York. Translated correspondence and reports from branch office in Paris. Acted as interpreter in Public Relations Department and liaison between French engineers and New York office staff.

1985–1987   French Teacher, Strauss High School, New York.

EDUCATION

M.A., 1987, French—Middlebury College, Vermont
B.A., 1985, French—Middlebury College, Vermont

SPECIAL SKILLS

Fluency in French, Spanish, German
IBM, Macintosh, Windows, MS Word, and others
Writing and Editing

REFERENCES

Furnished upon request.

Gail R. Geltzer
310 West 30th Street
New York, New York 10001
(212) 694-0074

Experience

St. Vincent's Hospital—Assistant Director of Public Information
1989–present

Describe, interpret, promote, and publicize policies, patient care services, medical research, medical, nursing, and paraprofessional education programs of this hospital to its various publics to earn their understanding, support, and acceptance. (Publics include patients, contributors, staff, faculty, and students, trustees, volunteers, other agencies, general and local community.) As editor of an award-winning internal-external house organ, develop ideas, do bulk of writing, total layout, and production of five-times-a-year, 16,000 circulation publication. Responsibilities include heavy press liaison with science, and hospital reporters on daily papers, television and radio stations, news, medical, health, and hospital magazines, government press officers, freelance writers, educational film producers. Write releases, arrange press conferences. Extensive liaison with public relations officers of affiliated institutions, other health and welfare agencies, city, state, and federal health agencies, etc., in joint efforts, exchange of information. Give public relations' counsel, editorial help to professional staff. Work with hospital's development office on fund-raising events.

The Salvation Army—Public Information Associate
1980–1989

Planned, wrote, produced major publications interpreting this noted agency's program of family counseling, social action, and welfare research to a variety of publics: annual report, a monthly bulletin to contributors, internal staff house organ, bimonthly newsletter for board and committee members, fund-raising campaign literature, brochures. Wrote radio and television spots, speeches as needed. Wrote and/or placed news and feature stories ranging from pilot demonstration study results to appraisals of legislation in fields of health, housing, aging, family and child welfare, narcotics addiction, courts, etc. Wrote case stories for *Times* Neediest Cases, of which agency was a major beneficiary. Job required keeping abreast of entire social welfare field and being able to translate into lay language, technical, often complicated concepts of caseworks, medicine, psychiatry, community organization, and legalities.

The American Nursing Association—Publication and Public Relations Consultant
1977–1980

Disseminated information about ANA's Department of Hospital Nursing to membership, allied professional groups (American Health Care Association, etc.), and public through articles, books, brochures, press releases, and promotional materials. Planned, wrote, produced pamphlets, newsletters, including national newsletter for psychiatric aides and technicians funded by a pharmaceutical company.

(Continued)

American Paramedical Association—Director of Public Information
1976–1977

Directed recruitment program for occupational therapists under grant from National Foundation. Created recruitment literature, supervised distribution nationally to prospective students, universities, guidance counselors, hospital and medical groups assisting with recruitment. Worked with newspapers, magazines, radio, television nationally. Traveled extensively to spur recruitment activities on state and local level; extensive liaison work with federal agencies.

Bridgeport University—Public Relations, School of Nursing
1973–1976

As branch officer of Bridgeport Information Bureau, planned and directed student recruitment program. Wrote, placed news and feature stories; produced recruitment literature; established contacts with prospective students, faculty, guidance personnel, alumnae. Responsible for fundraising activities for an endowed university chair in nursing.

New York's Children's Hospital—Assistant to Director of Public Relations
1970–1973

Presented stories of services, achievements, needs of hospital, working with newspapers, magazines, radio, television, educational films. Wrote, produced bimonthly staff house organ and semiannual magazine for contributors. Developed and wrote handbooks, pamphlets for patients, staff, donors, nursing school applicants and nursing staff. Assisted staff in preparing manuscripts for professional publications. Helped plan special events, tours.

Professional Memberships

American Association of Writers, East Coast Chapter; New York Public Relations Association.

Education

M.A., Political Science, Cornell University
B.A., Journalism, Queens College

References: Upon request.

IRENE C. NEWMEYER

HOME ADDRESS: 84-84 Dalny Road • Jamaica, New York 11432 • (718) 523-1904

JOB OBJECTIVE	A position offering challenge and responsibility in consumer affairs, marketing, or advertising research.
EDUCATION	THE UNIVERSITY OF CALIFORNIA
1997–20XX	Graduating in May 20XX with a B.A. Degree in MARKETING AND CONSUMER BEHAVIOR. DEAN'S LIST DISTINCTION.

Field of study includes: marketing and advertising theory and research, economics, business law, calculus, mass communications, statistics, psychology, sociology, and research methodology.

BERKELEY COURSES: Social and Managerial Concepts in Marketing, Consumer Behavior, Product Policy, Advertising Theory, and Policies, Sales Force Management, Marketing Research.

SENIOR RESEARCH SEMINARS AND PROJECTS:
- Children and Advertising
- Marketing Research—Cash vs. Credit Retail Analysis
- Portrayal of Women in Magazine Advertising (Role Model)
- Persuasive Impact of Liquor Ads in Print Media
- The Male Contraceptive Pill: Product Development and Marketing Strategies, including Advertising
- Independent study on <u>advertising effectiveness</u>

WORK EXPERIENCE Summers 2000	CALIFDATA CORPORATION—San Diego, California Administrative assistant in Sales Department. Trained in basic sales and organizational procedures. Responsible for record keeping, expense reports, public relations correspondence, inventory updates, and billing.
1999	GRAHAM MILLS—La Jolla, California Basic sales and management training. Responsible for billing, orders, inventory maintenance, shipping arrangements, deliveries.
1998	THE PRESS CLUB (Office)—San Diego, California Extensive experience in inventory control, contracts, billing, correspondence, and public relations.

(Continued)

EXTRA-
CURRICULAR
ACTIVITIES

<u>Down South</u>—responsible for soliciting advertising as well as writing copy and layout for "Intro to California."
Active with Freshman Orientation Programs. <u>UCSD Marketing and Management Club</u>—involved with structuring innovative lecture series in career opportunities in related fields and designing community "Intern" Program. California Consumer Board—Volunteer.

REFERENCES

Available on request.

HOWARD K. DONALDSON
1170 East Sycamore Lane
Nashville, Tennessee 37204
(615) LO-3-5341

EXPERIENCE:

11/94–present **NBC News,** Atlanta, Georgia.

Work on a freelance basis assisting in the process of public opinion polling. Wrote reports for management on the administration of the polling operation.

Prior to 1994 **M & M Pharmacy,** Atlanta, Georgia.

Worked in all phases of neighborhood retail pharmacy except professional services for a period of nine years on both a part-time basis during the school year and full-time basis during the summer.

Summer 1993 Volunteer work at the South Side Legislative Service Center for Assemblyman Tyson. Duties included handling constituent problems, with heavy emphasis on writing correspondence and knowledge of city and state agency functions.

EDUCATION:

1992–1994 **University of Richmond,** Richmond, Virginia.

Awarded B.A. in Political Science with Honors in January 1989.

1990–1992 **University of Georgia,** Atlanta, Georgia.

In 1991, participated in Georgia State Assembly Internship Program as a legislative research assistant in the office of then Deputy Minority Leader John Tyson.

Participated in Atlanta Government Internship Program working in the office of Councilman Thomas Sample.

References will be furnished upon request.

Paul R. Joseph
2803 Chesapeake St., NW
Washington, DC 10008
(202) 345-9876

Employment Objective

To manage dinner-trade continental restaurant in a suburban setting.

Employment Record

1993–present   Green Door Restaurant, Silver Springs, MD
<u>Assistant Manager</u> to owner-manager. Supervise kitchen, dining, and bar staff of 35. Approve menus, maintain food and linen stocks. Initiated wine listing and cellar.

1989–1993   Eight O'Clock Cafes, Washington, DC, VA, and MD
<u>Assistant Quality Control Director</u> for cafe chain. Assessed and maintained performance standards at seven (originally three) breakfast cafes: food, service, etc. Prepared reports and made recommendations for improvements.

1986–1989   Red Clock Luncheonette, Baltimore, MD
<u>Lunchtime Manager</u>. Supervised lunchtime trade at busy neighborhood-type restaurant; filled in as cook, as needed. Maintained receipts.

1982–1986   Rose's Inn, Elkton, MD
<u>Cook</u>. Prepared American/Continental meals in small, family-type restaurant.

Education   Completed two years at University of Maryland, Accounting major. Northeast High School, Baltimore, MD—Academic Diploma, 1982.

References   Available upon request.

Cheryl Newman
1231 Orchid Street
Los Angeles, California 90068
Phone: (213) 989-2406

JOB OBJECTIVE

Management of American/Continental restaurant in Greater Los Angeles area.

EXPERIENCE

June 1990– **The French Chef**
Present

Assistant Manager—General food service and managerial assistance in this eighty-table restaurant. Oversee luncheon and dinner kitchen and dining staffs. Maintain wine and food stocks. Have developed novel seasonal menus in consultation with chef, which have significantly increased volume of business.

September 1988– **The Oasis Hotel**
May 1990

Assistant Banquet Manager—Responsibility for planning and coordination of 100 banquets and private parties per year for from 10–500 guests (business meetings, personal celebrations, community events). Meal planning and "theme" development in consultation with banquet hosts.

June 1986–
September 1988

Waitress and Cashier at the Oasis Hotel, in both luncheonette and formal dining room.

EDUCATION

1991 Successful completion of Restaurant Management course, offered by Restaurant Associates of the United States, Inc., Los Angeles, California

1987 A.S. in Food Services, Dallas Junior College, Dallas, Texas
1985 Commercial diploma, Dallas Vocational High School, Dallas, Texas

OTHER ACTIVITIES

Vice Chairman, Los Angeles Restaurant Council

Chairman, Committee for Neighborhood Development, Los Angeles Chamber of Commerce

REFERENCES

Available upon request.

Jeremy Gibbons
186 Intracoastal Highway
Boca Raton, Florida 33448
(305) 965-9328

Nine years' professional experience in engineering salesmanship.

OBJECTIVE

To serve initially in sales engineering capacity (sophisticated mechanical equipment) and ultimately enhance responsibilities toward engineering management.

EXPERIENCE

Senior
Consultant

The Southern Sun Inc., Boca Raton, Florida—1994–present.
This position involves the professional selection and sales of real estate investments, requiring knowledge of tax laws and shelters as well as applicable real estate laws and geographical growth trends.

Sales
Engineer

Hobart Air Compressor Corporation, Highland Beach, Florida—1992–1994.

Responsible for the sales of industrial air compressors and their intrinsic components. These components included regulating, drive, and air drying systems and their auxiliary support accessories. As technical salesman, incorporated the attributes of an applicable engineer, sales representative, and field service engineer. A successful sale required the paralleling of stipulated specifications with the most reliable, effective, and economical systems. Frequently assisted with engineering, assembling, and authoring of facility expansion or new plant construction specifications. Often, the installation of new equipment demanded the coordination, instruction, and supervision of mechanical and electrical contractors. Subsequent start-up and troubleshooting required the establishment of a working relationship with plant and maintenance personnel.

Student
Trainee

Miami Naval Laboratories, Miami, Florida—1988–1992.
As part of five-year cooperative program, participated in developing, assembling, plotting, and recording data while working with engineers in the research and development of shipboard fire fighting systems, high-strength steels and titanium for submarine hulls, and damping materials for sonar dome application.

(Continued)

EDUCATION

Miami University, Miami, Florida—Mechanical Engineering
B.M.E. June 1988 (Dean's List).

AFFILIATIONS and
LICENSES

Associate Member American Society of Mechanical Engineers
F.A.A. Airframe Mechanics License
Florida Teaching Credential
Florida Real Estate Association

References furnished upon request.

CLAUDIA MORESCO
80 Central Park West
New York, New York 10014

Tel: 212-349-1138   Cell: 212-555-4818

SUMMARY   Major career achievements and satisfactions have come from
                   positions with responsibility for the identification and resolution of
                   problems. Skilled in decision making, including the organization and
                   analysis of data, evaluation of alternative solutions, selection of the
                   optimal approach, and negotiation for the implementation of the
                   decision. Experience in both line and staff positions and strong
                   interpersonal skills. Results-oriented, learn quickly, and enjoy
                   challenge. Accomplishments in all positions are substantiated by
                   rapid salary growth.

EXPERIENCE

July 1992–   Manager, Academic Market Development. Book and Information
Present   Services. Walton and Champion Companies, Walton, New York. Sales
                   analysis and strategic planning for existing academic market (college
                   and university libraries). New product development including market
                   research, evaluation of external new ventures proposals, initiation of
                   new products and services, financial analyses, and design of
                   marketing offer. Exploration and recommendation of new market
                   segmentation, development of marketing strategies for these
                   segments, preparation of financial projections, and implementation of
                   accepted proposals.

June 1989   Gift and Exchange Librarian, Barnard Libraries, Rochester, New York.
June 1992   Establishment of a department to administer the acceptance and
                   review of gifts to the University libraries. Preparation of a uniform gift
                   policy and procedure manual for ten campus libraries. Negotiation
                   and administration of the exchange of materials with foreign libraries,
                   particularly in the Soviet Union and Latin America. Negotiation with
                   dealers for the sale of unneeded material. Supervision of ten
                   employees.

                                                                      (Continued)

260   Sample Resumes

EDUCATION

M.S.L.S., DeWitt University, January 1991.
M.A.T., Manchester University, June 1987—Majors: History and Education.

HONORS

Dean's List all semesters
Phi Beta Kappa
Beta Phi Mu honorary

References

Available upon request.

SALES MANAGER
LUCY A. TORRES

12302 N.W. 44TH Street • Coconut Creek, FL 33076 • 954-555-4343

• DISTRICT MANAGER • SALES/RECRUITING •

Personnel Recruiter and District Manager with more than 20 years of progressive retail and wholesale management and merchandising experience, culminating in P & L responsibility for a 16-store multiunit operation. Extensive experience and expertise in developing and implementing sales and marketing strategies, merchandise planning, human resources management, buying, and in-store promotions.

Successful track record of driving revenue and profit growth for various major department store operations. Achieved and maintained #1 sales ranking in 3 separate store locations, producing no less than 20% increases for large discount retailer in the Northeast U.S. Skilled and adept in identifying and recruiting quality store management and staff and an excellent troubleshooter with a reputation for turning around marginally-performing store operations.

SUMMARY OF QUALIFICATIONS:
- Results-oriented experience in marketing store management, sales and customer service.
- Areas of expertise include: recruiting, training, team building, troubleshooting, loss prevention, corporate compliance, and merchandise management.
- Excellent communication and interpersonal skills.
- Ability to motivate and lead staff to achieve business and personal goals.
- Broad exposure and capabilities in development of product lines, vendor negotiations, pricing, and planning merchandise strategies.
- Extensive experience with special events, in-store promotions, creating visual displays, and managing inventory controls.

PROFESSIONAL EXPERIENCE:
GROCERS, INC., PALM BEACH/BROWARD COUNTY, FL/PUERTO RICO   4/02–PRESENT
District Director
- Direct the recruitment, training, and development of store managers and staff, as well as oversee the work performance of more than 100 employees.
- Increase sales production throughout district through initiation of personnel changes and enhanced professionalism of management, staff, and customer service level.
- Establish procedures, plans, and internal controls to guide operations and ensure compliance with corporate standards.
- Devise and implement better controls to reduce shortage problems as well as create more attractive visual standards.

DENVER RECRUITING GROUP, FT. LAUDERDALE, FL   4/01–4/02
Director of Client Services
- Devised innovative sales and marketing programs to expand occupational categories and acquire new clients.
- Recruited personnel to refer appropriate candidates to fill extensive employment listings obtained from clients.

JIFFY MILK N. BROWARD/PALM BEACH/MELBOURNE COUNTIES, FL   10/99–2/01
District Manager
- Complete P & L accountability for directing operations of 16 multistore units, with revenues exceeding $20 million.
- Served as troubleshooter to resolve both technical and nontechnical problems, including Human Resource and LP.
- Test District for AS 400 installation; developed and implemented District training to manage by P & L controllables.

BURDINES, MIAMI, FL   6/98–10/99
Regional Merchandise Liaison
- Complete responsibility for directing two divisions, Cosmetics and Intimate Apparel, with responsibility for establishing seasonal merchandise plans and developing prototype store layouts for each quarter.
- Combined annual sales revenues surpassed $130 million.
- Extensive travel to all 48 regional stores throughout Florida, training and directing the execution of standards, policies and product knowledge, as well as selling techniques to managers, counter managers, and beauty assistants.
- Coordinated activities with buying team, visual team, and merchandise planners, to develop seasonal themes.
- Part of Senior Executive Management team responsible for the management of opening two new store locations and eight department renovations, developing new floor plans, décor, and displays.

PROFESSIONAL EXPERIENCE:

TARGET, BROWARD COUNTY, FL   6/95–6/98
District Manager
- Complete P & L accountability for entire district.
- Managed 10 store units, with $60 million volume, after relocation by company to Florida.
- Improved sales for district by more than 25%, through improved merchandising, operations, customer service, and enhanced training.
- Developed bench program for District.
- Monitored SKU assortment and implemented floor plans, as well as inventory control and replenishment programs.
- Received outstanding merchant award for 3 consecutive years.

CALDOR STORES, NORWALK, CT.   10/92–5/95
Store Manager—Oceanside, NY
- Recruited to rectify serious production, staffing and image problems, in Oceanside, NY and restore operation to acceptable standards.
- Turned around situation through retraining and remotivation of staff, resulting in an increased sales volume of more than $5 million, as well as effectively reduced shrinkage from 9% to 2.2%.
- Developed 10 bench candidates for promotion.

Store Manager—Brooklyn, NY
- Promoted to Store Manager in Brooklyn, with responsibility to open this new location and start-up operations.
- Generated more than $40 million in sales revenues the first year, which surpassed sales plan by 20%.
- Conducted mass hiring and training of 230 store employees.

Store Manager—Glen Oaks, NY
- Managed a new store opening in Glen Oaks, NY, a 3-level freestanding building, which overachieved sales plan by 35% within 3 weeks of opening, and generated more than $35 million the first year.
- Received Softlines Presentation and Merchandising Award for each location.
- District Merchandising Trainer, with emphasis on softlines.

SAM & LIBBY, NEW YORK, NY   5/89–9/92
Corporate Sales Manager
- Managed the major department store accounts, including Macy's, Lord & Taylor, Bloomingdale's, and A & S, as well as 300 independent store accounts.
- Instrumental in opening the New York market for the company, driving sales from an initial $2 million to more than $10 million in two years.
- Initiated the "Shop in Shop" program in branch stores throughout the tri-state area and South to Virginia, managing 10 coordinators responsible for weekly maintenance of shops.
- Served as competitive shopping specialist and conducted design sourcing in Europe and major U.S. markets.

Account Executive—San Carlos, CA
- Supervised a key account, The Gap Stores, by special request of the Vice President of Merchandising.
- Developed and merchandised a new product line and styles sourced from Brazil and Taiwan.

Vice President of Production/Merchandise Manager—San Carlos, CA
- Supervised production Department, including monthly travel to Brazil and Taiwan, to review production quality and scheduling.
- Planned purchases for junior and children's divisions on a seasonal basis.

ROBINSON'S OF FLORIDA, ST. PETERSBURG, FL   6/86–3/89
Buyer—Women's Moderate Shoes
- Developed product lines, maintaining all gross margin components.
- Experienced in the use of merchandise plans, open to buy, gross margin, purchase journals, recaps, class and sales analysis.
- Maintained inventories, planned sales promotions, developed vendor relations, and selected markdowns.

EDUCATION:
FLORIDA STATE UNIVERSITY, TALLAHASSEE, FL
Bachelor of Science Degree
Major: Fashion Merchandising/Marketing

Edward Salson
144-30 Ford Brooks Road
Citadel, California 95610

**business
experience**

October 1993–
March 1998

Gibson Color Systems, Hudson, New Hampshire

Printing firm located in New Hampshire with a New York Sales Office.

Salesperson—Developing and servicing accounts handled out of the New York area. Estimating cost of preparatory work including separating and stripping job into position. Handling color correcting, press proofs, and detail work pertaining to a given job.

December 1986–
September 1993

Shank Graphics, Chicago, Illinois

Litho and gravure separator with a St. Paul Office.

Sales and Sales Service—Responsibilities included servicing established accounts and opening up new accounts. Did all the estimating for the St. Paul office.

February 1984–
December 1986

Baronet Litho Company, Jamestown, Virginia

Small commercial printer. Equipment included a 60-inch four-color press. Plant had complete facilities including stripping, plate making, and bindery and mailing department.

Assistant to Plant Manager—Handled all jobs received from salespeople. Made out job tickets and job layouts. Followed through on all jobs in various stages of production. Ordered paper and other items necessary to produce final product.

education

Rochester Institute of Technology

Earned B.S. in General Printing, 1984
Earned A.A.S. degree in Photographic Science, 1982

references

Will be furnished upon request.

GREGG D. LEWIS
1085 WARBURTON AVENUE, APARTMENT 808
YONKERS, NEW YORK 10701
914/423-5858

EXPERIENCE

MILLER PRODUCTS, DIVISION OF   **MAY 1994 TO PRESENT**
MILLER-WAILER, INC.

Sales Promotion Manager

> Coordinate promotions for brand and sales management. Includes:
> budgeting, planning, creative and complete implementations of plans.

> Manage department of four. Responsibilities for all sales promotional
> materials: artwork, printing, displays, premiums, sampling, and couponing.

> Negotiate for services of mailing and sampling executions, fulfillment
> houses, and coupon clearing organizations.

> Successfully introduced Dri XX Spray, Dri XX Roll-On Deodorant and Dew
> Drops with Fluoride: developed and executed promotion plan and strategy.

> Promotion budget of $10 million.

BEAUTIFUL HAIR, INC.   **FEBRUARY 1992 TO MAY 1994**

Product Promotion Manager

> Responsible for all retail promotion programs in the Hair Color and
> Toiletries Division: trade promotions, collateral material, pricing, sales
> objectives, and advertising plans by sales region.

> Developed promotion plans and executed them for new products: trade
> strategy, sampling, couponing, ad sales materials. New products include
> Essence Shampoo, which grew to number three in shampoo market.

> Worked closely with research, production planning, legal, graphic
> suppliers, and ad agency.

> Promotion budget of $12 million.

> Heavy business travel.

(Continued)

Assistant Product Promotion Manager

> Assisted the position "Production Promotion Manager" in all areas explained.

WILSON ASSOCIATES   **JANUARY 1988 TO FEBRUARY 1992**

Sales Representative

> Managed merchandise shows for company in local markets. Responsibility for sales volume in 150 direct and indirect accounts. Worked closely with company research in new product tests including: implementation of new product sales plans, weekly audits, and test analysis.

EDUCATION

> University of North Carolina, 1988
> B.S. in Business Administration/Marketing

REFERENCES

Available upon request.

ALBERTO ROSSI
One Top Stone Drive
Toledo, Ohio 43614
(419) 361-7444

EXPERIENCE

HIGHLY VISIBLE SOFTWARE CO., Toledo, Ohio

12/92 to Present   <u>National Account Manager</u>

Sell a variety of software to run on UNIX-based workstations, including E-Mail and word processing packages. Received 4 top sales awards; 1 of 2 salesmen in company to receive sales award for exceeding $2M in sales.

CREATIVE SOFTWARE, Los Angeles, California

6/91 to 12/92   <u>Regional Marketing Manager</u>

Responsible for all sales, marketing, staffing, and budgeting activity for four branch offices located within southern California, Arizona, and Colorado. Other activities included sales training, product positioning, product exposure, selling methodology, and sales manual development.

CSI/TEKNITRON, Greensboro, North Carolina

1981 to 1991   <u>Major Account Manager</u>

Marketing activity included direct sales to Fortune 1000 and California 100 companies. Succeeded in selling and installing over 150 CSI Data Processing Systems, qualifying me for numerous "100% Clubs." Involved in other projects such as competitive analysis, sales training, and sales compensation.

DELTA/MICROFILM BUSINESS SYSTEMS, Durham, North Carolina

1978 to 1981   <u>National Sales Manager</u>

Established a national sales organization to market computer output microfilm services. Responsible for all direct sales activity, sales training, and development of marketing policy.

EDUCATION

B.S. degree, Business Administration; Marketing Major, University of California, Northridge 1978

PERSONAL

Willing to relocate.

References available upon request.

Khanh Van Chen
488-1/2 State Street
San Francisco, California 94063
(415) 555-2345

Five years' professional and educational experience in counseling.

OBJECTIVE

To augment professional placement service by contributing expertise in interviewing, personnel, and guidance counseling.

AMPLIFICATION

To serve organization in private industry and ultimately develop skills for managerial position.

EXPERIENCE

Program
Coordinator

San Francisco Manpower Corporation, San Francisco, California—
1994 to present
Coordinated six dissimilar office skill training programs encompassing paraprofessional and professional personnel. As program coordinator and senior counselor, supervise thirty-four staff members and one hundred thirty trainees for each rotating cycle. Frequently instrumental in placing graduating trainees to applicable jobs and training them accordingly. Utilize public relations skills during heavy telephone work in contacting and solidifying prospective employers.

Publishing
Secretary

Santana Publishing Company, San Francisco, California—
1992 to 1994
This position required the screening and interpreting of telephone calls, written and oral communications concerning interoffice memorandums, and correspondences between management and accounting staff personnel.

Graduate
Assistant

University of Nebraska, Smokeville, Nebraska—1990 to 1991
In conjunction with work-study tuition program, arranged class schedules for students. Counseled foreign students with their academic, social, language adjustment, family, and immigration problems by applying principles of guidance.

EDUCATION

University of Nebraska, Smokeville, Nebraska—M.Ed., 1991
Major: Guidance and Counseling

University of Taiwan, Taiwan—B.A., 1989
Major: English

SPECIAL AWARDS

Scholarship to attend worldwide guidance and counseling convention. Coordinator of foreign students workshop. Champion debator, third year, college.

PUBLICATIONS

Editor—newsletter and brochure for San Francisco Manpower Corporation

REFERENCES

Available upon request.

CHARLOTTE KEANE
14 Waterview St.
Silver Springs, MD 41814
(301) 899-9248
(301) 791-2300

CAREER OBJECTIVE:

To work exclusively for a designer in a showroom presenting that designer's line to retail clothing buyers.

BUSINESS EXPERIENCE:

10/96–Present	PEGGY LANE & Co. Washington, DC Assistant manager for junior sportswear. Interviewed, trained, and supervised all new employees. Responsible for designing and implementing the weekly displays.
6/96–9/96	McGRAW'S Washington, DC Manager of restaurant and amusement complex. Designed menu, hired employees, worked with decorators to create proper ambiance in restaurant, managed inventories, controlled cash flow and budgets, and supervised all employees. $250,000 gross receipts during summer months.
6/95–9/95	CLASSIC CLOTHES Bethesda, MD Sales associate. Provided fashion consulting and helped to create window and store displays.

EDUCATION:

1993–1995	UNIVERSITY OF CONNECTICUT B.S. Degree Fashion Merchandising (May 1995) Member of Omicron Nu Honor Society
1991–1993	MARYMOUNT UNIVERSITY Arlington, VA Dean's List. President of Resident Dormitory

PERSONAL BACKGROUND:

Traveled in parts of Europe and the United States.

REFERENCES:

Provided upon request.

Dorothy Turner
415 Oakes Street
St. Paul, Minnesota 55149
(612) 654-1234

Experience

April 1995–present	**Medical Caseworker**, Catholic Churches, St. Paul, Minnesota. Interview patients and their families at St. Claire's Hospital to ascertain needs of home care; arrange for volunteer nursing and housekeeping and child care assistance.
June 1985–March 1995	**Family Caseworker**, K.H. Psychiatric Clinic, St. Paul, Minnesota. Conducted therapy sessions for teenagers, adults, and children; interviewed families of patients to determine financial competency and arranged for financial help.

Education

1985	M.S.W.—Columbia School of Social Work, New York City
1984	B.A.—University of Minnesota, St. Paul, Minnesota

References

Available upon request.

Adrienne Smithfield
22 Olive Tree Street
Kansas City, Missouri 64116

(816) 546-9865

EXPERIENCE

1990–present	**Children's Caseworker,** Angel of Mercy Home. Kansas City, Missouri. Interview children and families of children at Angel of Mercy Home. The home takes both orphans and children from inadequate homes. Do full investigations. Follow-up. Make recommendations concerning children.
1988–1990	**Family Caseworker,** Kansas City State Hospital. Interviewed members of families at the hospital or at their homes. Helped to make for better adjustment. Proposed plans for assisting patients.

EDUCATION

B.S., Social Work, Southern Missouri State College, Springfield, Missouri. Concentrated training in social work with an emphasis on psychiatric and pediatric.

PROFESSIONAL AFFILIATIONS

National Association of Social Workers

REFERENCES

References covering all phases of education and experience on request.

William Fredericks
14 San Fernando Avenue
Hohokus, New Jersey 07423   Telephone: (201) 456-4921

Past Experience:

1995 to present	Winkler, Cantor and Pomboy (Investments), New York, NY Experience similar to that stated for D.H. Blair and Co.

1988 to 1994
D.H. Blair and Co.
(Investments)
New York, NY

<u>As Supervisor</u> responsible for entire work output and efficiency of Order Room; proper execution of orders for brokers, banks, and institutional funds; assisted brokers in general operations; served as liaison with other brokerage firms on daily transactions and problems. Position required knowledge of stock exchange operations, figure aptitude, decision making, and absolute accuracy under extreme pressure.

1982 to 1988

<u>Senior Order Clerk</u> and supervisor of branch office of Tessel, Paturick and Ostrau, Inc.

1970 to 1982

<u>Cashier</u> with Merrill Lynch, New York, NY—handled large volumes of cash and securities; was bonded; supervised three cashier clerks; trained approximately 25 broker trainees in all phases of branch operations.

Education:

Special Schools: Finance Institutes for special courses in connection with banking and brokerage operations—1970.

References:

Available upon request.

CLYDE HENLEY
P.O. Box 92
Cranberry Lake, NJ
609-346-1130

RESUME CAPSULE   Twenty years' experience as Industrial Foreman, with superior
mechanical ability, production efficiency, leadership, and excellent
record in labor relations.

EXPERIENCE
1997–present   Foreman, Ginger Beverages Company, Marshall, NH. One of the
largest manufacturers of ginger beverages and crystallized ginger
products in the United States. Supervise work of eighteen employees
operating ginger presses, pulverizers, and separators, producing four
varieties of ginger-flavored beverages and confections. Full
responsibility for hiring and supervising employees, training
operators, and establishing work hours and shifts. Excellent rapport
with employees resulting in minimal grievances with union.

1996–1997   Foreman, Spartan Separators, Inc., Madison, NJ. One of America's
major manufacturers of separating equipment for use in food
processing. Worked in machine assembly department as night
supervisor with full responsibility for faultless assembly of food
processing equipment.

1992–1996   Tool and Die Maker, Waterford Machine Production Company.
Suggested design modifications, kept production moving. Worked as
assistant night superintendent during rush periods.

EDUCATION

Graduate Brooklawn High School, Brooklawn, NJ—1992.
(Mechanical)

REFERENCES

Upon request.

Kevin J. Hutchins
69 Marrietta Drive
Dallas, Texas 75234

Telephone: (214) 459-9345

Job Objective:	Systems Analyst

Experience:

1994– present	Programmer Supervisor Hartman Oil Company	Dallas, Texas

Write computer programs, developing block diagrams, utilizing available software and operating systems, and coding machine instructions. Originate block diagrams, working from outlines of proposed systems, develop file sizes, programming specifications. Determine appropriate use of tape or disk files, printer, etc. Select in-house software or subroutines to run in connection with program.

Write machine instructions, test, debug, and assemble program. Document overall system and develop data control procedures. Advise and instruct less-experienced programmers and prepare operating instructions.

1990–1994	Programmer Live Oak Electronics	Houston, Texas

As a trainee for six months, became proficient in HTML programming. Coded well-defined systems logic flowcharts into computer machine instructions using HTML. Coded subroutines following specifications, file size parameters, block diagrams. Performed maintenance tasks and patching to established, straightforward programs. Documented all programs as completed. Tested, debugged, and assembled programs.

Education:	Houston Community College—1988–1990. Completed two-year course.
References:	Provided on request.

ROSETTA BROWN
55 Atlanta Avenue
Roselle, New York 14512

716-366-9032

EXPERIENCE

1992–present   Elementary Teacher, Greendale Public Schools, Greendale, New York. Taught fourth and fifth grades. Complete responsibility for the writing, reading, and research for a Teacher's Kit—Children's Literature. (A synopsis, discussion questions, and enrichment multimedia activities for over 55 outstanding children's novels.)

1988–1992   Elementary Teacher, Greendale Public Schools, Greendale, New York. Taught second and third grades. Participated in much curriculum work, area of upgraded classes and inter-age grouping.

1987–1988   Receptionist, Robinson and Sons, New York City.

1986–1987   Saleswoman, The Tog Shop, New York City.

1985–1986   Reservationist, Landover Air Lines, New York, New York.

EDUCATION

M.A., June 1988—Adelphi University. Elementary Education.

Permanent Certification, 1987.
Common Branch Subjects (1–6).
The University of the State of New York.

B.A., June 1985—Russell College. English Major.

REFERENCES

Will be furnished upon request.

ALYSON REXDALE
60 West End Avenue
New York, NY 10023

(212) 866-5332

EXPERIENCE

1995–present   Teacher, Stuyvesant Elementary School, Rochester, NY. Took into account long-range goals of individual students as well as class as a unit, and developed and organized unit in consumer education utilizing visual and audio media. Created and developed working models for use of children to promote coordination and mental stimulation.

1991–1992   Tutored German children in English while at a German University in Stuttgart on Exchange Study Program.

EDUCATION

M.S., Elementary Education, Brampton College, Rochester, NY, 1995.

New York State Teacher's Certificate (N-6) #489664101, effective September 1995.

B.A., Psychology, State University of New York at Albany, 1993.

SPECIAL RECOGNITION

New York State Regents Scholarship—1989–1993

REFERENCES

Will be furnished upon request.

Robert R. Abbey
48 Mingus Circle
Bayonne, New Jersey 07002

OBJECTIVE: Appointment on teaching staff of small private institution in rural area,
                    preferably in New York State.

EXPERIENCE:

April 1994–   Teacher/Instructor in Charge of Training and
Present   Development, Eastern Academy, Fort Lee, New Jersey.

September 1993–   Assistant Dean of Students. Parkwood Junior College,
March 1994   Parkwood, New Hampshire. In charge of all student personnel programs,
                    including Career Counseling, Job Placement, Student Government,
                    Admissions Recruitment, Discipline, Athletics, Cultural Development, and
                    Student Welfare benefits.

September 1991–   Instructor, Glendale High School, Glendale, New York.
June 1993   Taught basic Art Courses and American History.

EDUCATIONAL
BACKGROUND:

M.A. (History/English), 1991—Wayne University, Michigan.

B.S. Education (History), 1990—St. Michael's College, New Jersey.

REFERENCES: Will be furnished upon request.

MARTHA KAYE
16 Court St.
Chicago, IL 24168

(213) 841-1286
(213) 911-4000

EXPERIENCE

November 1996
to
June 20XX

Travel agent with Valley & Williams & Co., Inc, established in 1879, one of the oldest and most prestigious New Chicago City travel agencies. Responsibilities encompassed counseling for FIT cruise and land travel arrangements, plus preparation of itineraries, tickets, and necessary travel documents. Valley & Williams sponsors cruise programs for cultural organizations and promotes allotments for Royal Viking Line and Windstar Cruises. The agency arranges cruise and land programs for the Metropolitan Museum of Art, The Chicago Art Institute, the Smithsonian, the Brooklyn Botanical Garden, and others. During my tenure, I was responsible for various departures—including selling and document processing. Valley & Williams utilizes PARS airline computer, Microsoft Word, and ITT telex.

January 1981
to
October 1996

Owned and managed Sante Travel Agency, St. Louis, Missouri. Sante Travel Agency is a prestigious St. Louis agency with a staff of fifteen and sales in excess of $3 million. During this time in the travel industry, successfully marketed domestic and international tours, wrote brochures, conducted tour groups, sold cruises, charters, and consulted with St. Louis cultural organizations for specialized sponsored tours: the Zoo, Art Museum, and Missouri Botanical Garden. Maintained a working knowledge of computers, agency business practices, cost and profitability factors. Planned and processed FIT travel arrangements for clients to every part of the world. Traveled extensively worldwide, and have a personal knowledge of touring and hotel facilities in the following countries: United States, England, Scotland, France, Germany, Italy, Portugal, New Zealand, Australia, New Guinea, China, Yugoslavia, Indonesia, Egypt, India, South America, South and East Africa, Scandinavia, Russia, Greece, Morocco, Israel, and the Caribbean. Sante Travel Agency utilized Sabre airline computer system.

EDUCATION

1985 Completed ICTA course and received certification as a CTC.
1977–1981 Washington University, St. Louis, B.A. degree.
1977 Graduated Mary Institute, a St. Louis girls' preparatory day school.

REFERENCES

To be furnished on request.

Lindsay Marie Wells
35 46 Swarr Run Road
Lancaster, Pennsylvania 17603
(717) 955-2937

EXPERIENCE:

May 1992–
present

NATIONAL INSTITUTE OF CERTIFIED PUBLIC ACCOUNTANTS
Manager, Salary Administration—Responsible for administration of salary increase program including promotional increases, adjustments, monthly merit increase reviews, performance appraisal program, and job evaluation. Conducting compensation surveys to determine necessity of adjusting exempt and nonexempt salary ranges. Participating in various compensation surveys. Maintaining employee budget. Developing and revising policies and procedures. Counseling employees. Advising personnel employees on job-related problems. Administration and supervision of personnel department in Director's absence.

January 1991–
May 1992

BOOKER AND BOOKER
Personnel Assistant—Responsible for smooth running of personnel; functions on a day-to-day basis included interviewing and hiring of administrative staff, obtaining temporary personnel, supervising work-study employees, and keeping personnel records. Prepared and filed various governmental reports including Veteran Reports. Processed some benefits claims and administered the salary increase program.

June 1987–
December 1990

WATERMAN HOUSE, INC.
Wage and Salary Specialist—Responsible for maintaining an equitable salary administration program, including meeting with department managers in order to study and analyze jobs, preparation of job descriptions, evaluation of jobs using established system to determine grades and prepare records of validity. Developed new evaluation system for exempt and nonexempt employees, prepared and maintained merit increase budget and rate schedules, and organization charts and listings for all divisions.

EDUCATION:

1991–1994

Various AMA and Commerce and Industry Courses dealing with Personnel.

1985–1987

Pitt Community College—A.A. Degree (Psychology).

REFERENCES:

Available upon request.

Judy Lee Foster
56 Highland Avenue
Louisville, KY 40223
Telephone: (502) 498-8874

<u>Job Objective—Word Processing Supervisor</u>

<u>Experience</u>

1992–present   Word Processor: Blue Grass Enterprises, Inc.—Louisville, KY.

Worked under the direction of the Group Head inputting data from various departments, following standardized procedures and instructions. Learned to handle jobs without specific instructions. Extensive knowledge of WordPerfect. Assisted other word processors who were in training.

1991–1992   Transcribing Machine Operator: Colonel Harvey Foods—Louisville, KY.

Typed a variety of recorded material, including complex, technical, and sometimes confidential reports. Required to make the proper choice of layout and form and to be sure punctuation and grammar were correct.

1989–1991   Clerk Typist: All State Manufacturing Company—Lexington, KY.

Used dictaphone to type letters; typed reports from typewritten drafts. Did some statistical typing and typed invoices and purchase orders. Answered call director and helped receptionist. Operated embossograph to cut name plates and used adding machine.

1988–1989   File Clerk: First National Bank—Lexington, KY.

Arranged, sorted, and filed invoices, correspondence, and other miscellaneous material. Retrieved and refiled items as requested. Performed some typing assignments.

<u>Education</u>

Lexington Mason High School, Business Studies Diploma, 1988

<u>References</u>

Provided on request.

Sylvia Martinson
16 Beverly Place
Los Angeles, CA 41825
(519) 845-7633

BUSINESS EXPERIENCE:

2/92–Present   B.B. & K. Sales, Inc.
       Brooklyn, NY

       Word Processor
       Duties include typing contracts, reviewing title searches, contacting clients
       for timely return of documents, scheduling dates for closing with parties and
       attorneys, accepting binders determining prospective clients' eligibility,
       preparing contractors' worksheets, making judgments as to what repairs
       needed immediate attention before property could be made available for
       sale or rent, proofreading, and editing contracts, manuscripts, and
       correspondence.

3/87–1/92   Baker & Ross, Inc.
       Brooklyn, NY

       Administrative Assistant
       Duties included reviewing tenants' files, conducting recertification of
       tenants' eligibility to determine rate of rent, verifying prospective tenants'
       living quarters, maintaining log of payments, payments past due, and
       supervising the repairs of apartments and the building in general.

EDUCATION:

9/86–6/88   New York Technical College. Associates degree. Major in Liberal Arts.

6/81–6/85   Thomas Jefferson High School, Academic degree.

SKILLS: Typing: 65 wpm
       Windows 95 for PC
       EXCEL, MS Word.

REFERENCES: Furnished upon request.

Dorothy Turner
415 Oakes Street
St. Paul, Minnesota 55149
(612) 654-1234

<u>Objective</u>	Secure a position as a technical writer.
<u>Education</u>	M.A. (English), University of Illinois, 1986 B.S. (Education), University of Illinois, 1985

<u>Experience</u>

<u>St. Paul High School</u>   1991–Present
High School English Teacher

Responsible for teaching English (writing, grammar, and literature) and history in secondary school.

<u>Geigo Terminal Systems</u>, Minneapolis, Minnesota   1985–1991

<u>Senior Technical Editor</u> (1988–1991)

Responsible for editing user manuals, programming guides, and feature summaries for Geigo terminals and related computer equipment.

Additionally responsible for the quality control of technical documentation; assisted writers with writing and editing problems, and instructed writers individually and in seminars; also on-call to edit other corporation documents.

Instrumental in providing the company with accuracy, precision, and consistency in documentation by researching, compiling, and editing a glossary of standard terms used by Geigo in reference to its products. (This glossary and my guidelines for technical writing are still used by Geigo.)

<u>Software Technical Writer</u>   (1985–1988)

Responsible for researching, writing, and producing system operation and programming guides, and feature summaries; assisted in designing the documents from inception through production. Interfaced with engineering, marketing, and graphic arts.

(Continued)

Freelance Writer and Consultant   1984–1985

Employed by several computer and publishing firms, as follows:

C.B.S. Data Corporation—Wrote abstracts of articles from commercial banking publications; wrote critiques of competitors' advertising.

John Wiley & Sons—Proofread and copyedited portions of high school texts.

Loeb Publishing—Wrote exercises for college grammar text; proofread and copyedited the K-8 reading series.

Kodak Corporation—Edited scientific articles and user manuals.

I.E.E.E.—Proofread and edited hardware and software documents and textbooks.

Related Experience	Wrote reviews and feature articles for corporation newspaper; wrote some advertising copy; wrote a critical biography; wrote courses of study.
	Conducted workshops and seminars in technical writing and expository composition; chaired committees on curriculum development.
	Evaluated compositions for College Entrance Examinations Board.
	Taught grammar and writing in college and adult education.
References	On Request.

Barbara Berkman
47 East 72nd Street
New York, New York 10027

OBJECTIVE   Technical Writer

PROFESSIONAL
ACCOMPLISHMENTS

Software   ■ Designed and implemented programs in BASIC, ASSEMBLY, and
                    HTML
                  ■ Created text files and source programs using EMACS

Writing   ■ Completed 200 hours of technical writing instruction
                  ■ Wrote technical documents:
                    —JCL Reference Manual
                    —EMACS Reference Guide
                  ■ Designed instructional materials including:
                    —3 videocassette training aids for welfare workers
                    —course syllabus with 30 content units
                    —2 chapters of an instructional booklet
                    —evaluation questionnaires

Training   ■ Prepared and delivered training program to clerical staff of NY
                    State Welfare Department
                  ■ Designed and delivered classroom lectures
                  ■ Trained and supervised instructional staff of 15
                  ■ Utilized a wide variety of audiovisual equipment including films,
                    slides, overheads, videocassettes, and slide tapes
                  ■ Performed needs analyses and implemented programs based on
                    results of analyses

Management   ■ Acted as department coordinator; supervised faculty
                  ■ Interviewed, evaluated, and recommended candidates for
                    university faculty positions
                  ■ Negotiated learner contracts at community agencies
                  ■ Chaired Course Development Committee
                  ■ Coordinated social services to a diverse community population

(Continued)

EDUCATION
- Technical Writing Program, Brooklyn Community College, 1993
- Personnel Development: Design of Training Programs, Hofstra University, 1986
- M.S. in Social Work, Hofstra University, 1985, GPA 3.9
- B.A. in English, SUNY, Stony Brook, 1983, Magna Cum Laude

EXPERIENCE
- Staff Social Worker, St. Joseph's Hospital, Long Island, NY, 1991–20XX
- Instructor, Parent Education. St. Joseph's Hospital, Long Island, NY, 1988–1991
- Assistant Professor, School of Social Services. Long Island University, 1985–1991

PROFESSIONAL
ORGANIZATION   Society for Technical Communication

REFERENCES   References and writing sample available upon request.

10

Which Job Do I Take?

You've spent weeks on the hunt and you've received two or three job offers. Now your thoughts change from "How do I get the job I want?" to "Which one shall I accept?" What? You think that's an easy decision and that you'd take the job that offers the most money? Well, maybe yes, and maybe no. There's more to be considered than just money.

Say you're a recent college graduate who's never worked full time before. You've come to a large metropolis because you know that's where your future lies. You don't know anybody. After weeks of searching, you have had two job offers. In one, the higher paid of the two, you will be working in a small office with one or two other people; in the other, with 5 percent less pay, you'll be a member of a large staff and will have the opportunity to meet lots of people.

Because you've come to the city to start a whole new life, you must consider that a job that offers an opportunity to expand your social life might offer something as valuable as money. That is one of the many intangibles you must consider in the job selection process. Here are some others:

Some companies provide training programs; others are willing to pay part (or all) of the costs of specialized university courses for you to add to your skills and knowledge. How valuable is that? What will that additional education be worth in the future? This is another area to consider.

The geographical location of a job will also influence your decision. If it would require you to relocate, should you? Have you thought about the cost of living in a different city? Remember, to judge the worth of your salary properly, it must be compared to the cost of living. What about cultural activities in the new city? And how important are they to you?

Even without relocation, you must consider the location of your job. Perhaps you are one of those people who seeks some diversion during the lunch hour—visiting a museum or doing some shopping. In that case, a job in a rural area that offers a few dollars more than a job close to a cultural or shopping area might not interest you. One requiring 15 minutes of travel—a short walk from your home—could be preferable to another with a higher salary and an hour's bus or subway ride away. Often, a slight difference in salary is more than eaten up by transportation costs. Besides, time going to and from work is not exactly leisure time!

When making your decision, be sure that you consider the importance of being happy with your new job. Our agency advises entry-level job seekers to take the job they instinctively feel good about. We've found that being happy in a job almost guarantees better job performance and, hence, promotion. We've also found that most companies promote from within and will consider their staff members for each new job opportunity. Our philosophy is "Proximity is the mother of opportunity," and, therefore, the wrong job in the right company often or usually becomes the right job in the right company.

A beginner should consider growth potential in a first job. Your first job should be considered as a place to learn, to get experience, and to prove yourself.

The many intangibles in selecting which job offer to take also apply to every job seeker. For example, is there a company cafeteria? Many company cafeterias offer good, nutritious food to their employees at low cost. Considering that in many instances a full meal at the company cafeteria will cost less than a hamburger and beverage at a luncheonette or fast-food counter, you might be able to save some money. Between economic advantages and convenience, it's certainly worth thinking about!

The company health plan offered is another important factor. Young people often tend to disregard a firm's hospital and major medical plans—they consider themselves immortal! But anyone, of any age, can suddenly find himself or herself confronted with a stay in the hospital, resulting in large medical bills.

If you are married with children, you probably are more aware of the value of a good medical plan, but do you know that some companies offer psychiatric and dental coverage as well? How many parents of a troubled teenager would welcome psychiatric coverage! Perhaps you have a child who will need orthodontic work in two or three years. If among your job offers a company offers no dental plan at all, and another company offers all or a percentage of dental costs, you must weigh carefully just how important such a plan is to you.

If you're over 40 years old and expect to stay in this job until your retirement, try to find out which offer will give you the most career advancement. One of the firms that has offered you a job may hire employees your age or younger to fill the levels above your position. But

Which Job Do I Take?

another firm might be able to offer you a position as soon as the immediate supervisor reaches retirement age. How quickly can you get promoted? How high can you go in the company?

Just as job searching is a thinking process, so is job selection. There's much to think about in selecting which job offer to accept. It is never solved by simply flipping a coin. You must really think about what is important to you, about which job you think will best use your skills, talents, and abilities, and where you will be the happiest.

Once you make the decision, stick to it, and commit yourself completely. Getting the job is just the first step. The next step is making the job into *your* job. By giving it your all and approaching it with integrity and imagination, you will change your job into a challenging career.

Index

About the Authors

Gene Corwin has been an owner/manager, placement counselor and recruiter in the Employment Agency field for more than 25 years. Since 1991, he has been Director of Career Blazers Resume Services in Boca Raton, Florida, and has written or cowritten several guides for job-seekers.

Gary Joseph Grappo is founder and former president of CareerEdge, and has been a consultant and human resource executive for many national and international corporations.

Adele Lewis has coauthored and contributed to numerous career and resume titles for more than 20 years.